G000124338

NOT FOR TOURISTS™

Guide to Manhattan

2000

Happy Mazza Media LLC

•

New York

published and designed by: Happy Mazza Media LLC

NFT™ - NOT FOR TOURISTS™ - GUIDE TO MANHATTAN - 2000
www.notfortourists.com

Printed in China

ISBN# 0-9672303-0-6 $19.95

Concept by
Jane Pirone

Information Design
Jane Pirone
Rob Tallia

Editor
Jane Pirone

Project Manager
Rob Tallia

Writing and Editing
Rob Tallia
Jane Pirone
Kristina Feliciano

Graphic Design and Production
Gabe Ashkenazi
Barry Caul
Dominique Vitali
Barbara Vasquez
Miss Jenni
Rie Sugai
Adriana Cordero

Proof Reader
Doug French

Research and Data Entry
Cecilia Amrute
Chris Gardella
Mike Ha

Peter Hollitscher
Howard Lee
Warren Leung
Donna Lichaw
Gabrielle Prisco
Kevin Rose
Jack Schieffer
Chris Thomas
Jordan Zaretsky

Very Special Thanks
Alex Daily
Clare Jacobson
Jodie Ousley
reitdesign
Sabrina Smith

Dear NFT User:

Two years ago, we began work on the most practical, portable, encyclopedic, and just plain good-looking guidebook to Manhattan that we could possibly imagine. We called it NFT—"Not For Tourists." We were tired of trying to cull practical information about Manhattan from a mind-numbingly wide range of sources, including "practical" guides, "insider" guides, tourist books, out-of-date magazine articles, the internet, faded newspaper clippings, radio spots, esoteric city offices, torn maps, and the (almost) wordless mutterings of thousands of commuters, straphangers, and similarly frustrated city dwellers.

Well, we did it. Here is the inaugural issue of NFT-Manhattan, a guidebook that we think will lighten the load of those folks who, like ourselves, have tried to find an ATM in TriBeCa, a parking lot in the East Village, or a liquor store in Chelsea—and who haven't had the luxury of being able to simultaneously lug around the Yellow Pages. It's the main goal of NFT—to provide already-savvy New Yorkers, commuters, business travelers (and even tourists!) with the kind of information they'd love to have while sitting on a street-corner in Midtown in the rain—but in a format that will fit in their back pocket.

A few comments about NFT: one, we'd love to have your feedback on this book. If something is not in NFT that you think should be, or if we've claimed something exists that no longer does, we want to know about it. And while we've made the best possible effort to make sure that x store really is in y location, if we've placed it wrong the first time around, tell us about it and we'll get it right next year. Second, the proliferation of "deli" ATMs in the last year has radically changed the number of places one can withdraw money in Manhattan. However, we figured that if you knew that your bank was only another block away, you'd probably walk to it instead and avoid the surcharge. Hence, we've only listed the major financial institution's ATMs in our book—at least, for this version of it.

These and other innumerable, annoying, nit-picky, and ultimately boring issues were ours to decide. Now it's time for you to take over. We're looking forward to hearing from you.

Here's hoping you find what you need.

Jane Pirone
Editor, NFT–Manhattan
www.notfortourists.com

Table of

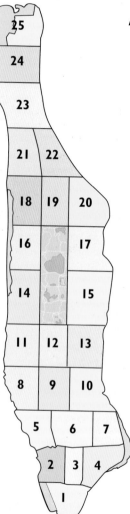

Contents

Financial District MAP

Vesey St

7 WTC

6 WTC

5 WTC

Ann St

Beekman St

SOUTH BRIDGE
RESIDENTIAL
TOWER

Pearl St

Peck Slip

SOUTH ST SEAPORT
HISTORICAL DISTRICT

Fulton St

Dey St

WORLD TRADE
CENTER

CONCOURSE

Cortlandt St

John St

Dutch St

3 WTC

4 WTC

2 WTC

Liberty St

Church St

Liberty Pl

Maiden Ln

Platt St

Gold St

Ryders Al

Cliff St

Water St

Front St

Beekman St

Fulton St

Burling Slip

Cedar St

Thames St

Liberty St

Legion
Mem Sq

Cedar St

Pearl St

Fletcher St

Maiden Ln

Albany St

Carlisle St

Trinity Pl

Broadway

Nassau St

Pine St

Water St

Front St

South St

Rector St

Wall St

Wall St

Pier 13

Washington St

Greenwich St

Exchange Alley

Broad St

Exchange Pl

Hanover St

Gouverneur Ln

FDR DRIVE

Edgar St

New St

William St

Hanover
Sq

Old Slip

Old Slip

Pier 11

Morris St

Beaver St

Mill Ln

West St

Morris St

Marketfield St

S William St

Stone St

Coenties Slip

Pier 9

Battery Pl

Stone St

Bridge St

Pearl St

VIETNAM
VETERANS
PLAZA

ROBERT F.
WAGNER JR.
PARK

Bowling
Green

Whitehall St

Moore St

Water St

Broad St

Heliport Auth.

Pier A

Battery Pl

State St

Peter Minuit Plz

East
River

BATTERY
PARK

Battery Park Underpass

STATEN ISLAND
FERRY TERMINAL

Hudson River
(North River)

Brooklyn Battery Tunnel

A thicket of skyscrapers mask an astounding amount of old, wonderful buildings in this area, such as Federal Hall, Trinity Church, the Cunard Building, and the Customs House. The American International Building, at 70 Pine Street, is the least-known great Art Deco building in the world.

💲 ATMs

- 1. Apple • 88 Pine St.
- 2. Atlantic • 15 Maiden Lane
- 3. Bank of New York • 20 Broad St.
- 4. Bank of New York • 48 Wall St.
- 5. Bank of Tokyo • 100 Broadway
- 6. Chase • 4 New York Plaza
- 7. Chase • 14 Wall St.
- 8. Chase • 52 Broadway
- 9. Chase • 55 Water St.
- 10. Chase • 1 Chase Plz.
- 11. Chase • 2 WTC
- 12. Chase • 5 WTC
- 13. Chase • 214 Broadway
- 14. Citibank • 120 Broadway
- 15. Citibank • 1 WTC Concourse
- 16. Citibank • 107 William St.
- 17. Citibank • 1 Broadway
- 18. Citibank • 111 Wall St.
- 19. Commercial • 120 Broadway
- 20. EAB • 120 Broadway
- 21. Fleet • 130 Liberty St.
- 22. Fleet • 150 Broadway
- 23. Fleet • 175 Water St.
- 24. Fuji • 2 WTC
- 25. Marine Midland (HBSC) • 140 Broadway
- 26. Marine Midland (HBSC) • 70 Pine St.
- 27. Marine Midland (HBSC) • 5 WTC
- 28. Marine Midland (HBSC) • 212 Broadway
- 29. Marine Midland (HBSC) • 110 William St.
- 30. Republic National • 100 Maiden Lane
- 31. Republic National • 26 Broadway

⬤ Bagels

- Bagelicious • 3 Maiden Lane
- Le Bagle Inc 2 • 25 John St.

🏥 Hospital

- The Floating Hospital • Pier 11

★ Landmarks

- American International Building • 70 Pine St.
- Battery Maritime Building • 11 South St.
- Bowling Green • Broadway & State St.
- Cunard Building • 25 Broadway
- Customs House/Museum of the American Indian • 1 Bowling Green
- Federal Hall • 26 Wall St.
- The Federal Reserve Bank • 33 Liberty St.
- New York Stock Exchange • 20 Broad St.
- South Street Seaport
- St. Paul's Chapel & Cemetery • B'way & Fulton St.
- Trinity Church & Cemetery • B'way & Wall St.
- Vietnam Veterans Plz. • Coenties Slip & Water St.
- World Trade Center

24 Hour Pharmacy

- Duane Reade • 7 WTC

✉ Post Offices

- Bowling Green • 25 Broadway
- Church St. Station • 90 Church St.
- Peck Slip • 1 Peck Slip
- Wall Street • 73 Pine St.

🅢 School

- Greater New York Chapter • 80 Maiden Lane

GRID 1   Financial District MAP

Vesey St

7 WTC

6 WTC

5 WTC

Ann St

Beekman St

Peck St

Pearl St

SOUTH BRIDGE
RESIDENTAL
TOWER

SOUTH ST SEA
HISTORICAL DIS

Fulton St

1 WTC

WORLD TRADE
CENTER

CONCOURSE

Dey St

2 WTC

4 WTC

John St

Dutch St

Ryders Al

Cliff St

Water St

Beekma

Front St

Cortlandt St

Liberty Pl

Maiden Ln

Platt St

Gold St

Pearl St

Fulton St

Liberty St

Church St

Liberty St

Legion
Mem Sq

Burling Slip

Fletcher St

Cedar St

Thames Pl

Nassau St

Maiden Ln

Albany St

Trinity Pl

Cedar St

Water St

Front St

South St

Carlisle St

Broadway

Pine St

Rector St

Washington St

Greenwich St

Wall St

Wall St

FDR DRIVE

Pier

Exchange Alley

Exchange Pl

Hanover St

Gouverneur Ln

Pier 11

Edgar St

Broad St

William St

Hanover
Sq

Old Slip

Old Slip

Pier 9

Morris St

New St

Morris St

Beaver St

Mill Ln

Marketfield St

S William St

Stone St

Coenties Slip

VIETNAM
VETERANS
PLAZA

West St

Stone St

Bridge St

Pearl St

Bowling
Green

Battery Pl

Whitehall St

Moore St

Water St

Broad St

Heliport Auth

ROBERT F.
WAGNER JR.
PARK

State St

Pier A

Peter Minuit Plz

BATTERY
PARK

Battery Park Underpass

STATEN ISLAND
FERRY TERMINAL

East
River

Hudson River
(North River)

Brooklyn Battery Tunnel

Mayor Guiliani is valiantly trying to convince people that downtown is an excellent place to live. There's nothing here. It's totally dead at night.

C 24-Hour Copy Centers

- Kinko's • 100 Wall St.
- National Reproductions • 130 Cedar St.

Gyms

- Bally Sports Club • 25 Broadway
- Dolphin Fitness Club • 156 William St.
- Executive Fitness Center • 3 WTC
- HRC Tennis & Yacht • Piers 13 & 14
- Liberty Club MCB • 200 Rector Pl.
- NY Health & Racquet Club • 39 Whitehall St.
- New York Sports Clubs • 30 Cliff St.
- NY Sports Club • 30 Wall St.
- Plus One Fitness Clinic • 200 Liberty St.
- Wall Street Boxing Fitness • 76 Beaver St.

T Hardware Stores

- Apple Specialties • 19 Rector St.
- Dick's Hardware • 205 Pearl St.
- Fulton Supply & Hardware • 74 Fulton St.
- Wolff Hardware • 127 Fulton St.

Liquor Stores

- Arber Liquors • 28 John St.
- Famous Wines & Liquor • 27 William St.
- Fulton Wines & Spirits • 110 Fulton St.
- G's Wine & Spirits • 95 Trinity Place
- Maiden Lane Wine & Liquor • 6 Maiden Lane
- New York Wine Exchange • 9 Beaver St.
- Water Street Wine & Spirit • 79 Pine St.

Video Rentals

- Ann St. Entertainment Center • 21st Ann St.
- Thunder Video • 100 Greenwich St.

There is no such thing as street parking until after 7 p.m., and only then near the Fulton Fish Market. Be careful about driving on South Street in the early morning, since it is usually blocked off for fish market business. Good luck driving during the day.

Subways

① ⑨	South Ferry
① ⑨	Rector St.
① ⑨	Cortlandt St. /WTC
② ③	Wall St.
ⓒ ⓔ	WTC
Ⓐ ⓒ ⓙ Ⓜ ② ③ ④ ⑤	Fulton St.
ⓙ Ⓜ ⓩ	Broad St.
Ⓝ ⓡ	White Hall /South Ferry
Ⓝ ⓡ	Rector St.
Ⓝ ⓡ	Cortlandt St.
④ ⑤	Bowling Green
④ ⑤	Wall St.

Bus Lines

1	Fifth and Madison Aves.
6	7th Ave./B'way/Ave. of the Americas
9	Ave. B/E. B'way
10	7th/8th Aves./Douglas Blvd.
15	First/Second Aves.
22	Madison/Chambers St.

⊙ Car Rental
• Hertz • 20 Morris St.

Ⓟ Parking Garages
• 45 Wall St. Parking • 45 Wall St.
• 111 KKG • 111 Washington St.
• Downtown Parking • 56 Fulton St.
• Edison Parking Corp • 151 Maiden Lane
• Kinney • 55 Water St.
• Meyers Parking System • 1 Water St.
• Pine-Water Garage • 80 Pine St.
• Rickshaw Garage • 38 Broadway
• Ropetmar Garage • 80 Gold St.
• Ropetmar Garage • 299 Pearl St.
• State Pearl Garage • 1 Battery Park Plaza

TriBeCa ESSENTIALS

If anywhere in New York actually warrants insanely high real estate prices, it must be TriBeCa. Tons of gorgeous loft spaces and the surprising quietude of Duane Park make it highly desirable. Still perhaps a bit too solitary at night.

ATMs

- 1. Bank of New York • 233 Broadway
- 2. Chase • 281 Broadway
- 3. Chase • 423 Canal St.
- 4. Chase • 407 Broadway
- 5. Citibank • 108 Hudson St.
- 6. Citibank • 415 Broadway
- 7. Citibank • 250 Broadway
- 8. Fleet • 260 Canal St.
- 9. Marine Midland (HBSC) • 110 W. Broadway
- 10. Marine Midland (HBSC) • 268 Canal St.
- 11. Municipal Credit Union • 125 Barclay St.
- 12. Republic National • 265 Broadway
- 13. Skyline Federal Credit Union • 32 Ave. of the Americas

★ Landmarks

- City Hall • Park Row & Broadway
- Duane Park • Duane St.
- Harrison St. Houses • Harrison & Greenwich St.
- The Dream House • 275 Church St.
- Tweed Courthouse • Chambers St. & Broadway
- Walker's • 16 North Moore St.

Library

- New Amsterdam • 9 Murray St.

Police Precinct

- 1st Precinct • 16 Ericsson Pl.

Post Offices

- Canal Street • 350 Canal St.
- Church St. Station • 90 Church St.

Schools

- Audrey Cohen College • 75 Varick St.
- Chelsea Vocational High School • 131 Ave. of the Americas
- College of Insurance • 101 Murray St.
- Drake Schools of Manhattan • 225 Broadway
- Manhattan Comm. College • 199 Chambers St.
- New York Law School • 57 Worth St.
- PS 234 Independence School • 292 Greenwich St.
- Satellite Academy Program • 51 Chambers St.
- Stuyvesant High School • 345 Chambers St.

TriBeCa MAP

Watts St

Desbrosses St

Vestry St

Laight St

Washington St

Hubert St

Collister St

Beach St

Greenwich St

Hubert St

HUDSON SQ

Ericsson Pl

Varick St

St. Johns Lane

Ave of The Americas

Thompson St

W. Broadway

Wooster St

Greene St

Mercer St

Grand St

Canal St

Lispenard St

Walker St

White St

Franklin St

Leonard St

Worth St

Thomas St

Duane St

Reade St

Chambers St

Warren St

Murray St

Park Pl

Barclay St

North Moore St

Franklin St

W. Broadway

Harrison St

Jay St

Staple St

Hudson St

Chambers St

Warren St

Park Pl

Ball Fields

West St

TRIBECA BRIDGE

End Ave

Church St

Franklin

Broadway

Trimble

CIVIC CENTER

CITY HALL

CITY HALL PARK

Park Row

TriBeCa not only has one of Manhattan's great theaters, The Screening Room, but it also has the multi-use, ultra-hip Knitting Factory on Leonard Street to boast of.

24-Hour Copy Centers
- Blumberg Excelsior Copy • 66 White St.
- Kinko's • 105 Duane St.

Gyms
- Hardcore Muscle & Fitness • 25 Park Pl.
- New York Sports Clubs • 151 Reade St.
- Oishi Judo Club • 79 Leonard St.
- Tribeca Gym • 79 Worth St.

Hardware Stores
- ACE Hardware • 160 W. Broadway
- Central Industrial Supply • 446 Broadway
- CK & L Hardware • 307 Canal St.
- CNL • 378 Canal St.
- Tribeca Hardware • 154 Chambers St.

Laundromats
- Ecomat • 39 N. Moore St.
- PJ Chinese Laundry • 30 Grand St.

Liquor Stores
- Brite Buy Wines & Spirits •
  11 Ave. of the Americas
- City Hall Wines & Spirits • 108 Chambers St.
- Commerce Wine Merchant Inc. • 160 Chambers St.
- Down Town Liquor Store • 90 Hudson St.
- Hecht Liquors Inc. • 237 W. Broadway

Movie Theatres
- Hudson River Park Conservancy •
  Pier 25 at North Moore St.
- The Screening Room • 54 Varick St.
- Void • 16 Mercer St.
- Knitting Factory • 74 Leonard St.

Video Rentals
- 323 Canal Video Inc. • 323 Canal St.
- Ann St. Entertainment Center • 21st Ann St.
- Greenwich Street Video • 368 1/2 Greenwich St.

Parking and driving are usually quite decent here, except for the fact that Greenwich Street bears a striking resemblance to Dresden, circa 1945.

Subways

① ⑨	Canal St.
① ⑨	Franklin St.
① ② ③ ⑨	Chambers St.
② ③	Park Pl.
Ⓝ Ⓡ	City Hall
Ⓐ Ⓒ Ⓔ Ⓝ Ⓡ	Canal St.
Ⓐ Ⓒ	Chambers St.
Ⓖ Ⓔ	WTC

Bus Lines

1	Fifth & Madison Aves.
6	7th Ave./B'way/Ave. of The Americas
9	Ave. B/E. Broadway
10	Abingdon Sq.
15	8th/9th St. Crosstown
22	7th Ave./Ave. of the Americas/Broadway
103	5th Ave./Ave. of the Americas/Riverside Dr.

⊙ Car Rentals

- National Car Rental • 138 Reade St.
- United Car Rental • 74-76 Ave. of The Americas

Ⓟ Parking Garages

- 512 Parking • 280 Church St.
- Bill-Dom Parking • 31 Vestry St.
- Central Parking System • 75 Park Pl.
- Edison • 15 Worth St.
- Edison • 343 Broadway
- Greenwich St. Parking • 377 Greenwich St.
- Izadi Enterprises • 108 Leonard St.
- Katz Parking System • 86 Warren St.
- Kinney • 56 North Moore St.
- Marna Parking • 14 White St.
- Park Right • 35 Reade St.
- Reade Parking • 75 Reade St.

City Hall MAP

Delancey St

Kenmare St

Broome St

Grand St

Wooster St

Greene St

Mercer St

Howard St

Centre Market Pl

SARA D ROOSEVELT PK

Forsyth St

Eldridge St

Hester St

Chrystie St

Bowery

Lispenard St

Walker St

Mulberry St

Baxter St

Centre St

Canal St

Mott St

Elizabeth St

Canal St

White St

Franklin St

Cortlandt Alley

Lafayette St

Benson Pl

Franklin St

MANHATTAN BRIDGE

Forsyth St

Leonard St

Worth St

Catherine Lane

Bayard St

CONFUCIUS PLAZA

Church St

Broadway

Thomas St

Duane St

Hogan St

D.M.V.

Worth St

Pell St

Doyers St

Division St

E. Broadway

Moscow St

Chatham Sq

Catherine St

Henry St

Madison

Reade St

Chambers St

FEDERAL PLAZA

Catherine Lane

Foley Sq

N.Y. COUNTY COURTHOUSE

Pearl St

Oliver St

Warren St

Murray St

Park Pl

Barclay St

Trimble Pl

Cardinal Hayes Pl

U.S. COURTHOUSE

Park Row

CHATHAM GREEN HOUSES

Pearl St

James St

St. James Pl

MUNICIPAL BLDG

POLICE PLAZA

Madison St

GOV. ALFRED E. SMITH HOUSES

TWEED COURTHOUSE

CITY HALL

CITY HALL PARK

House Sq

Ave of the Finest

Robert F. Wagner Sr. Pl.

Park Row

Theatre Alley

Spruce St

BROOKLYN BRIDGE

Frankfort St

Pearl St

Beekman St

SOUTH BRIDGE RESIDENTAL TOWER

FDR DRIVE

Fulton St

Nassau St

William St

Ann St

Gold St

SOUTH ST SEAPORT HISTORICAL DISTRICT

Peck Slip

RLD TRADE CENTER

If you haven't had the crab soup dumplings at Joe's Shanghai on Pell Street, you should.

💲 ATMs

- 1. Abacus • 181 Canal St.
- 2. Bank of New York • 233 Broadway
- 3. Chase • 281 Broadway
- 4. Chase • 180 Canal St.
- 5. Chase • 214 Broadway
- 6. Chase • 407 Broadway
- 7. Chase • 423 Canal St.
- 8. Citibank • 164 Canal St.
- 9. Citibank • 2 Mott St.
- 10. Citibank • 415 Broadway
- 11. Citibank • 250 Broadway
- 12. Dime • 221 Canal St.
- 13. Fleet • 50 Bayard St.
- 14. Fleet • 260 Canal St.
- 15. Marine Midland • 110 W. Broadway
- 16. Marine Midland • 212 Broadway
- 17. Marine Midland • 254 Canal St.
- 18. Marine Midland • 268 Canal St.
- 19. Marine Midland • 27 E. Broadway
- 20. Marine Midland • 29 Bowery
- 21. Marine Midland • 50 Bowery
- 22. Republic National • 17 Chatham Sq.
- 23. Republic National • 265 Broadway

🌼 Community Gardens

- Forsyth St. Garden • Delancey and Forsyth
- Fishbridge Park • 338-340 Pearl St.

🏥 Hospital

- NYU Downtown Hospital • 170 William St.

★ Landmarks

- Bridge Cafe • Corner of Dover & Water St.
- Chinatown Ice Cream Factory • Bayard St
- City Hall • Park Row and Broadway
- Doyers St. (Bloody Angle) • Doyers St.
- Hall of Records • Chambers and Park Row
- Happy Mazza Media • 2 E. Broadway
- Municipal Building • Chambers and Park Row
- The Dream House • 275 Church St.
- Tweed Courthouse • Chambers and Broadway

📖 Libraries

- New Amsterdam • 9 Murray St.
- Chatham Square • 33 E.Broadway

👮 Police Precinct

- 5th Precinct • 19 Elizabeth St.

✉ Post Offices

- Canal St • 350 Canal St.
- Chinatown • 6 Doyers St.
- Church St. Station • 90 Church St.
- Peck Slip • 1 Peck Slip

🎓 Schools

- Drake Business School • 225 Broadway
- IS 131 Dr. Sun Yat Sen School • 100 Hester St.
- Murray Bergtraum High School • 411 Pearl St.
- On The Record School • 225 Broadway
- PS 124 • Confucius Plaza
- PS 126 • Catherine St.
- PS 130 DeSoto School • 143 Baxter St.
- Pace University • 1 Pace Plaza
- Satellite Academy Program • 51 Chambers St.
- Stenotype Academy • 15 Park Row

City Hall MAP

© 24-Hour Copy Centers

- Blumberg Excelsior Copy • 66 White St.
- Kinko's • 105 Duane St.

Gyms

- Hardcore Muscle & Fitness • 25 Park Pl.
- New York Sports Clubs • 30 Cliff St.
- New York Sports Clubs • 151 Reade St.
- Oishi Judo Club • 79 Leonard St.
- Tribeca Gym • 79 Worth St.
- Xie He Jian Kang Center • 302 Broome St.

Hardware Stores

- 831 VCD Shop • 13 Elizabeth St.
- Central Industrial Supply • 446 Broadway
- Centre Plumbing & Hardware • 233 Centre St.
- Chinatown 25 Cents Store • 7 Elizabeth St.
- CK & L Hardware • 307 Canal St.
- Design Source • 107 Bowery
- EK Fastener • 41 Warren St.
- East Broadway Appliance Hardware • 59 E. Broadway
- Grand Hardware • 99 Chrystie St.
- Kessler Hardware • 229 Grand St.
- Lendy Electric Equipment • 176 Grand St.
- Lucky Home Center • 100 Lafayette St.
- Mott Hardware • 52 Kenmare St.
- T&Y Hardware • 101 Chrystie St.
- Wei Qiang Zheng • 55 Chrystie St.
- Weinstein & Holtzman Inc • 29 Park Row
- World Construction Inc • 78 Forsyth St.

Laundromats

- 121 Elizabeth St. Laundromat • 121 Elizabeth St.
- Chinese Hand Laundry • 149 Canal St.
- Kaos Laundry • 66 Frankfort St.
- Long Giang Dang Laundromat • 168 Elizabeth St.
- New Laundromat • 81 Canal St.
- PJ Chinese Laundry • 30 Grand St.
- Wonder Wash & Dry • 10 Elizabeth St.

Liquor Stores

- Bowery Discount Wine & Liquors • 133 Bowery
- Brite Buy Wines & Spirits • 11 Ave. of the Americas
- Eighty Eight Wines & More Inc. • 57 Grand St.
- Sam Wai Liquor Store • 17 E. Broadway
- Walker Liquors • 101 Lafayette St.
- Wine Wo Liquor Discount Ctr • 24 Bowery

Pet Store

- Aqua Star Pet Shop • 172 Mulberry St.

Video Rentals

- 323 Canal Video Inc. • 323 Canal St.
- 831 VCD Shop • 13 Elizabeth St.
- Charming Video Inc • 200 Centre St.
- J & R Music World • 23 Park Row
- JNK Video • 202 Mott St.
- Laser Video Center • 97 Chrystie St.
- Terence Video • 282 Grand St.
- USA Shenchow Trading Corp • 125 Canal St.
- UE Enterprises Center • 153 Centre St.
- UE Enterprises Inc. • 118 Mott St.

Kenmare St

Broome St

Centre Market Pl

Grand St

Broadway

Thompson St

Wooster St

Greene St

Mercer St

Howard St

Hester St

Lispenard St

Walker St

White St

Franklin St

Leonard St

Worth St

Thomas St

Duane St

Reade St

Chambers St

Warren St

Murray St

Park Pl

Barclay St

Fulton St

Dey St

Church St

Trimble

W. Broadway

Ave of the Americas

Benson Pl

Cortlandt Alley

Catherine Lane

Lafayette St

Canal St

Baxter St

Mulberry St

Mott St

Elizabeth St

Bayard St

Pell St

Moscow St

Doyers St

Division St

Hogan St

D.M.V.

Worth St

N.Y. COUNTY COURTHOUSE

Pearl St

U.S. COURT HOUSE

Cardinal Hayes Pl

Park Row

FEDERAL PLAZA

Foley Sq

TWEED COURTHOUSE

MUNICIPAL BLDG

CITY HALL

NR

CITY HALL PARK

House Sq

Park Row

POLICE PLAZA

CONFUCIUS PLAZA

Chatham Sq

CHATHAM GREEN HOUSES

Madison St

Pearl St

E. Broadway

Henry St

Catherine St

Oliver St

St. James Pl

James St

GOV. ALFRED E. SMITH HOUSES

Ave of the Finest

BROOKLYN BRIDGE

Robert F. Wagner Sr. Pl

Spruce St

Beekman St

William St

Ann St

Gold St

Frankfort St

SOUTH BRIDGE RESIDENTIAL TOWER

Pearl St

Peck Slip

SOUTH ST SEAPORT HISTORICAL DISTRICT

FDR Dr

Theatre Alley

Nassau St

WORLD TRADE CENTER

WTC

SARA D ROOSEVELT PK

Forsyth St

Eldridge St

Christie St

Bowery St

MANHATTAN BRIDGE

Chatham Square is a quiet, pastoral intersection that allows plenty of time for relaxation during the day, since you'll be sitting in a shockingly hellish traffic snarl (due to the fact that it is the intersection of NINE streets, four bus lines, and every police and fire vehicle in the city). The Brooklyn Bridge is best approached from Pearl Street. Be careful about driving east on Canal Street—you have to make a right on Bowery or else you'll drive over the Manhattan Bridge (Canal Street is one-way going west between Bowery and Chrystie). Forget about parking during the day.

Subways

① ② ③ ⑨	Chambers St.
① ⑨	Franklin St.
① ⑨	Cortlandt St.
② ③	Park Pl.
② ③ ④ ⑤	Fulton St. - Broadway Nassau
Ⓐ Ⓒ Ⓙ Ⓜ Ⓩ	Fulton St. - Broadway Nassau
④ ⑤ ⑥	Brooklyn Bridge
⑥ Ⓝ Ⓡ Ⓙ Ⓜ Ⓩ	Canal St.
Ⓐ Ⓒ	Chambers St.
Ⓐ Ⓒ Ⓔ	Canal St.
Ⓑ Ⓓ Ⓠ	Grand St.
Ⓒ Ⓔ	Cortlandt St.
Ⓙ Ⓜ	Bowery
Ⓙ Ⓜ Ⓩ	Chambers St.
Ⓝ Ⓡ	City Hall

Bus Lines

⑥①/⑤①	Lafayette & Canal Sts.
①	Broadway & Centre St.
⑥	Church St. and Broadway
⑨	Park Row
⑩	W. Broadway
⑮	E. Broadway & Park Row
㉒	Chambers & Madison St.
⑩③	Bowery & Park Row

⊙ Car Rental
• National Car Rental • 138 Reade St.

Ⓟ Gas Station
• Park On Auto Service • 75 Kenmare St.

Ⓟ Parking Garages
• Central Parking • 169 William St.
• Chatham Parking • 180 Park Row
• Clara Parking • 61 Chrystie St.
• Edison • 343 Broadway
• Edison • 174 Centre St.
• Edison • 10 Peck Slip
• Edison • 142 Grand St.
• Edison • 204 Lafayette St.
• Edison • 288 Pearl St.
• Edison • 167 Front St.
• Ivory Car Park • 332 Pearl St.
• Izadi Enterprises • 108 Leonard St.
• MTP Chrystie Corp • 89 Chrystie St.
• Park On Auto • 196 Mulberry St.
• Park Right • 35 Reade St.
• Rapid Park Industries • 25 Beekman St.
• Reade Parking • 75 Reade St.

Rivington St

Suffolk St

Clinton St

Attorney St

Ridge St

SAMUEL GOMPERS HOUSES

WILLIAMSBURG BRIDGE

Ped. BR

CORLEARS HOOKS

Delancey St

Broome St

Pitt St

Willett St

Abraham Kazan St

Cannon St

Lewis St

HILLMAN HOUSES

Allen St

Orchard St

Ludlow St

Essex St

Norfolk St

Grand St

Samuel Dickstein Plz

VLADECK HOUSES

CORLE. HOO. PARK

Seward Park Houses

SEWARD PARK HOUSES

Jackson St

Gouverneur St

Hester St

W.H. SEWARD PARK

E. Broadway

Henry St

Madison St

Montgomery St

Gouverneur St

Eldridge St

Canal St

Jefferson St

Margin

Division St

Pier

LA GUARDIA HOUSES

Forsyth St

Pike St

Ruttgers St

Cherry St

FDR DRIVE

RUTGERS HOUSES

South St

Pier 42

RUTGERS PARK

MANHATTAN BRIDGE

East River

Market St

Monroe St

KNICKER-BOCKER VILLAGE

Water St

Catherine St

GOV. ALFRED E. SMITH HOUSES

BROOKLYN BRIDGE

The Lower East Side is the home of Kossar's Bialys on Grand Street between Essex and Norfolk—they make the best bialys ever, period.

💰 ATMs
- 1. Banco Popular • 134 Delancey St.
- 2. Chase • 108-109 Delancey St.
- 3. Citibank • 411 Grand St.
- 4. Emigrant • 465 Grand St.
- 5. Fleet • 318 Grand St.

🅑 Bagels
- Kossar's Bagels and Bialys • 367 Grand St.
- Kossar's Bagels and Bialys • 39 Essex St

✿ Community Gardens
- Lower East Side People Care • 25 Rutgers St.
- P.S. 134 • 293 E. Broadway

🄷 Hospital
- Gouverneur Hospital • 227 Madison St.

★ Landmarks
- Bialystoker Synagogue • 7-11 Willet St.
- Eldridge St. Synagogue • 12 Eldridge St.
- Lower East Side Tenement Museum • 90 Orchard St.

📖 Library
- Seward Park • 192 E. Broadway

℞ 24-Hour Pharmacy
- Rite Aid • 408 Grand St.

🄿 Police Precinct
- 7th Precinct • 19 1/2 Pitt St.

✉ Post Offices
- Knickerbocker • 130 E. Broadway
- Pitt Station • 185 Clinton St.

🄢 Schools
- IS 131 Dr. Sun Yat Sen School • 100 Hester St.
- JHS 056 Corlears School • 220 Henry St.
- PS 001 Alfred E. Smith School • 8 Henry St.
- PS 002 Meyer London School • 122 Henry St.
- PS 020 Anna Silver School • 166 Essex St.
- PS 042 Benjamin Altman School • 71 Hester St.
- PS 110 F. Nightingale School • 285 Delancey St.
- PS 124 Yung Wing School • 40 Division St.
- PS 126 Jacob Riis School • 80 Catherine St.
- PS 134 Henrietta Szold School • 293 E. Broadway
- PS 137 John L Bernstein School • 327 Cherry St.
- PS 142 Amalia Castro School • 100 Attorney St.
- Seward Park High School • 350 Grand St.
- Mesivta Tifereth Jerusalem • 141 E. Broadway

Lower East Side MAP

Rivington St

Samuel Gompers Houses

Delancey St

WILLIAMSBURG BRIDGE

CORLE HOO

Broome St

Pitt St

Willett St

Abraham Kazan St

Cannon St

Lewis St

HILLMAN HOUSES

Suffolk St

Clinton St

Attorney St

Ridge St

Orchard St

Ludlow St

Essex St

Norfolk St

Grand St

SEWARD PARK HOUSES

SAMUEL DICKSTEIN PLZ

VLADECK HOUSES

Jackson St

CO

Allen St

Forsyth St

SEWARD PARK HOUSES

Clinton St

Henry St

Madison St

Gouverneur St

Montgomery St

Gouverneur St

Hester St

W.H. SEWARD PARK

E. Broadway

Jefferson St

LA GUARDIA HOUSES

Eldridge St

Canal St

Division St

Rutgers St

Cherry St

Pike St

South St

FDR DRIVE

Pier 42

Forsyth St

RUTGERS HOUSES

MANHATTAN BRIDGE

RUTGERS PARK

Market St

Monroe St

KNICKER-BOCKER VILLAGE

Catherine St

Water St

GOV. ALFRED E. SMITH HOUSES

East River

BROOKLYN BRIDGE

Gym

- Xie He Jian Kang Center • 302 Broome St.

Hardware Stores

- East Broadway Appliance Hardware • 59 E. Broadway
- Fung Chung Hardware • 154A E. Broadway
- General Machinery • 358 Broome St.
- Grand Home Center • 302 Grand St.
- HH Hardware • 95 Rivington St.
- International Electrical • 77 Allen St.
- Karlee Hardware • 98 E. Broadway
- Kessler Hardware • 229 Grand St.

Laundromats

- 101 Allen Laundrymat • 101 Allen St.
- AK Laundromat • 95 Rivington St.
- City Laundry • 48 Hester St.
- Fairy Laundry • 90 Pitt St.
- Mayco Fashion • 62 Orchard St.
- New Laundromat • 81 Canal St.
- O'Henry Laundromat • 37 Henry St.
- Tai Looney Laundromat • 299 Broome St.

Liquor Stores

- Good Time Liquor • 135 Division St.
- Ivory Wines & Liquors • 563 Grand St.
- Jade Fountain Liquor • 123 Delancey St.
- Loon Chun Liquor • 47 Pitt St.
- Sam Wai Liquor Store • 17 E. Broadway
- Seward Park Liquors Inc • 393 Grand St.

Pet Stores

- Petland • 85 Delancey St.
- Sammy Aquarium • 11 Essex St.
- Pet Projects Unlimited • 75 Montgomery St.

Video Rentals

- Blockbuster Video• 237 Cherry St.
- City Video • 79 Allen St.
- Loeung Sik Chi • 14 Orchard St.
- Magic King Video • 403 Grand St.
- Terence Video • 282 Grand St.
- The Video Store • 128 Rivington St.
- U S A Shenchow Trading Corp • 125 Canal St.
- Yang Ying • 88 E. Broadway
- Yeung Chi Ho • 70A Canal St.

Lower East Side MAP

TOWERS

Rivington St

SAMUEL
GOMPERS
HOUSES

WILLIAMSBURG BRIDGE

Ped. BR

J M Z

Delancey St

CORLEARS
HOOKS

Broome St

HILLMAN HOUSES

Pitt St

Willett St

Abraham Kazan St

Cannon St

Lewis St

Norfolk St

Grand St

14

Clinton St

SAMUEL
DICKSTEIN
PLZ

500

Seward St

Essex St

Ludlow St

Orchard St

Allen St

SEWARD
PARK
HOUSES

SEWARD
PARK
HOUSES

VLADECK
HOUSES

CORLEARS
HOOK
PARK

Jackson St

15

W.H.
SEWARD
PARK

Hester St

East Broadway

Henry St

Madison St

Montgomery St

Gouverneur St

Gouverneur St

Eldridge St

Canal St

Jefferson St

F

LA GUARDIA
HOUSES

Margin

Division St

G

Pier

Forsyth St

15

22

Rutgers St

Cherry St

FDR DRIVE

Pier 42

Pike St

RUTGERS
HOUSES

South St

South St

RUTGERS
PARK

MANHATTAN BRIDGE

Monroe St

Market St

Catherine St

Water St

GOV.
ALFRED E. SMITH
HOUSES

*East
River*

BROOKLYN BRIDGE

If they ever finish working on the Williamsburg Bridge, it'll be great—four lanes in either direction and a reconstructed J/M/Z line (currently not running across the bridge). Until then, it will suck, just like it always has.

Subways

(B)(D)(Q) .... Grand St.

(F) .... Delancey St.

(J)(M)(Z) .... Essex St.

Bus Lines

[21/51] ....Forsyth St.

[15/39] ....Delancey St.

[9] .... E. Broadway & Essex St.

[14] .... Grand St.

[15] .... Allen St.

[22] .... Madison St.

Gas Station

• Mobil • 2 Pike St.

(P) Parking Garages

• Area Garage Corp • 275 Delancey St.
• Central Parking • 135 Delancey St.
• Kinney • 105 Essex St.
• Municipal Lot • Broome & Ludlow Sts.
• Parking • 40 Henry St.
• Square Plus Operating • 47-59 Henry St.
• Water & South Garage • 223 South St.

West Village MAP

W 15th St

W 14th St

Little W 12th St

Gansevoort St

Horatio St

Jane St

W 12th St

Bethune St

Bank St

W 11th St

Perry St

Charles St

W 10th St

Christopher St

Grove St

Commerce St

Barrow St

Morton St

Leroy St

Clarkson St

W Houston St

King St

Charlton St

Van Dam St

Spring St

Dominick St

Broome St

Canal St

HOLLAND TUNNEL

Hudson River

WEST SIDE HIGHWAY

Ninth Av

Eighth Av

Washington St

Greenwich St

West St

Charles Ln

Washington St

Greenwich St

Hudson St

Varick St

W 13th St

Greenwich Av

Waverly Pl

W 4th St

Bleecker St

Seventh Av South

Jones St

Cornelia St

Bedford St

Carmine St

Sheridan Sq

Gay St

Washington Pl

W 12th St

W 11th St

W 10

W 9th St

W 8th St

Waverly

W 4th St

W 3rd St

Minetta La

Bleecker St

MacDougal St

Sullivan St

Prince

Spring

Avenue of The Americas (Sixth Av)

St. Luke's Pl

JAMES J. WALKER PARK

Bloomfield St

Renwick St

Hamersley St

💰 ATMs
- 1. Chase Manhattan • 158 W. 14th St.
- 2. Chase Manhattan • 20 W. 4th St.
- 3. Chase Manhattan • 302 W. 12th St.
- 4. Chase Manhattan • 245 Hudson St.
- 5. Citibank • 75 Christopher St.
- 6. Dime Savings • 340 Ave. of the Americas
- 7. Republic National • 101 W. 14th St.

⭕ Bagels
- Bagel Buffet • 406 Sixth Ave.
- Bagelry • 510 Hudson St.
- Famous Bagel Buffet • 510 Ave. of the Americas
- Murray's Bagels • 500 Ave. of the Americas
- New World Coffee • 448 Ave. of the Americas

✳️ Community Garden
- City-As-School HS (EIG) • 16 Clarkson St.

🅷 Hospitals
- St. Vincent's Hospital & Medical Center • 153 W. 11th St.
- St. Vincent's AIDS Center • 412 Ave. of the Americas

★ Landmarks
- Jefferson Market Courthouse • 425 Ave. of the Americas
- Chumley's • 86 Bedford St.
- The Ear Inn • Washington & Spring
- Stonewall • 53 Christopher St.
- White Horse Tavern • 567 Hudson St.
- Westbeth Building • Washington & Bethune

📖 Libraries
- Hudson Park • 66 Leroy St.
- Jefferson Market • 425 Ave. of the Americas

℞ 24-Hour Pharmacy
- Duane Reade • 378 Sixth Ave.

🅿 Police Precinct
- 6th Precinct • 233 W. 10th St.

✉ Post Offices
- Village • 201 Varick St.
- West Village • 527 Hudson St.

🅢 Schools
- Chelsea Vocational High School • 131 Sixth Ave.
- Empire State College-State University of New York • 225 Varick St.
- Executive High School Internship Program • 16 Clarkson St.
- Joffrey Ballet School • 434 Ave. of the Americas
- Merce Cunningham Studio • 463 West St.
- PS 3 The Charette School • 490 Hudson St.
- PS 41 Greenwich Village School • 116 W. 11th St.
- PS 721 Manhattan Occupational Training School • 250 W. Houston St.
- St. Vincent's Hospital Medical School • 153 W. 11th St.
- St. Vincent's Hospital School of Nursing • 27 Christopher St.

West Village MAP

W 15th St
W 14th St
W 13th St
Ninth Av
Little W 12th St
Gansevoort St
Horatio St
Jane St
W 12th St
Bethune St
Bank St
W 11th St
Perry St
Charles St
W 10th St
Christopher St
Grove St
Barrow St
Morton St
Leroy St
Clarkson St

Abingdon Sq
Greenwich Av
Waverly Pl
W 4th St
Eighth Av
Bleecker St
PATH
Commerce St
Bedford St
St. Luke's Pl
JAMES J.
WALKER PARK

W 12th St
W 11th St
W 10th St
W 9th St
W 8th St
Sheridan Sq
Waverly Pl
Washington Pl
Seventh Av South
Jones St
Cornelia St
W 4th St
W 3rd St
Minetta La
Carmine St
Bleecker St
MacDougal St
Sullivan St
Prince St

Avenue of The Americas (Sixth Av)

Gay St

Washington St
Charles Ln
Greenwich St

WEST SIDE HIGHWAY

Hudson River

West St

W Houston St
Hudson St
King St
Charlton St
Van Dam St
Spring St
Varick St

Dominick St
Broome St
Watts St
Canal St
Renwick St
HOLLAND TUNNEL
Spring St
Grand St

400 460 300 400 300 200 150 100 70 62 60
240 2 138 130 180 90 244 16 236

24-Hour Diners
- French Roast • 78 W. 11th St.
- Gray's Papaya • 402 Sixth Ave.
- Florent • Gansevoort St.

Gyms
- Crunch Fitness • 666 Greenwich St.
- New York Sports Club • 125 Seventh Ave. South
- Printing House Fitness & Racquet Club • 421 Hudson St.
- Revolution Studios • 104 W. 14th St.
- Serge Gym • 451 West St.
- West Village Workout • 140 Charles St.

Hardware Stores
- Alternative Housewares & Hardware • 710 Greenwich St.
- Barney's Hardware • 467 Sixth Ave.
- Blaustein Paint & Hardware • 304 Bleecker St.
- Chelsea Hardware & Supply • 104 Charlton St.
- Garber Hardware • 49 Eighth Ave.
- Hardware Mart • 151 W. 14th St.
- Lock-It-Hardware • 59-61 Carmine St.
- Nanz Custom Hardware • 20 Vandam St.
- Nocetti Hardware • 11 Carmine St.

Laundromats
- Bank St. Laundromat • 296 W. 4th St.
- BK Jackson Heights Laundromat • 48 Carmine St.
- Brigton Clean • 267 W. 15th St.
- Broome St. Laundromat • 512 Broome St.
- Chelsea Laundromat • 156 W. 15th St.
- Chin's Chinese Laundromat • 149 W. 13th St.
- Greenwich Laundromat • 112 Greenwich Ave.
- Jerri's Cleaners & Launders • 444 Ave. of the Americas
- Kim Grace Laundromat & Dry Cleaners • 71 Seventh Ave. South
- L&S Chinese Laundry & Dry Cleaning • 643 Hudson St.
- Lee Ngun Mui • 304 W. 4th St.
- Lina Laundromat • 256 W. 15th St.
- R&S Bedford Laundry • 62 Bedford St
- RS Laundry • 72 Bedford St.
- SMG Laundry • 328 W. 15th St.
- Suds Cafe Laundromat • 141 W. 10th St.
- Superior Laundry • 227 Waverly Pl.
- Village Cleaners • 66 Carmine St.
- Village Dry Clean Laundromat Service • 321 W. 11th St.

- Village Laundercenter • 146 W. 4th St.
- Waterworks 2 • 24 Charles St.
- You's Cornelia Street Laundromat • 30 Cornelia St.

Liquor Stores
- Casa Liquor & Wine • 258 Sixth Ave.
- Castle Wines & Liquors • 168 Seventh Ave. S
- Christopher St. Liquor Shoppe • 45 Christopher St.
- Crossroads Wine & Liquor • 55 W. 14th St.
- Golden Rule Wine & Liquor • 457 Hudson St.
- Imperial Liquors • 579 Hudson St.
- Manley's Liquor Store • 35 Eighth Ave.
- North Village Wine & Liquor • 254 W. 14th St.
- Sea Grape Wine & Spirits • 512 Hudson St.
- Spring Street Wine Shop • 187 Spring St.
- Village Vinter • 448 Ave. of the Americas
- Village Wine & Spirits • 486 Ave. of the Americas
- Young's Liquor Store • 135 Waverly Pl.

Movie Theatres
- Art Greenwich • 97 Greenwich Ave.
- Film Forum • 209 W. Houston St.
- Tripod Room • 515 Greenwich St.
- Clearview's Waverly Twin • 323 Sixth Ave.
- Hudson Park Conservancy • Pier 54 at 13th St.

Pet Stores
- Beasty Feast • 237 Bleecker St.
- Beasty Feast • 680 Washington St.
- Beasty Feast • 630 Hudson St.
- Groom-O-Rama • 496 Ave. of the Americas
- Pet Palace • 109 W. 10th St.
- Pet's Kitchen • 116 Christopher St.
- Petland Discounts • 389 Avenue of Americas
- Urban Pets • 18 Christopher St.

Video Rentals
- Cin Video • 354 West St.
- Crazy Fantasy Video • 333 Sixth Ave.
- Evergreen Video • 37 Carmine St.
- Kim's Video III • 144 Bleecker St.
- Mrs. Hudson's Video Take-Away • 573 Hudson St.
- The Hellfire Club • 673 Hudson St.
- Video Diner Club Limited • 357 West St.
- Video Oyster • 137 W. 12th St.
- World of Video • 51 Greenwich Ave.

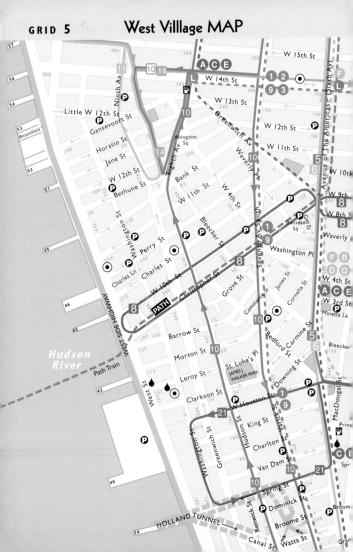

As more and more people flow into the West Village, the tougher it's becoming to park anywhere east of Washington St. The Holland Tunnel is almost always jammed, especially from the Varick St. approach. Try the Broome St. approach instead.

Subways

1 **9**	Christopher St. at Sheridan Sq.
1 **9**	Hudson St. at Varick St.
1 **2** **3** **9**	14th St. at 7th Ave.
C **E**	Spring St. at 6th Ave.
A **C** **E** **B** **D** **F** **Q**	W. 4th St. at 6th Ave.
A **C** **E** **L**	14th St. at 8th Ave.
F **L**	14th St. at 6th Ave.

Bus Lines

10	7th Ave./8th Ave./Central Park West
11	9th Ave./10th Ave.
14	14th St. Crosstown
10	Abingdon Sq.
8	8th/9th St. Crosstown
21	Houston St. Crosstown
6	7th Ave./Ave. of the Americas/Broadway
5	5th Ave./Ave. of the Americas/Riverside Dr.

⊙ Car Rentals

- Autorent Car Rental • 412 West St.
- Dollar Rent A Car • 99 Charles St.
- Hertz Car Rental • 18 Morton St.
- United Car Rental • 575 Washington St.
- Zuppa Brothers Downtown Office • 145 W. 14th St.

◆ Car Washes

- Two Guys General Auto Repair Inc. • 160 Leroy St.
- Village Car Wash & Lube • 359 West St.
- Carz-A-Poppin Carwash • 124 Ave. of the Americas

P Gas Stations

- Getty • 63 Eighth Ave.
- Mobil • 140 Ave. of the Americas

P Parking Garages

- 3 Sheridan Square Parking • 3 Sheridan Sq.
- 756 Parking • 756 Washington
- Apple West 11th St. Garage • 332 W. 11th St.
- Broome-Thompson S. Garage • 520 Broome St.
- Chivian Garage • 101 W. 12th St.
- Clara Parking • 243 Hudson St.
- Dover Garage 2 • 534 Hudson St.
- Edison NY Parking • 161 Varick St.
- Edison NY Parking • 10 Ninth Ave.
- Elfy Parking • 97 Charles St.
- Flannery Parking System • 388 Hudson St.
- Garage Management • 160 W. 10th St.
- Garage Management • 122 W. 3rd St.
- Jan-Bar Parking • 122 Varick St.
- Kinney System • 20 Morton St.
- Mayor Parking • Pier 40 West St. & W. Houston St.
- Meat Mkt Garage • 26 Little W. 12th St.
- Metro Parking Systems • 214 W. Houston St.
- Mutual Parking • 166 Perry St.
- R S F Parking • 134 W. 10th St.
- United Parking • 575 Washington St.
- Varick Parking • 214 W. Houston St.

PATH Path Stations

- 9th St.-Hoboken & Journal Square • 9th St. at Sixth Ave.
- Christopher St.-Hoboken & Journal Square • Christopher St. west of Hudson St.

This area is the most diverse section of Manhattan and is filled with contradiction. Milano's vs. the B-Bar, Barnes & Noble vs. The Strand, The Back Fence vs. CBGB, etc. Also an architectural "greatest hits." All the purple squares are part of NYU.

$ ATMs

- 1. Amalgamated Bank • 11-15 Union Sq. W.
- 2. Apple Bank • 145 Fourth Ave.
- 3. Chase • 32 University Pl.
- 4. Chase • 756 Broadway
- 5. Chase • 766 Broadway
- 6. Chase • 255 First Ave.
- 7. Chase • 525 Broadway
- 8. Chase • 623 Broadway
- 9. Citibank • 555 LaGuardia Pl.
- 10. Citibank • 72 Fifth Ave.
- 11. Dime • 130 Second Ave.
- 12. Dime • 340 Ave. of the Americas
- 13. EAB • 105 Second Ave.
- 14. Fleet • 72 Second Ave.
- 15. Fleet • 528 Broadway
- 16. Flushing Savings Bank • 33 Irving Pl.
- 17. Marine Midland (HBSC) • 245 First Ave.
- 18. Marine Midland (HBSC) • 10 Union Sq. E.
- 19. Republic National • 1 E. 8th St

⬤ Bagels

- Bagel Bob's Campus • 51 University Pl.
- Bagel Buffet • 406 Ave. of the Americas
- David's Bagels • 220 First Ave.
- Famous Bagel Buffet • 510 Ave. of the Americas
- Murray's Bagels • 500 Ave. of the Americas
- New World Coffee • 488 Ave. of the Americas

✿ Community Gardens

- Albert's Garden • 16-18 E. 2nd St.
- LaGuardia Garden • Bleecker & La Guardia
- M' finda Kalunga Garden • Forsyth & Stanton
- East Side Greenspace • 404-16 E. 12th St.
- PS 19 • 185 First Ave.
- Forsyth St. Garden • Delancey & Forsyth

⊞ Hospitals

- New York Eye and Ear Infirmary • 310 E. 14th St.
- St Vincent's AIDS Ctr • 412 Ave. of the Americas

★ Landmarks

Bayard-Condict Building • 65 Bleecker St.
CBGB & OMFUG • Bowery & Bleecker Sts.
Colonnade Row • 428 Lafayette St.
Cooper Union • 30 Cooper Sq.
Grace Church • 802 Broadway
Great Jones Fire House • Great Jones & Bowery
Milano's • W. Houston & Mott Sts.
Old Merchant's House • 29 E. 4th St.
The Public Theater • 425 Lafayette St.
Salmagundi Club • 47 Fifth Ave.
Singer Building • 561 Broadway
St. Mark's-in-the-Bowery Church • 131 E. 10th St.
The Strand Bookstore • Broadway & 12th St.
Washington Square Park • Washington Square
Washington Mews • University Pl. (entrance)

▭ Libraries

- Jefferson Market • 425 Ave. of the Americas
- Ottendorfer • 135 Second Ave.

® 24-Hour Pharmacy

- Duane Reade • 378 Ave. of the Americas

▣ Police Precinct

- 9th Precinct • 321 E. 5th St.

✉ Post Offices

- Cooper • 93 Fourth Ave.
- Patchin • 70 W. 10th St.
- Prince • 103 Prince St.

ⓢ Schools

- Allied Health Program in Orthopedics • 310 E. 14th St.
- Chelsea Vocational High School • 131 Fourth Ave.
- Cooper Union • 30 Cooper Sq.
- Eugene Lang College • 65 W. 11th St.
- Institute of Audio Research • 64 University Pl.
- Joffrey Ballet School • 434 Ave. of the Americas
- New Museum • 65 Fifth Ave.
- New School For Social Research • 66 W. 12th St.
- New York University • 70 Washington Sq. S.
- Nikolais And Louis Dance Lab • 375 W. Broadway
- Parson's School of Design • 66 Fifth Ave.
- Pratt Institute • 295 Lafayette St.
- PS 019 Asher Levy School • 185 First Ave.
- PS 751 Career Development Ctr • 113 E. 4th St.

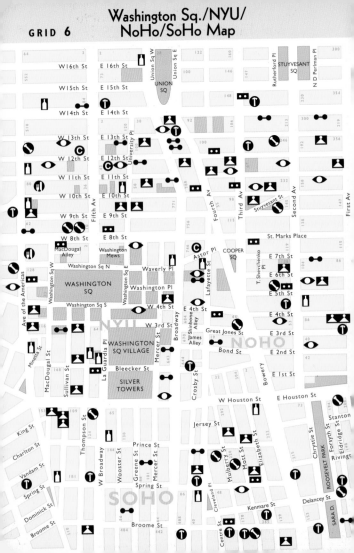

Washington Sq./NYU/ NoHo/SoHo Map

GRID 6

C 24-Hour Copy Centers
- The Village Copier • 20 W. 13th St.
- Kinko's • 24 E. 12th St.
- Kinko's 13-25 Astor Pl.

24-Hour Diners
- French Roast • 78 W. 11th St.
- Gray's Papaya • 402 Sixth Ave.

Gyms
- Crunch Fitness • 404 Lafayette St.
- Crunch Fitness • 54 E. 13th St.
- Crunch International • 88 University Pl.
- David Barton Gym • 623 Broadway
- Dolphin Fitness • 242 E. 14th St.
- Kickboxing Self-Defense USA • 52 E. 7th St.
- Lucille Roberts • 80 Fifth Ave.
- NY Health & Racquet Club • 24 E. 13th St.
- One-on-One Training • 63 Greene St.
- One-on-One Training • 826 Broadway
- Pamela Warshay Fitness • 80 E. 11th St.
- Peter Anthony Fitness • 113 Mercer St.
- Plus One Fitness • 106 Crosby St.
- Shidogakuin • 252 Lafayette St.
- Sol Goldman YM-YWHA • 344 E. 14th St.
- World Gym • 665 Broadway
- Wu Mei Kung Fu • 21 Mott St.
- Xie He Jian Kang Center • 302 Broome St.

Hardware Stores
- 14th St. Hardware • 211 E. 14th St.
- Ace Hardware • 130 Fourth Ave.
- Allied Hardware • 59 Second Ave.
- Barney's Hardware • 467 Sixth Ave.
- Bowery Discount Hardware • 183 Bowery
- Brickman and Sons • 55 First Ave.
- Butler Hardware • 75 Spring St.
- Centre Plumbing & Hardware • 233 Centre St.
- Colon Ross • 129 Allen St.
- East Hardware • 79 Third Ave.
- General Machinery • 358 Broome St.
- H & W Hardware • 220 First Ave.
- Metropolitan Hardware • 175 Spring St.
- Mike's Lumber Store • 7 E. 14th St.
- Mott Hardware • 52 Kenmare St.
- Nanz Custom Hardware • 20 Vandam St.
- OK Hardware • 438 Broome St.
- Saifee Hardware • 114 First Ave.
- Shapiro Hardware • 63 Bleecker St.
- T&Y Hardware • 101 Chrystie St.

Laundromats
- 121 Elizabeth St. Laundromat • 121 Elizabeth St.
- 97 2nd Ave. Launderette • 97 Second Ave.
- Aphrodite French Cleaners • 30 University Pl.
- Chow & Lam • 204 E. 10th St.
- East Village Launderette • 100 First Ave.
- Erasmo's Laundromat • 175 First Ave.
- Greenwich Laundromat • 177 Thompson St.
- Hartz Automatic Laundry • 59 First Ave.
- Home Service Laundromat • 280 Mulberry St.
- ICD • 336 E. 13th St.
- Jerri's Cleaners • 444 Ave. of the Americas
- KT Laundry & Dry Cleaning • 120 W. Third St.
- Lafayette Laundry • 238 Lafayette St.
- Lafayette Laundry & Cleaners • 31 University Pl.
- Launder Center • 60 Third Ave.
- Laundrobot • 202 E. 6th St.
- Laundromat Broome St. • 512 Broome St.
- Laundry on Fourth • 114 Fourth Ave.
- Laundry on Fourth • 70 E. 12th St.
- Long Giang Dang Laundromat • 168 Elizabeth St.
- Louie Benny • 32 E. 13th St.
- MacDougal Laundromat • 56 MacDougal St.
- Mario Laundromat • 211 Thompson St.
- Mercer Launderette • 208 Mercer St.
- Mott St. Cleaners • 242 Mott St.

- Stavros Laundromat • 78 W. 3rd St.
- Tom Yip Han • 219 E. 10th St.
- Village Bleachers • 34 E. 11th St.
- Village Laundercenter • 146 W. 4th St.
- Wash Rite • 112 E. 4th St.
- Weiping Chinese Laundry • 132 Fourth Ave.
- West Lake Laundromat • 149 Sullivan St.
- Wong Kwong Laundry • 147 Sullivan St.

Liquor Stores
- Anthony Liquors • 52 Spring St.
- Astor Wines & Spirits • 12 Astor Pl.
- Casa Liquor & Wine • 258 Sixth Ave.
- Crossroads Wine & Liquor • 55 W. 14th St.
- East Village Wines • 138 First Ave.
- Elizabeth & Vine • 253 Elizabeth St.
- S & P Liquor & Wine • 300 E. 5th St.
- Soho Wine & Spirits Inc. • 461 W. Broadway
- Spring Street Wine Shop • 187 Spring St.
- Thompson Wine & Spirits • 222 Thompson St.
- Union Square Wine & Spirits • 33 Union Sq W
- Village Vintner • 448 Ave. of the Americas
- Village Wine & Spirits • 486 Ave. of the Americas
- Warehouse Wines & Spirits • 735 Broadway
- Washington Sq. Wine & Liquor • 545 La Guardia Pl.
- Zeekman B&S • 47 University Pl.

Movie Theatres
- Angelika Film Center • 18 W. Houston St.
- Anthology Film Archives • 32 Second Ave.
- Astor Place Theatre • 434 Lafayette St.
- Black Star Bar • 92 Second Ave.
- Cinema Classics • 332 E. 11th St.
- Cinema Village • 22 E. 12th St.
- City Cinemas: Village East • 189 Second Ave.
- Clearview's Waverly Twin • 323 Sixth Ave.
- Fez • 380 Lafayette St.
- King Juan Carlos I Center • 53 Washington Sq. S.
- Loews Village • 66 Third Ave.
- Millennium • 66 E. 4th St.
- New School • 66 W. 12th St.
- NY Open Cine • De Salvo Pk, Mulberry & Spring St.
- NYU Cantor Film Center • 36 E. 8th St.
- Quad Cinema • 34 W. 13th St.
- St. Mark's-in-the-Bowery Archives • 131 E. 10th St.
- United Artists: Union Sq 14 • Broadway at 13th St.

Pet Stores
- Afishionado • 28 W. 8th St.
- Animal Cracker • 26 First Ave.
- Aqua Star Pet Shop • 172 Mulberry St.
- Creature Features • 3 Great Jones St.
- Groom-O-Rama • 496 Ave. of the Americas
- JBJ Discount Pet Shop • 151 E. Houston St.
- New World Aquarium • 5 W. 8th St.
- Pacific Aquarium & Plant Inc. • 46 Delancey St.
- Pet Bar • 132 Thompson St.
- Pet Canteen • 219 Mulberry St.
- Pet Club • 244 E. 13th St.
- Pet's Garden • 239 E. 5th St.
- Petland Discounts • 389 Avenue of Americas
- Whiskers • 235 E. 9th St.
- Win Tropical Aquariums • 169 Mott St.

Video Rentals
- Blockbuster Video • 780 Broadway
- Charming Video • 200 Centre St.
- Club Video • 239 E. 5th St.
- Couch Potato Video • 9 E. 8th St.
- Crazy Fantasy Video • 333 Sixth Ave.
- Hollywood Video • 46 Third Ave.
- JNK Video • 202 Mott St.
- Kim's Video • 6 St Mark's Pl.
- Kim's Video III • 144 Bleecker St.
- Kozmo.com • 111 E. 12th St.
- Third Avenue Adult Videos • 127 Third Ave.
- Tla Video • 54 W. 8th St.
- Tower Video • 383 Lafayette St.

Considering how exciting and vibrant this section of the city is, parking should be way worse than it is. Contains one of the subway system's weirdest anomalies—you can only transfer to the B, D, F, Q from the 6 train's downtown track—there is no free transfer from the uptown side.

Subways

6 .... Astor Place
6 .... Bleecker St.
6 .... Spring St.
4 **5** **6** **N** **R** **L** .... Union Square
N **R** .... Eighth St.
N **R** .... Prince St.
C **E** .... Spring St.
A **C** **E** **B** **D** **F** **Q** .... W. 4th St.
L **F** .... 14th St. & Sixth Ave.
L .... 14th St. & Third Ave.
L .... 14th St. & First Ave.
B **D** **F** **Q** .... Broadway- Lafayette
F .... Second Ave.

Bus Lines

1 .... Fifth and Madison Aves.
2 .... Fifth and Madison Aves./Powell Blvd.
3 .... Fifth and Madison Aves./St. Nicholas Ave.
5 .. Fifth Ave./Ave. of the Americas/Riverside Dr.
6 .... 7th Ave./Broadway/Ave. of the Americas
7 .... Columbus Ave./Amsterdam Ave./
Lenox Ave./6th/7th Aves./Broadway
8 .... 8th/9th Sts. Crosstown
9 .... Avenue B/E. Broadway
14 .... 14th St. Crosstown
15 .... First/Second Aves.
21 .... Houston St./Avenue C
101 ... Third Ave./Lexington Ave./Amsterdam Ave.
102 ... Third Ave./Lexington Ave./Malcolm X Blvd.
103 .... Third Ave./Lexington Ave.

Car Rentals

- A1 Rent Car • 303 Bowery
- AA Exotic Rental/Village Rent-A-Car•19 E. 12th St.
- Autorent Car Rental • 307 E. 11th St.
- Avis Rent-A-Car • 68 E. 11th St.
- Enterprise Rent-A-Car • 221 Thompson St.
- Mirkin Alex • 298 Mulberry St.
- National Car Rental • 21 E. 12th St.
- Nationwide Rent-A-Car • 220 E. 9th St.

Car Washes

- Broadway Hand Car Wash • 614 Broadway
- Carz-A-Poppin Carwash • 124 Ave. of the Americas

Gas Stations

- Amoco • 610 Broadway
- Downtown Automotive • 326 Bowery
- Gaseteria • Lafayette & Houston St.
- Mobil • 140 Ave. of the Americas
- Mobil • 24 Second Ave.
- Park On Auto Service • 75 Kenmare St.
- Sunoco • Bowery & E. 3rd St.

Parking

- 395 Parking Corp • 395 Broome St.
- 503 Broadway Parking • 501 Broadway
- Aran • 97 E. Houston St.
- Barcadi Parking • 321 Bowery
- Broome-Thompson St. • 520 Broome St.
- Champion Broadway Parking • 60 E. 8th St.
- Chelnik • 3 Washington Sq. Village
- Chivian Garage • 101 W. 12th St.
- Clara Parking • 61 Chrystie St.
- Edison • 375 Lafayette St.
- Edison • 204 Lafayette St.
- Edison • 174 Centre St.
- Eighth St. Parking • 11 Fifth Ave.
- Flannery Parking • 48 W. 15th St.
- Garage Management • 122 W. 3rd St.
- Garage Management • 21 E. 12th St.
- Garage Management • 2 Fifth Ave.
- Kaladop Park • 557 Broadway
- Kinney System • 310 E. 11th St.
- Kinney System • 224 Mulberry St.
- Manhattan Parking • 73-84 Third Ave.
- Matel • 303 E. 6th St.
- Mercer Parking • 165 Mercer St.
- Randi Parking • 76 E. 13th St.
- Rebuilders Supply • 85 Fourth Ave.
- Smart 66 Parking • 12 E. 13th St.
- Stable Parking • 14 Kenmare St.
- Stewart House • 70 E. 10th St.
- Thompson Street Parking • 221 Thompson St.
- Valet Parking • 7 W. 14th St.

East Village MAP

STUYVESANT TOWN

JOHN MURPHY PARK

East River

E 15th St

E 14th St

E 13th St

E 12th St

E 11th St

E 10th St

E 9th St

E 8th St

E 7th St

E 6th St

E 5th St

E 4th St

E 3rd St

E 2nd St

E 1st St

E. Houston St

Avenue A

Avenue B

Avenue C

Avenue D

Szold Pl

JACOB RIIS HOUSES

Ped. BRIDGE

FDR Drive

JACOB RIIS HOUSES

EAST RIVER PARK

Ped. BRIDGE

LILLIAN WALD HOUSES

TOMPKINS SQUARE PARK

First Av

Marks

VILLAGE VIEW HOUSES

FIRST HOUSES

Mangin

Baruch Pl

BARUCH HOUSES

HAMILTON FISH PARK

Sheriff St

Columbia St

MASARYK TOWERS

SAMUEL GOMPERS HOUSES

Stanton St

Rivington St

Delancey St

Norfolk St

Suffolk St

Clinton St

Attorney St

Ridge St

Pitt St

Eldridge St

Allen St

Orchard St

Ludlow St

Essex St

Lewis St

Broome St

WILLIAMSBURG BRIDGE

Ped. BRI

Thanks to the hard work of many activists, it looks as if we won't have to delete all these community garden icons in the East Village. However, a Citibank on 7th Street and Avenue B would be nice.

💰 ATMs

- 1. Banco Popular • 134 Delancey St.
- 2. Chase • 108-109 Delancey St.
- 3. Chase • 255 First Ave.
- 4. Co-Op • Ave. B and 3rd St.
- 5. EAB • 50 Ave. A
- 6. Marine Midland • 245 First Ave.

⬤ Bagels

- The Bagel Zone • Ave. A between 3rd & 4th Sts.
- David's Bagels • 220 First Ave.

✿ Community Gardens

- 11th St. Block Assoc. • 422 E. 11th St.
- 13th St. Community Garden • 520-522 E. 13th St.
- 368 E. 8th St. Gardening Club •372-374 E. 8th St.
- 55 Avenue C-HDFC • 293-297 E. 4th St.
- 600 B/C E. 9th Block Assoc. • 632-636 E. 9th St.
- 6BC Botanical Garden • 624-628 E. 6th St.
- 6th St. & Ave. B Garden • 78-92 Ave. B
- 9th St. Community Garden • 144 Ave. C
- 9th St. Community Garden • 703 E. 9th St.
- All Peoples Garden • 293-295 E. 3rd St.
- All The Way • 350-54 E. 4th St.
- Allied Productions • 247 E. 2nd St.
- Ave. B Block Association • 209 Ave. B
- Avenue B Community Garden • 200-198 Ave. B
- Bello Amanecer Borincano • 117-121 Ave. C
- Brisas Del-Caribe • 237 E. 3rd St.
- CAMPOS • 640-644 E. 12th St.
- Children's Garden • S/W Corner 12th St. & Ave. B
- Comm. of Poor People in Action • 171 Stanton St.
- Coradan Evaeden • 603 E. 11th St.
- Creative Little Garden • 530 E. 6th St.
- De Colores • 311-313 E. 8th St.
- Earth People • 333-335 E. 8th St.
- East 2nd Street Block Assoc. • 236-238 E. 2nd St.
- East Side Comm. High School • 404-16 E. 12th St.
- East Side Story • 276 E. 3rd St.
- East Third (A-B) Block Assoc. • 194-196 E. 3rd St.
- El Jardin Del Paradiso • 706-716 E. 5th St.
- El Jardin Del Paradiso •
  718 E. 5th St./ 311-321 E. 4th St.
- El Sol Brillante • 522-528 E. 12th St.
- El Sol Brillante HDFC • 537 E. 12th St.
- Fifth St. Slope Garden Club • 626-27 E. 5th St.
- Firemen's Memorial Garden • 358-364 E. 8th St.
- Green Oasis Comm. Gardens • 376-382 E. 9th St.
- Hope Garden • 193 E. 2nd St.
- Iglesia Pentecostal Arca De Salvacion •
  174 Suffolk St.
- Jardin De La Esperanza • 223-225 E. 7th St.
- JHS 22- Environmental School • 415 E. Houston St.
- Kenkeleba House • 212 E. 3rd St.
- Kenkeleba House • 220 E. 2nd St.
- Lower East Side Ecology Center • 215 E. 7th St.
- Pargue De Tranquilidad • 314-318 E. 4th St.
- PS 140 • 123 Ridge St.

- PS 142 • 100 Attorney St.
- PS 019 • 185 First Ave.
- PS 196 • E. Houston St/FDR Dr.
- PS 034 Schoolyard Garden • 730 E. 12th St.
- PS 063 • 121 E. 3rd St.
- Tenants of 268 E. 4th St. • 270-272 E. 4th St.
- The Earth School • 600 E. 6th St.
- The Serenity Gardeners • 626 E. 11th St.
- Urban Botanica Society • 237 E. 7th St.

🏥 Hospital

- New York Eye & Ear Infirmary • 310 E. 14th St.

★ Landmarks

- Bialystoker Synagogue • 7-11 Willet St.
- Charlie Parker House • Ave. B at Tompkins Sq Pk
- Lower Eastside Tenement Museum • 90 Orchard St.
- Tompkins Square Park • Ave. A and 9th St.

📖 Libraries

- Hamilton Fish Park • 415 E. Houston St.
- Tompkins Square • 331 E. 10th St.

🅿 Police Precincts

- 7th Precinct • 19 1/2 Pitt St
- 9th Precinct • 321 E. 5th St.

✉ Post Offices

- Peter Stuyvesant • 432 E. 14th St.
- Tompkins Square • 244 E. 3rd St.

🅢 Schools

- JHS 022 G. Straubenmuller School •
  111 Columbia St.
- JHS 060 Ottilia M. Beha School • 420 E. 12th St.
- JHS 025 Marta Valle School • 145 Stanton St.
- Lower East Side Prep School • 145 Stanton St.
- Manhattan Night Comprehensive HS. •
  240 Second Ave.
- PS 015 Roberto Clemente School • 333 E. 4th St.
- PS 019 Asher Levy School • 185 First Ave.
- PS 020 Anna Silver School • 166 Essex St.
- PS 034 F. D. Roosevelt School • 730 E. 12th St.
- PS 061 Anna Howard Shaw School •
  610 E. 12th St.
- PS 063 William McKinley School •
  121 E. 3rd St.
- PS 064 Robert Simon School • 600 E. 6th St.
- PS 094 • 442 E. Houston St.
- PS 097 Mangin School • 525 E. Houston St.
- PS 140 Nathan Straus School •
  123 Ridge St.
- PS 142 Amalia Castro School •
  100 Attorney St.
- PS 188 John Burroughs School •
  442 E. Houston St.

We think that David's Bagels on First Avenue rocks. We also think that Kim's Video and Two Boots Video have the best selection of movies in Manhattan.

24-Hour Copy Center
• Kinko's • 250 E. Houston St.

24-Hour Diners
• Odessa • Ave A. between 7th & 8th Sts.
• 7A • 7th St. & Ave. A
• Sidewalk Restaurant • 94 Ave. A
• Yaffa Café • 97 St. Mark's Place

Farmer's Market
• Tompkins Square Park • Ave. A and 7th St.

Gyms
• De Mause, Alan • 63 Ave. A
• Dolphin Fitness Club • 155 E. 3rd St.
• Gladiator's Gym • 503 E. 6th St.
• Sol Goldman YM-YWHA • 344 E. 14th St.

Hardware Stores
• Brickman and Sons • 55 First Ave.
• CHP Hardware • 96 Ave. C
• Colon Rosa • 129 Allen St.
• East Side Lumber • 421 E. 13th St.
• H&W Hardware • 220 First Ave.
• HH Hardware • 95 Rivington St.
• I. Rothstein • 56 Clinton St.
• International Electrical • 77 Allen St.
• JR Hardware • 129 Ave. C
• Los Hispanos Floor Covering • 47 Clinton St.
• Rosa Hardware • 85 Pitt St.
• Saifee Hardware • 114 First Ave.

Laundromats
• 01 Allen St. Laundromat • 101 Allen St.
• 14th St. Laundromat • 426 E. 14th St.
• AK Laundromat • 136 Ludlow St.
• Ave. A Laundry King • 97 Ave. A
• Chow & Lee Laundromat • 534 E. 14th St.
• Clinton Laundromat • 19 Clinton St.
• E.V. Laundromat • 286 E. 10th St.
• East Village Launderette • 166 Ave. B
• East Village Launderette • 100 First Ave.
• East Village Launderette • 153 E. 3rd St.
• Erasmo's Laundromat • 175 First Ave.
• Fairy Laundry • 90 Pitt St.
• Hartz Automatic Laundry • 59 First Ave.
• Kim's Laundromat • 208 Ave. A
• KT Laundry & Dry Cleaning • 120 W. 3rd St.
• Launderific • 222 Ave. B
• Power Laundromat • 49 Ave. B
• Sun Sun Dry Cleaning • 116 Stanton St.
• Up & Up Laundromat • 13 Ave. A

Liquor Stores
• Ave. A Wine & Liquor • 196 Ave. A
• Ave. C Liquor • 193 Ave. C
• Bee Liquors • 225 Ave. B
• East Village Wines • 138 First Ave.
• Fung Sing • 138 First Ave.
• Jade Fountain • 123 Delancey St.
• Loon Chun Liquor • 47 Pitt St.
• Nizga Liquors • 58 Ave. A
• Sale Price Liquor • 24 Ave. C
• Vazac Liquor • 178 E. 7th St.

Movie Theatres
• Cinema Classics • 332 E. 11th St.
• Cine-Noir Film Society • Pink Pony, 176 Ludlow St.
• La Vista • 303 E. 8th St.
• Nyurican Poets Café • 236 E. 3rd St.
• Tonic • 107 Norfolk St.

Pet Stores
• Animal Cracker • 26 First Ave.
• Little Creatures • 126 St. Mark's Pl.
• Mikey's Pet Shop • 130 E. 7th St.
• Pacific Aquarium & Plant Inc. • 46 Delancey St.
• Petland • 85 Delancey St.

Video Rentals
• Accidental CD's Records & Tapes • 131 Ave. A
• Alpha Video • 134 Ave. C
• Blockbuster Video • 250 E. Houston St.
• Bus Stop Video Shop • 3 Ave. D
• Kim's Video • 85 Ave. A
• The Video Store • 128 Rivington St.
• Two Boots Video • Ave. A b/w Third & Fourth Sts.

Parking is usually pretty good except for Friday and Saturday night, when the Bridge & Tunnel crowd invades. The East Village badly needs a subway line that has a Tompkins Square Park stop, but it will never happen, no matter how gentrified the neighborhood gets. So you can just forget it.

Subways

F ....Houston St. and 1st Ave.

F J M Z ....Delancey and Essex Sts.

L ....14th St. and 1st Ave.

Bus Lines

8 ....9th and 10th St

9 ....14th St and Ave. B

14 ....14th St and Ave. A/D

15 .... First Ave.

21 ....1st St and Ave. C

8 39 .... Delancey St.

Gas Stations

- Mobil • 253 E. 2nd St.
- Gaseteria • Ave. B/Houston St

Parking

- Area Garage • 275 Delancey St.
- Central Parking System • 135 Delancey St.
- Edison Park Fast • 215 E. Houston St.
- Kinney System • 105 Essex St.

Chelsea MAP

★ Jacob K. Javits Convention Center

Twelfth Av

W 37th St
W 36th St
W 35th St
W 34th St
W 33rd St

WEST SIDE HIGHWAY

★ Post Office ✉ ★

W 31st St ✉ Ⓢ
W 30th St
W 29th St

W 28th St
Chelsea Park Ⓢ
W 27th St

Penn

Station

Eleventh Av

Tenth Av

Ninth Av

Ⓗ South

W 26th St
W 25th St

Houses

W 24th St

W 23rd St
W 22nd St
W 21st St Ⓢ   Ⓢ
W 20th St
W 19th St
W 18th St
W 17th St   Ⓢ
W 16th St ✉
W 15th St
W 14th St

Eighth Av

Hudson River

Chelsea Piers

More services are desperately needed, especially by the Javits Center area (unless you count the services of transvestite prostitutes as "essential"). It's a ghost town at night. Perhaps the future site of Yankee Stadium? Stranger things have happened…

💰 ATMs

- 1. Carver Federal Savings • 261 Eighth Ave.
- 2. Chase Manhattan • 475 W. 23rd St.
- 3. Chase Manhattan • 238 Eighth Ave.
- 4. Citibank • 322 W. 23rd St.
- 5. Citibank • 111 Eighth Ave.
- 6. Fourth Federal Savings • 242 W. 23rd St.

🥯 Bagels

- Chelsea Bagels • 300 W. 23rd St.
- Jo-Jo's Bagel • 346 Ninth Ave.
- Ruthie's Cheesecake & Rugalach • 75 Ninth Ave.

🏥 Hospital

- St. Vincent's Senior Health at Penn South • 365 W. 25th St.

★ Landmarks

- Penn Station • 31th St. and Eighth Ave.
- J.A. Farley Post Office • 30th St. and Eighth Ave.
- Jacob K. Javits Convention Center • 36th St. and Eleventh Ave.

📖 Library

- Muhlenberg • 209 W. 23rd St.

℞ 24-Hour Pharmacy

- Rite Aid • 282 Eighth Ave.

🅟 Police Precinct

- Mid-Town South • 357 W. 35th St.

✉ Post Offices

- JA Farley General • 421 Eighth Ave.
- Morgan General • 341 Ninth Ave.

💲 Schools

- General Theological Seminary • 175 Ninth Ave.
- IS 70 O'Henry School • 333 W. 17th St.
- New York School Of Astrology • 545 Eighth Ave.
- PS 11 William T Harris School • 320 W. 21st St.
- PS 33 Chelsea School • 281 Ninth Ave.
- Tech Career Institutes • 320 W. 31st St.
- Technical Career Institute • 500 Eighth Ave.

Even though this area has several of New York's most happening dance clubs and has seen an amazing increase in the number of art galleries, it's time for Blockbuster to head west towards Eleventh Avenue!

24-Hour Diners
- Moonstruck Diner • 400 W. 24th St.
- Skylight Diner • 402 W. 34th St.
- Tick Tock Diner • 481 Eighth Ave.

Gyms
- American Fitness Centers • 128 Eighth Ave.
- Chelsea Gym • 267 W. 17th St.
- Gleason's Gym • Chelsea Piers-Pier 62
- Origins Feel Good Health Spa • Chelsea Piers-Pier 62
- Sports Center at Chelsea Piers • Chelsea Piers-Pier 60

Hardware Stores
- Busy Bee Hardware • 527 W. 36th St.
- Convenience Travel • 219 Ninth Ave.
- Convention Hardware Center • 191 Ninth Ave.
- Diener Park Lumber & Bldg Supply • 194 Eighth Ave.
- Greenspan Simon Hardware • 261 W 35th St.
- London Paints and Servistar Hardware • 191 Ninth Ave.
- MJ Hardware & Electric • 520 Eighth Ave.
- Mercer Sq. Hardware • 286 Eighth Ave.
- NF Hardware • 219 Ninth Ave.
- Scheman & Grant • 575 Eighth Ave.
- SGS Hardware • 157 Eighth Ave.
- Silver's Hardware • 88 Tenth Ave.
- United Equipment and Supply • 419 Ninth Ave.
- Young Hardware Inc. • 399 Eighth Ave.

Laundromats
- Alice's Laundromat • 164 Eighth Ave.
- Brigton Clean • 267 W. 15th St.
- Chelsea Laundromat • 364 W. 23rd St.
- Everbest Laundromat • 302 W. 21st St.
- Hamid Laundry World • 233 Ninth Ave.
- Lina Laundromat • 256 W. 15th St.
- Lings Laundry • 186 Ninth Ave.
- Princeton Laundry • 450 W. 31st St.
- SMG Laundry • 328 W. 15th St.
- Well More Laundromat • 204 Eighth Ave.

Liquor Stores
- 34th Street Winery • 460 W. 34th St.
- 9th Ave. Wine & Liquor • 474 Ninth Ave.
- Brian's Liquor • 336 Ninth Ave.
- Chelsea Liquor • 114 Ninth Ave.
- Delauren Wines & Liquors • 332 Eighth Ave.
- Grand Liquors • 2049 Eighth Ave.
- Harry's Liquors • 270 W. 36th St• House of Cheers • 261 W. 18th St.
- London Terrace Liquor • 221 9th Ave.
- North Village Wine & Liquor • 254 W. 14th St.
- Philippe Wine & Liquor • 312 W. 23rd St.

Movie Theatres
- Clearview Chelsea • 260 W. 23rd St.
- Gavin Brown's Enterprise • 436 W. 15th St.
- The Kitchen • 512 W. 19th St.

Pet Store
- Barking Zoo • 172 Ninth Ave.

Video Rentals
- Adult Entertainment Center • 448 Eighth Ave.
- Alan's Alley Video • 207A Ninth Ave.
- Blockbuster Video • 128 Eighth Ave.
- Penn Visual • 252 W. 31st St.
- Rina Inc. • 364 W. 23rd St.
- Video Blitz •144 Eighth Ave.

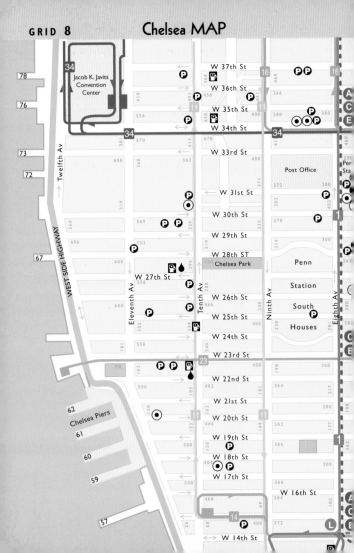

Parking and driving in this area is quite bad during the day and quite good at night, although there just aren't many spots at all above 30th Street.

Subways

Ⓐ Ⓒ Ⓔ Ⓛ ....14th St. at 8th Ave.

Ⓐ Ⓒ Ⓔ ......34th St. at 8th Ave. (Penn Station)

Ⓒ Ⓔ ....23rd St. at 8th Ave.

Bus Lines

⑩ ....7th Ave./8th Ave./Central Park West

⑪ ....9th Ave./10th Ave.

⑭ ....14th St. Crosstown

⑯ ㉞ ....34th St. Crosstown

㉓ ....23rd St. Crosstown

⊙ Car Rentals

• Allstar Rent-A-Car • 325 W. 34th St.
• Autorent Car Rental • 464 W. 18th St.
• Berma Limousine • 537 W. 20th St.
• Hertz Car Rental • 1 Penn Plaza
• Midtown Rent-A-Car • 230 W. 31st St.
• Nationwide Rent-A-Car • 241 W. 26th St.
• New York Rent-A-Car • 325 W. 34th St.
• New York Rent-A-Car • 230 W. 31st St.
• U-Save Auto Rental • 333 Tenth Ave.

◆ Car Washes

• Steve's Detailing & Tires • 516 W. 27th St.
• 235 10th Ave. Car Wash • 235 Tenth Ave.

℗ Gas Stations

• Amoco • 436 Tenth Ave.
• Citigas • Tenth Ave. & 27th St.
• Exxon • 165 Tenth Ave.
• Gaseteria • Tenth Ave. & 36th St.
• Getty • 239 Tenth Ave.
• Getty • 63 Eighth Ave.

℗ Parking

• 15th St. Garage • 422 W. 15th St.
• 509 W. 34 St. Garage • 509 W. 34th St.
• 514 W. 23rd St. Garage • 514 W. 23rd St.
• Albatross Parking • 346 W. 37th St.
• Allied Parking Systems • 451 Tenth Ave.
• Central Parking System • 254 W. 31st St.
• Edison Park Fast • 249 W. 28th St.
• Edison Parking • 524 W. 23rd St.
• Edison Parking • 451 Ninth Ave.
• Fur Parking • 241 W. 28th St.
• George Gibson Parking • 545 W. 25th St.
• Impact Parking • 333 W. 26th St.
• Kaz Systems • 282 Eleventh Ave.
• 320 West 30th St. Garage • 320 W. 30th St.
• 37th Street Parking • 510-515 W. 37th St.
• Meyers Parking Garage • 325 W. 34th St.
• Public Parking • 343 Tenth Ave.
• Public Parking • 516 W. 30th St.
• Public Parking • 530 W. 30th St.
• Rocket 18 Parking • 438 W. 18th St.
• Smart 19 Parking • 438 W. 19th St.
• Square Plus Operating • 1 Penn Plaza
• Square Plus Parking • 300 W. 31st St.
• 349 W. 37th St Garage • 349 W. 37th St.
• United Parking • 249 Tenth Ave.
• United Parking • 279 Tenth Ave.
• Wizard Parking • 320 W 36th St.

If you stand in the middle of traffic at the junction of Broadway, Fifth Avenue, and 24th Street and turn slowly around, you'll see the Flatiron Building, the Met Life Building, the New York Life Building, and the Empire State Building. It's perhaps the single most awe-inspiring spot in all of Manhattan, if you don't get run over.

$ ATMs

- 1. Amalgamated • 11-15 Union Sq. W.
- 2. Atlantic • 100 W. 32nd St.
- 3. Atlantic • 960 Sixth Ave.
- 4. Atlantic • 620 Sixth Ave.
- 5. Bank Leumi • 1400 Broadway
- 6. Bank of New York • 162 Fifth Ave.
- 7. Bank of New York • 350 Fifth Ave.
- 8. Broadway National • 250 Fifth Ave.
- 9. Carver Federal Savings • 261 Eighth Ave.
- 10. Chase Manhattan • 305 Seventh Ave.
- 11. Chase Manhattan • 399 Seventh Ave.
- 12. Chase Manhattan • 33 E. 23rd St.
- 13. Chase Manhattan • 71 W. 23rd St.
- 14. Chase Manhattan • 5 W. 19th St.
- 15. Chase Manhattan • 245 Fifth Ave.
- 16. Chase Manhattan • 349 5Fifth Ave.
- 17. Chase Manhattan • 158 W. 14th St.
- 18. Chase Manhattan • 86 Fifth Ave.
- 19. Chase Manhattan • Penn Station
- 20. Chase Manhattan • 2 Penn Plaza
- 21. Chase Manhattan • 238 Eighth Ave.
- 22. Chase Manhattan • 221 Park Ave. S.
- 23. Chase Manhattan • 386 Park Ave. S.
- 24. Chase Manhattan • 390 Park Ave. S.
- 25. Cho Hung • 241 Fifth Ave.
- 26. Citibank • 201 W. 34th St.
- 27. Citibank • 717 Ave. of the Americas
- 28. Citibank • 411 Fifth Ave.
- 29. Citibank • 326-334 5th Ave.
- 30. Citibank • 72 Fifth Ave.
- 31. Citibank • 1 Park Ave.
- 32. Citibank • 111 Eighth Ave.
- 33. Commercial Bank of New York • 2 Park Ave.
- 34. Commercial Bank of New York • 1407 Broadway
- 35. Commercial Bank of New York • 404 Fifth Ave.
- 36. EAB • 1107 Broadway
- 37. EAB • 5 Penn Plaza
- 38. EAB • 475 Park Ave. S.
- 39. Fleet • 116 Fifth Ave.
- 40. Fleet • 350 Fifth Ave.
- 41. Fleet • 4 Penn Plaza
- 42. Fleet • 515 Seventh Ave.
- 43. Fourth Federal Savings • 242 W. 23rd St.
- 44. Greenpoint • 358 Fifth Ave.
- 45. Greenpoint • 1 Penn Plaza
- 46. Korea Commercial • 1250 Broadway
- 47. Marine Midland (HBSC) • 10 Union Sq. E.
- 48. North Fork • 1001 Ave.of the Americas
- 49. Republic National • 101 W. 14th Ave.

Bagels

- Chelsea Bagels • 300 W. 23rd St.
- Famous Buffet • 510 Ave. of the Americas
- Hot Bagels • 688 Ave. of the Americas
- Le Bon Bagel • 980 Ave. of the Americas
- Nathan Café & Deli • 319 Fifth Ave.
- Pick "A" Bagel On Sixth • 601 Ave. of the Americas

H Hospitals

- American Ass. For Bikur Cholim Hospital • 156 Fifth Ave.
- Beth Israel Medical Center: Phillips Ambulatory Center/ Cancer Center • 10 Union Sq. E.
- New York Foundling Hospital • 590 Ave. of the Americas

★ Landmarks

- Chelsea Hotel • 23rd St. btwn 7th and 8th Aves.
- Empire State Building
- Flatiron Building • 175 Fifth Ave.
- Flower District • 28th St. btwn. 6th and 7th Aves.
- Garment District • West 30's south of Herald Square
- Macy's Herald Square • 151 W. 34th St.
- Madison Square Garden • 4 Pennsylvania Plaza
- Madison Square Park • 23rd St.
- Metropolitan Life Insurance Co. • 1 Madison Ave.
- Theodore Roosevelt Birthplace • 28 E. 20th St.
- Union Square • 14th St.-Union Sq.

Libraries

- Andrew Heiskell Library for The Blind • 40 W. 20th St.
- Muhlenberg • 209 W. 23rd St.
- Science, Industry, and Business Library • 188 Madison Ave.

Ⓡ 24-Hour Pharmacies

- Rite Aid • 282 Eighth Ave.
- Town Total Health • 45 E. 30th St.

Ⓟ Police Precinct

- 10th Precinct • 230 W. 20th St.

✉ Post Offices

- Central Parcel Post • 325 W. 15th St.
- Empire State • 19 W. 33rd St.
- Greeley Square • 40 W. 32nd St.
- J.A. Farley • 421 8th Ave.
- Old Chelsea • 217 W. 18th St.

Ⓢ Schools

- American Academy Of Dramatic Arts • 120 Madison Ave.
- Bourel Technical • 50 W. 34th St.
- Empire State College-SUNY • 229 W. 28th St.
- Fashion Institute of Technology • 227 W. 27th St.
- High School of Fashion Industries • 225 W. 24th St.
- Katharine Gibbs School • 200 Park Ave.
- Liberty High School • 250 W.18th St.
- Mabel Dean Bacon Vocational HS.•127 E.22 St.
- New Museum • 65 Fifth Ave.
- NY College of Optometry • 100 E. 24th St.
- NY Institute of Credit • 71 W. 23rd St.
- NY School of Astrology • 545 Eighth Ave.
- Norman Thomas • 111 E. 33rd St.
- NY City • 135 E. 22nd St.
- Parsons School of Design • 66 Fifth Ave.
- PS 723 Manhattan Trans Ctr • 22 E. 28th St.
- Studio Semester • 229 W. 28th St.
- Technical Career Institute • 500 Eighth Ave.
- Touro College • 27 W. 23rd St.
- West Side • 500 Eighth Ave.

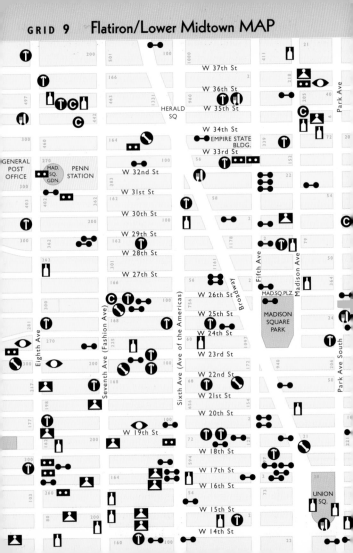

W 37th St

W 36th St

W 35th St

HERALD SQ

W 34th St

EMPIRE STATE BLDG.

W 33rd St

W 32nd St

W 31st St

GENERAL POST OFFICE

MAD. SQ. GDN.

PENN STATION

W 30th St

W 29th St

W 28th St

W 27th St

W 26th St

MAD.SQ.PLZ.

W 25th St

MADISON SQUARE PARK

W 24th St

W 23rd St

W 22nd St

W 21st St

W 20th St

W 19th St

W 18th St

W 17th St

W 16th St

W 15th St

UNION SQ.

W 14th St

Eighth Ave

Seventh Ave (Fashion Ave)

Sixth Ave (Ave of the Americas)

Broadway

Fifth Ave

Madison Ave

Park Ave South

Park Ave

The Flatiron/Lower Midtown area contains two of New York's most famous business districts, the Garment District (in the west 30's south of Herald Square) and the Flower District (28th Street between 6th and 7th Avenues).

24-Hour Copy Centers

- Kinko's • 191 Madison Ave.
- Kinko's • 245 Seventh Ave.
- On-Site Sourcing, Inc. • 443 Park Ave. S.
- Sir Speedy • 225 W. 34th St.
- Sir Speedy • 234 W. 35th St.

24-Hour Diners

- Coffee Shop • Union Sq. W.
- Kang Suh • 1250 Broadway
- L'Express • 249 Park Ave. S.
- Tick Tock Diner • 481 Eighth Ave.
- Woo Chon • 8-10 W. 36th St.

Gyms

- 19th St. Gym • 22 W. 19th St.
- 5th Ave. Black Belt Center • 251 Fifth Ave.
- Adolphus Fitness • 5 E. 17th St.
- American Fitness Centers • 128 Eighth Ave.
- Anderson's Martial Arts • 42 W. 30th St.
- Athletic Complex • 3 Park Ave.
- Bally Sports Club • 139 W. 32nd St.
- Bally Total Fitness • 641 Ave. Americas
- Blue Velvet Boxing Club • 23 W. 24th St.
- Body Perfection • 123 E. 24th St.
- Body Sculpture • 50 W. 34th St.
- Chau's Wu Mui Kung Fu Int'l • 159 W. 25th St.
- Chelsea Gym • 267 W. 17th St.
- Chelsea Racquet & Fitness Club • 45 W. 18th St.
- Crunch Fitness • 38th & Broadway
- David Barton Gym • 552 Ave. of the Americas
- Definitions • 139 Fifth Ave.
- Duomo • 11-13 E. 26th St.
- Episode • 18 W. 27th St.
- Equinox Fitness Club • 897 Broadway & 19th St.
- Fitness Results • 137 Fifth Ave.
- Johnny Lats Gym Inc. • 7 E. 17th St.
- Kodokan Judo & Self Defense • 152 W. 26th St.
- Kyokushin USA • 284 Fifth Ave.
- La Salud Hispania • 303 Fifth Ave.
- Lotus Health Studio • 15 Penn Plaza
- Lucille Roberts Health Club • 80 Fifth Ave.
- Middletown Health Club • 290 Fifth Ave.
- New York Budo • 12 W. 27th St.
- New York Sports Clubs • 200 Madison Ave.
- New York Sports Clubs • 303 Park Ave. S.
- Peak Performance Sport & Fitness Center • 106 E. 19th St.
- Pex Personalized Exercise • 924 Broadway
- Pierre Roman • 208 W. 29th St.
- Revolution Studios • 104 W. 14th St.
- School of Tai Chi Chuan • 5 E. 17th St.
- Scott Judith • 412 Ave. of Americas
- Steel Gym • 146 W. 23rd St.
- Synergy Fitness Clubs • 4 Park Ave.
- Workout Partners • 29th St.
- YMCA of Greater NY: McBurney • 215 W. 23rd St.
- Zone Studios 121 • 31 E. 31st St.

Hardware Stores

- 727 Hardware • 727 Ave. of the Americas
- A&M 28th St. Hardware • 15 E. 28th St.
- Adco Hardware • 23 W. 35th St.
- Admore Hardware & Lock • 11 E. 33rd St.
- Astro Industrial Hardware • 3 E. 17th St.
- B&N Hardware • 12 W. 19th St.
- Diener Park Lumber • 194 Eighth Ave.
- Elm Electric & Hardware • 884 Sixth Ave.
- Greenspan Simon Hardware • 261 W. 35th St.
- Halmor Hardware and Supply • 48 W. 22nd St.
- Hardware Mart • 151 W. 14th St.
- Harris Hardware • 17 W. 18th St.
- J&M Hardware & Locksmiths • 238 Park Ave. S.
- Jamali Hardware & Garden Supplies • 149 W. 28th St.
- KDM Hardware • 150 W. 26th St.
- Kove Brothers Hardware • 189 Seventh Ave.
- Mercer Sq. Hardware • 286 Fifth Ave.
- Young Hardware Inc. • 399 Eighth Ave.

- Midcity Hardware • 130 W. 25th St.
- Mike's Lumber Store • 7 E. 14th St.
- MJ Hardware & Electric • 520 Eighth Ave.
- Scheman & Grant • 575 Eighth Ave.
- SGS Hardware • 157 Eighth Ave.
- Spacesaver Hardware • 132 W. 23rd St.
- Whitey's Hardware • 37 W. 32nd St.

Laundromats

- Alice's Laundromat • 164 Eighth Ave.
- Berkeley Sutton Cleaners • 47 E. 34th St.
- Chelsea Cleaner • 125 & 1/2 Seventh Ave.
- Chelsea Laundromat • 156 W. 15th St.
- Chelsea Laundromat & Dry Cleaning • 156 W. 15th St.
- Chelsea New Wave Laundromat • 178 Seventh Ave.
- Empire State Laundromat • 16 E. 30th St.
- Kwik Wash • 211 W. 16th St.
- Lina Laundromat • 256 W. 15th St.
- Madison St. Laundromat & Dry • 209 Madison Ave.
- NY Cleaners • 104 W. 17th St.
- NY Laundromat • 105 W. 16th St.
- SMG Laundry • 328 W. 15th St.
- Well More Laundromat • 204 Eighth Ave.

Liquor Stores

- Bombay Spirits • 224 W. 35th St.
- Casa Oliveira Wines & Liquors • 98 Seventh Ave. S.
- Crossroads Wine & Liquor • 55 W. 14th St.
- Delauren Wines & Liquors • 332 Eighth Ave.
- Franks Liquor Shop • 46 Union Sq.
- Gramercy Park Wines & Spirits • 121 E. 23rd St.
- Harry's Liquors • 270 W. 36th St.
- Honig's Wines and Liquors • 61 W. 23rd St.
- Horan Liquor • 33 Seventh Ave.
- House of Cheers • 261 W. 18th St.
- J L Wine & Liquors • 60 E. 34th St.
- Kessler Liquors • 23 E. 28th St.
- Landmark Wine & Spirit • 167 W. 23rd St.
- Madison Ave. Liquors • 244 Madison Ave.
- North Village Wine & Liquor • 254 W. 14th St.
- Old Chelsea Wine & Liquor Store • 86 Seventh Ave.
- Quality House • 2 Park Ave.
- Royal Wine & Liquor Store • 45 Madison Ave.
- Sonest Liquors • 878 Sixth Ave.
- Wine Gallery • 576 Ave. of the Americas
- Yuk Cheun Liquor • 195 Madison Ave.
- Union Square Wine & Spirits • 33 Union Sq W

Movie Theatres

- A Different Light • 151 W. 19th St.
- Clearview's Chelsea • 260 W. 23rd St.
- Clearview's Chelsea West • 333 W. 23rd St.
- Loews 19th St. East • 890 Broadway
- Morgan Library • 29 E. 36th St.

Pet Stores

- Blue Ribbon Dog Company • 20 W. 22nd St.
- Doggone Purrrty • 151 W. 25th St.
- Furry Paws • 120 E. 34th St.
- Outsect • 147 W. 22nd St.
- Petco • 860 Broadway
- Petland Discounts • 312 W. 23rd St.

Video Rentals

- 155 Video Center • 155 W. 33rd St.
- 603 Video Store • 603 Ave. of the Americas
- AM • 36 Fifth Ave.
- Adult Entertainment Center • 448 Eighth Ave.
- Blockbuster Video • 128 Eighth Ave.
- Blockbuster Video • 424 Park Ave. S.
- Koryo Video • 7 W. 32nd St.
- International Express Video • 219 Madison Ave.
- Palmer Video • 295 Park Ave. S.
- Penn Visual • 252 W. 31st St.
- Perez Nelson • 244 W. 16th St.
- Rina Inc. • 364 W. 23rd St.
- Video Blitz • 144 Eighth Ave.

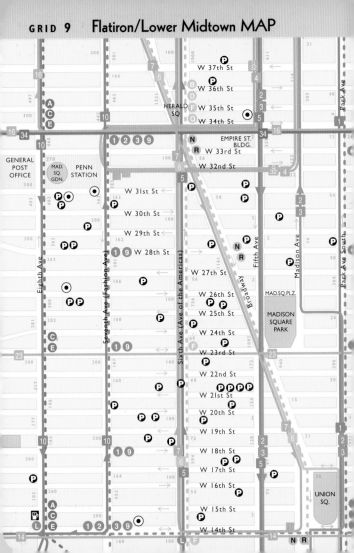

W 37th St
W 36th St
HERALD SQ
W 35th St
W 34th St
EMPIRE ST. BLDG.
W 33rd St
W 32nd St
GENERAL POST OFFICE
MAD. SQ. GDN.
PENN STATION
W 31st St
W 30th St
W 29th St
W 28th St
W 27th St
W 26th St
W 25th St
MAD. SQ. PLZ
MADISON SQUARE PARK
W 24th St
W 23rd St
W 22nd St
W 21st St
W 20th St
W 19th St
W 18th St
W 17th St
W 16th St
UNION SQ.
W 15th St
W 14th St

Eighth Ave
Seventh Ave (Fashion Ave)
Sixth Ave (Ave of the Americas)
Broadway
Fifth Ave
Madison Ave
Park Ave South
Park Ave

Parking during the day and on weekends is extremely difficult in this area, due to the number of business districts and commercial enterprises that are here. Driving isn't much better, since Lincoln Tunnel traffic has far-ranging repercussions.

Subways

Ⓐ Ⓒ Ⓔ ....34th St. at 8th Ave. (Penn Station)

Ⓐ Ⓒ Ⓔ Ⓛ ....14th St. at 8th Ave.

Ⓑ Ⓓ Ⓕ Ⓞ Ⓝ Ⓡ ....34th St. at 6th Ave.

Ⓒ Ⓔ ....23rd St. at 8th Ave.

Ⓕ Ⓛ ....14th St. at 6th Ave.

Ⓐ Ⓕ Ⓕ Ⓝ Ⓡ Ⓛ .... 14th St. at Broadway
................(Union Square)

Ⓕ ....23rd St. at 6th Ave.

Ⓝ Ⓡ .... 23rd St. at Broadway

Ⓝ Ⓡ .... 28th St. at Broadway

① ② ③ ...34th St. at 7th Ave. (Penn Station)

① ⑨ ....28th St. at 7th Ave.

① ⑨ ....23rd St. at 7th Ave.

① ⑨ ....18th St. at 7th Ave.

① ⑨ ② ③ ....14th St. at 7th Ave.

⑥ ....33rd St. at Park Ave. S.

⑥ ....28th St. at Park Ave. S.

⑥ ....23rd St. at Park Ave. S.

Bus Lines

① ② ③ .... 5th Ave./Madison Ave.

④ ....5th Ave./Madison Ave./Broadway

⑤ ....5th Ave./Ave.of the Americas/Riverdale Dr.

⑥ ....7th Ave./Broadway/Ave. of the Americas
Columbus Ave./Amsterdam Ave./Lenox/

⑦ .... 6th Ave./7th Ave./Broadway
7th Ave./8th Ave. (Central ParkWest)/
.... Frederick Douglass Blvd.

⑩ ....14th St. Crosstown

⑭ ....23rd St. Crosstown

㉓ ....34th St. Crosstown

⑯ ....Penn Station -Jackson Heights, Queens

⊙ Car Rentals

- Eldan Rent-A-Car • 350 Fifth Ave.
- Hertz Car Rental • 1 Penn Plaza
- Nationwide Rent-A-Car • 241 W. 26th St.
- New York Rent-A-Car • 230 W. 31st St.
- Zupa Bros. • 145 W. 14th St.

⊞ Gas Station

- Brothers Sale & Service • 63 Eighth Ave.

Ⓟ Parking

- 6 E. 17th St. Parking • 6 E. 17th St.
- 52 W. 36th St. Parking • 59 W. 36th St.
- 53 W. 25th St. Parking • 52 W. 26th St.
- 60 W. 23rd St. Parking • 60 W. 23rd St.
- 112 W. 25th St. Parking • 112 W. 25th St.
- 136 W. 19th St. Garage • 136 W. 19th St.
- Central Parking System • 254 W. 31st St.
- Champion Parking • 41 W. 17th St.
- Champion Parking • 28 W. 18th St.
- Champion Parking • 31 W. 37th St.
- Chelnik Parking • 29 W. 25th St.
- Crosstown Parking • 14 W. 31st St.
- Edison Park Fast • 249 W. 28th St.
- Edison Parking • 398 Park Ave. S.
- Ezey • 10 W. 29th St.
- Ezey 38th St. • 217 W. 29th St.
- Ezey Parking Systems • 9 W. 31st St.
- Fine Parking • 21-25 W. 20th St.
- Flannery Parking • 39 W. 21st St.
- Flannery Parking • 129 W. 21st St.
- Flannery Parking • 48 W. 15th St.
- Fran Parking • 60 E. 20th St.
- Fur Parking • 241 W. 28th St.
- Garage Management • 7 W. 21st St.
- Kingly Parking • 39 W. 23rd St.
- Kinney System • 29 W. 28th St.
- Kinney System • 60 Madison Ave.
- LPS Management • 371 Seventh Ave.
- Martinton • 226 W. 18th St.
- Meyers Parking System • 111 Eighth Ave.
- Meyers Parking System • 254 W. 31st St.
- Mutual Parking • 7 W. 21st St.
- Rapid Park Industries • 124 W. 20th St.
- Rapid Park Industries • 10 E. 30th St.
- S P I Operating • 132 W. 27th St.
- Safe Haven Parking • 260 W. 126th St.
- Servwel Parking • 150 W. 20th St.
- Square Plus Operating • 1251 Broadway
- Square Plus Operating • 153 Seventh Ave.
- Square Plus Operating • 20 E. 16th St.
- Square Plus Operating • 252 W. 26th St.
- Stavros Parking •
  736 Avenue of the Americas
- Term Parking • 605-11 Sixth Ave.
- Unique Parking • 47 E. 21st St.

⊞ Path Stations

- 33 St.-Hoboken & Journal Square •
  33rd St. at Sixth Ave.
- 23 St.-Hoboken & Journal Square •
  23rd St. at Sixth Ave.
- 14 St.-Hoboken & Journal Square •
  14th St. at Sixth Ave.

This area is home to one of Manhattan's most pastoral and beautiful settings, Gramercy Park. It also contains two humongous and drab residential communities, Stuyvesant Town and Peter Cooper Village.

💲 ATMs

- 1. Amalgamated Bank • 301 Third Ave.
- 2. Chase Manhattan • 400 E. 23rd St.
- 3. Chase Manhattan • 400 Second Ave.
- 4. Chase Manhattan • 255 First Ave.
- 5. Chase Manhattan • 450 Third Ave.
- 6. Chase Manhattan • 386 Park Ave. S.
- 7. Chase Manhattan • 390 Park Ave. S.
- 8. Citibank • 481 First Ave.
- 9. Citibank • 1 Park Ave.
- 10. Citibank • 399 Park Ave.
- 11. Citibank • 262 First Ave.
- 12. Citibank • 25 Waterside Plaza
- 13. Commercial Bank of New York • 2 Park Ave. at 33rd St.
- 14. EAB • 475 Park Ave. South
- 15. Greenpoint • 254 E. 34th St.
- 16. Independence Savings • 250 Lexington Ave.
- 17. Marine Midland (HBSC) • 245 First Ave.
- 18. Marine Midland (HBSC) • 10 Union Sq. East

⬤ Bagels

- Bagel & Schmear • 166 E. 28th St.
- Bagel De Juer • 478 Third Ave.
- Bagelry • 425 Third Ave.
- Bagels Around the Clock • 637 Second Ave.
- Daniel's Bagel Corp. • 569 Third Ave.
- David's Bagels • 331 First Ave.
- Ess-A -Bagel • 359 First Ave.
- La Bagel • 263 First Ave.
- Pick A Bagel On Third • 297 Third Ave.
- Shaun's Bagel Café Inc. • 178 Lexington Ave.

🏥 Hospitals

- Bellevue Hospital Center • 462 First Ave.
- Beth Israel Medical Center • 281 First Ave.
- Beth Israel Medical Center • 10 Union Sq. E.
- Cabrini Medical Center • 227 E. 19th St.
- Hospital For Joint Diseases • 301 E. 17th St.
- NYU Medical Center: Tisch Hospital • 560 First Ave.
- New York Eye & Ear Infirmary • 310 E. 14th St.
- V.A. Hospital • 408 First Ave.

★ Landmarks

- Con Edison Building • 145 E. 14th St.
- Gramercy Park • Irving Place at 20th St.
- National Arts Club • 15 Gramercy Park South
- Pete's Tavern • 129 E. 18th St.
- Sniffen Court • 36th St. at Third Ave.
- The Players • 16 Gramercy Park South

📖 Libraries

- Epiphany • 228E. 23rd St.
- Kips Bay • 446 Third Ave.

℞ 24-Hour Pharmacy

- CVS Pharmacy • 342 E. 23rd St.

🅿 Police Precinct

- 13th Precinct • 230 E. 21st St.

✉ Post Offices

- Madison Square • 149 E. 23rd St.
- Murray Hill • 205 E. 36th St.
- Peter Stuyvesant • 432 E. 14th St.
- Station 138 (Macy's) • 151 34th St.

🄢 Schools

- Baruch College • 151 E. 25th St.
- Beth Israel Medical Center • 307 First Ave.
- Katharine Gibbs School • 200 Park Ave.
- Manhattan Night Comprehensive High School • 240 Second Ave.
- New York College Of Optometry • 100 E. 24th St.
- NYU Dental School • First Ave. and 24th St.
- NYU Medical Center • 30th St. and First Ave.
- Phillips-Beth Israel School of Nursing • 310 E. 22nd St.
- PS 040 Augustus St. Gaudens • 319 E. 19th St.
- PS-JHS 047 School for the Deaf • 225 E. 23rd St.
- PS 106 Bellevue Hospital • 27th St. & First Ave.
- PS 116 Mary L. Murray School • 210 E. 33rd St.
- PS 226 • 345 E. 15th St.
- School Of Visual Arts • 209 E. 23rd St.
- Washington Irving High • 40 Irving Pl.

Murray Hill/Stuyvesant Town/
Gramercy MAP

GRID 10

East River

Queens-Midtown Tunnel

Avenue C

E 37th St
E 36th St
E 35th St
E 34th St
E 33rd St
E 32nd St
E 31st St
E 30th St
E 29th St
E 28th St
E 27th St
E 26th St
E 25th St
E 24th St
E 23rd St
E 22nd St
E 21st St
E 20th St
E 19th St
E 18th St
E 17th St
E 16th St
E 15th St
E 14th St

E 16th St
E 15th St

Sniffen Ct.
Lexington Av
Third Av
Second Av
First Av
Park Av South
Broadway Alley
Irving Place
Union Sq E
Rutherford Pl
Stuyvesant Square
Nathan D Perlman Pl
Asser Levy Pl
Franklin D Roosevelt Drive
Marginal St
Avenue C

KIPS BAY PLAZA

NYU MEDICAL CENTER

BELLEVUE HOSPITAL CENTER

WATERSIDE PLAZA

VET. ADM. MEDICAL CENTER

MARINA & SKYPORT

PETER COOPER VILLAGE

GRAMERCY PARK

STUYVESANT TOWN

It shouldn't be too difficult to find what you need here...

24-Hour Diners

- Gemini Restaurant • 641 Second Ave.
- Gramercy Restaurant • 184 Third Ave.
- L'Express (Bistro) • 249 Park Ave. South
- Sarge's Deli • 548 Third Ave.

Gyms

- 5th Ave. Black Belt • 220 E. 32nd St.
- Aerobox Athletics Enterprises Inc. • 10 Waterside Plaza
- Athletic Complex • 3 Park Ave.
- Body Perfection • 123 E. 24th St.
- Club 29 • 155 E. 29th St.
- Dolphin Fitness Clubs • 201 E. 23rd St.
- Dolphin Fitness East Inc. • 242 E. 14th St.
- New York Sports Clubs • 614 Second Ave.
- Luye Aquafit • 310 E. 23rd St.
- Manhattan Place Condominium Health Club • 630 First Ave.
- New York Sports Clubs • 131 E. 32nd St.
- New York Sports Clubs • 303 Park Ave. South
- Peak Performance Sport & Fitness Center • 106 E. 19th St.
- Rivergate Fitness Center • 401 E. 34th St.
- Sol Goldman YM-YWHA • 344 E. 14th St.
- Synergy Fitness Clubs • 4 Park Ave.
- Ultimate Image • 67 Irving Pl.
- Waterside Swim & Health Club • 35 Waterside Plaza at FDR Dr.

Hardware Stores

- 14th Street Hardware Inc. • 211 E. 14th St.
- Gurell Hardware • 132 E. 28th St.
- Homefront Hardware & Lumber • 202 E. 29th St.
- J & M Hardware & Locksmiths Inc. • 238 Park Ave. South
- Kips Bay Hardware Co. • 601 Second Ave.
- Lumberland Hardware • 400 Third Ave.
- Render of 72nd • 485 Third Ave.
- Simon's Hardware & Bath • 421 Third Ave.
- Town & Village Hardware • 345 E. 18th St.
- Vercesi Hardware • 152 E. 23rd St.
- Warshaw Hardware & Electrical • 248 Third Ave.

Laundromats

- 14th St. Laundromat • 426 E. 14th St.
- 235 Laundromat • 235 E. 25th St.
- 33rd St. Laundry & Dry Cleaners • 155 E. 33rd St.
- A & D Laundromat • 325 First Ave.
- Ace Luck of P & N, Inc. • 401 Third Ave.
- Brigton Clean • 267 W. 15th St.
- CH Century Corp. • 238 E. 24th St.
- Chen Laundromat • 350 E. 20th St.
- East 29 St. Laundry • 212 E. 29th St.
- Edwin Porras Launderette • 162 E. 37th St.

- Ever Ready Laundromat • 137 Lexington Ave.
- Giant Laundromat • 176 Third Ave.
- H&T Laundry and Cleaning • 356 E. 19th St.
- Ham Kum Chen • 352 E. 20th St.
- Hing's Laundromat • 229 E.21st St.
- KD Laundromat • 217 E. 26th St.
- Laundercoin • 311 E. 37th St.
- NY Yeh's Co., Inc. • 115 E. 31st St.
- Professional Dry Cleaners & Laundry • 486 Second Ave.
- P's Laundry Services • 240 E. 28th St.
- Super Laundromat & Cleaners • 105 Lexington Ave.
- Top Dog Laundry • 333 Third Ave.
- Trudy's Laundry • 238 E. 36th St.
- Vanity Fair Cleaners • 376 Third Ave.
- Wascomat • 489 Second Ave.

Liquor Stores

- Buy Rite Discount Liquors • 398 Third Ave.
- Choose It Wines & Spirits Co Inc. • 472 2nd Ave.
- Elman's Liquors • 279 Third Ave.
- First Ave. Wine & Spirits Supermarket • 383 First Ave.
- Franks Liquor Shop • 46 Union Sq. East
- Gramercy Park Wines & Spirits • 121 E. 23rd St.
- HS Wine & Liquors Inc. • 161 Third Ave.
- House of Wine & Liquor • 250 E. 34th St.
- Royal Wine Merchants Ltd. • 25 Waterside Plaza
- Stuyvesant Sq Liquors • 333 Second Ave.
- Wines On 1st • 224 First Ave.
- Winfield Flynn Liquors Ltd. • 558 Third Ave.
- Zeichner Wine & Liquor • 279 First Ave.

Movie Theatres

- Loews Kips Bay • Second Ave. & 32nd St.
- Sony 34th St. Showplace • 238 E. 34th St.

Pet Stores

- Animal World Inc. • 219 E. 26th St.
- Barking Zoo II • 283 Third Ave.
- Furry Paws Inc. • 120 E. 34th St.
- Greater N Y Aquarium • 215 E. 23rd St.
- Little Red Pet Shop • 202 E. 25th St.
- Petco • 550 Second Ave.
- Petland Discounts • 404 Third Ave.

Video Rentals

- Blockbuster Video • 278 Third Ave.
- Blockbuster Video • 312 First Ave.
- Blockbuster Video • 151 Third Ave.
- Blockbuster Video • 155 E. 34th St.
- Libra Varieties Inc • 483 Third Ave.
- Palmer Video • 295 Park Ave. S.
- Third Avenue Adult Videos • 127 Third Ave.
- Video Stop Inc • 367 Third Ave.

Murray Hill/Stuyvesant Town/ Gramercy MAP

GRID 10

E 37th St
E 36th St
E 35th St
Queens Midtown Tunnel
Sniffen Ct.

34
E 34th St
98

6
E 33rd St
E 32nd St
16
KIPS BAY PLAZA
E 31st St
NYU MEDICAL CENTER
E 30th St
E 29th St
E 28th St
6
E 27th St
Broadway Alley
21
BELLEVUE HOSPITAL CENTER
E 26th St
E 25th St
WATERSIDE PLAZA
VET. ADM. MEDICAL CENTER
E 24th St
6
23
E 23rd St

Park Av South
Lexington Av
Third Av
Second Av
First Av
Asser Levy Pl
Franklin D Roosevelt Drive
Marginal St

MARINA & SKYPORT
E 22nd St
15
1
E 21st St
101
102
GRAMERCY PARK
PETER COOPER VILLAGE
2
3
E 20th St
103
E 19th St
E 18th St
Irving Place
Rutherford Pl
4
E 17th St
STUYVESANT TOWN
5
6
E 16th St
Stuyvesant Square
Nathan D Perlman Pl
E 15th St
N
R
Union Sq E
E 14th St
9
14
L
L
L

Avenue C
E 16th St
E 15th St
East River

Avenue
E 16
E 15

Street parking sucks, but you can usually move around okay except for the area around the Queens Midtown Tunnel, and during the day on First Avenue out in front of Bellevue and NYU Medical Centers. The Gulf gas station that used to be on 23rd street doesn't service automobiles anymore. The reconstruction of the Union Square subway station looks to be taking about 20 years to finish.

Subways

Ⓛ	14th St. at 1st Ave.
Ⓛ	14th St. at 3rd Ave.
Ⓛ④⑤⑥ⓃⓇ	Union Square
⑥	23rd St. at Park Ave. South
⑥	28th St. at Park Ave. South
⑥	33rd St. at Park Ave. South

Bus Lines

①②③	5th Ave./Madison Ave.
⑨	Ave. B/East Broadway
⑭	14th St. Crosstown
⑮	1st/2nd Aves.
⑯	34th St. Crosstown
㉑	Houston St. Crosstown
㉓	23rd St. Crosstown
⑯	34th St. Crosstown
101	3rd Ave./Lexington Ave.
102	3rd Ave./Lexington Ave.
103	3rd Ave./Lexington Ave.

Ⓒ Car Rentals

- Dollar Rent A Car • 329 E. 22nd St.
- Hertz Car Rental • 150 E. 24th St.
- National Car Rental • 142 E. 31rd St.
- Renault USA Inc • 650 First Ave.

Ⓟ Parking

- 155 E. 34 Garage • 155 E. 34th St.
- 211 Garage• 211 E. 18th St.
- 245 Operating • 57-59 Irving Place
- Chelnik Parking • 200 E. 27th St.
- Consolidated Parking • 146 Third Ave.
- Ezey 31 • 171 Lexington Ave.
- Garage Management • 300 E. 34th St.
- Garage Management • 142 E. 31st St.
- Garage Management • 144 E. 17th St.
- Guardian 31 St. Parking • 151 E. 31st St.
- Jeff Parking • 329 E. 22nd St.
- Jo-Dash Parking • 488 Third Ave.
- Kinney's System • 202 E. 18th St.
- Kinney System • 329 E. 21st St.
- Kinney System • 340 E. 34th St.

- Corinthian Garage • 330 E. 38th St.
- Horizon Garage • 415 E. 37th St.
- Edison Parking • 398 Park Ave. South
- Fran Parking • 60 E. 20th St.
- Management Systems • 200 E. 32nd St.
- Manhattan Parking • 245 E. 19th St.
- Manhattan Parking • 90 Park Ave.
- Meyers Parking System • 240 E. 27th St.
- Meyers Stuyvesant Garages • 420 E. 20th St.
- Miller Parking • 50 Park Ave.
- NY Parking E. 24 St • 200 E. 24th St.
- Penny Garage • 242 E. 25th St.
- Precise Parking • 150 E. 18th St.
- Rapid Park Industries • 575 First Ave.
- Rapid Park Industries • 148 E. 33rd St.
- Salem Parking Garage • 145 E. 34th St.
- Shawit Garage • 201 E. 28th St.
- Square Plus Operating • FDR Drive & E. 34th St.
- YOR 24th • 214 E. 24th St.
- Zephyr Parking • 132 E. 35th St.

Hell's Kitchen MAP

The continuing gentrification of Hell's Kitchen (and name change to "Clinton") will doubtlessly increase the number of essential services, (for instance the number of banks). The area around the Port Authority Bus Terminal is still one of the most authentically seedy places in Manhattan.

💲 ATMs

- 1. Chase Manhattan • 524 W. 57th St.
- 2. Chase Manhattan • 821 Eighth Ave.
- 3. Chase Manhattan • 969 Eighth Ave.
- 4. Citibank • 401 W. 42nd St.
- 5. Citibank •1748 Broadway
- 6. Fleet • 428 W. 59th St.
- 7. Fleet • Port Authority Bus Terminal
- 8. Republic National • 661 Eighth Ave.
- 9. Republic National •1790 Broadway

🥯 Bagels

- Bagel House • 308 W. 50th St.
- Bagels & Co. • 243 W. 38th St.
- H & H Bagels • 639 W. 46th St.

✺ Community Gardens

- 11th Ave. Community Garden • 722 Eleventh Ave.
- Clinton Community Garden • W. 47th-48th Sts.
- Oasis 1 • 765 Tenth Ave.
- Oasis 2 • 511-19 W. 52nd St.
- PS 111 • 440 W. 53rd St.

🏥 Hospitals

- Roosevelt Hospital Center • 1000 Tenth Ave.
- St. Clare's Family Health Center • 350 W. 51st St.
- St. Clare's Hospital • 426 W. 52nd St.

★ Landmarks

- Intrepid Sea, Air, and Space Museum • 12th Ave. /45th St.
- Theater Row • 42nd St. / 9th and 10th Aves.

📖 Library

- Columbus • 742 Tenth Ave.

Ⓡ 24-Hour Pharmacies

- CVS Pharmacy • 1 Columbus Pl. (58th St. & Ninth Ave.)
- Duane Reade • 224 W. 57th St.
- Duane Reade • 625 Eighth Ave. (Port Authority)

🅿 Police Precinct

- Mid-Town North • 524 W. 42nd St.

✉ Post Offices

- Columbus Circle • 27 W. 60th St.
- Radio City • 322 W. 52nd St.
- Times Square • 340 W. 42nd St.

🅢 Schools

- Alfred Adler Institute • 1780 Broadway
- American Academy McAllister Institute • 450 W. 56th St.
- Creative Writing Center • 439 W. 49th St.
- HS Of Graphic Communication Arts • 439 W. 49th St.
- Interboro Institute • 450 W. 56th St.
- John Jay College • 899 Tenth Ave.
- New York School Of Astrology • 545 Eighth Ave.
- PS 017 Hudson River • 328 W. 48th St.
- PS 051 Elias Howe School • 520 W. 45th St.
- PS 058 Manhattan School • 317 W. 52nd St.
- PS 111 Adolph S. Ochs School • 440 W. 53rd St.
- Park West High School • 525 W. 50th St.

Again, as more money pours into Hell's Kitchen, more services should start to crop up along Tenth and Eleventh Avenues.

24-Hour Diner

- Market Diner • 43rd St. & Eleventh Ave.

Gyms

- Bally Sports Club • 350 W. 50th St.
- Body Sculpt • 300 W. 40th St.
- Crunch • 42nd St. & Eleventh Ave.
- Iowa Sports Management • 456 W. 43rd St.
- Manhattan Plaza Health Club • 482 W. 43rd St.
- Manhattan Sports Club • 350 W. 50th St.
- Mid-City Gym • 244 W. 49th St.
- New York Underground Fitness • 440 W. 57th St.
- Riverbank West Health Club • 555 W. 42nd St.
- The Strand Health Club • 500 W. 43rd St.

Hardware Stores

- Columbus Hardware Inc. • 852 Ninth Ave.
- Garden Hardware & Supply Co. • 785 Eighth Ave.
- HT Sales Co. True Value • 718 Tenth Ave.
- Lopez Sentry Hardware Inc. • 691 Ninth Ave.
- Metropolitan Lumber & Hardware •
  617 Eleventh Ave.
- MJ Hardware & Electric Corp. • 520 Eighth Ave.
- Mike's Lumber Store • 556 Columbus Ave.
- New Era Industrial Hardware Inc. •
  359 W. 54th St.
- Scheman & Grant Inc. • 629 575 Eighth Ave.
- Straight Hardware & Supply Co. • 613 Ninth Ave.

Laundromats

- Dennis Laundry • 617 Ninth Ave.
- Ding Dong Cleaners • 354 W. 51st St.
- Rainbow Cleaners • 453 W. 46th St.
- Second Wave Launder Center • 842 Ninth Ave.
- Superb Laundry Ltd. • 707 Ninth Ave.
- Vionette Laundromat • 750 Tenth Ave.
- Zanussi Automatic Laundry • 794 Ninth Ave.

Liquor Stores

- 9th Ave. Wine & Liquor • 474 Ninth Ave.
- Athens Wine & Liquor • 302 W. 40th St.
- B & G Wine & Liquor Store • 507 W. 42nd St.
- Cambridge Wine & Liquors Inc. • 594 Eighth Ave.
- Columbus Circle Liquor Store Inc. •
  1780 Broadway
- Fifty-Fifth Street Liquor Store • 410 W. 55th St.
- First Liquor Store • 840 Ninth Ave.
- Manhattan Plaza Winery Inc. • 589 Ninth Ave.

- Ninth Avenue Wine & Liquors • 860 Ninth Ave.
- Ray & Frank Liquor Store Inc. • 706 Ninth Ave.
- Reidy Wine & Liquor Inc. • 768 Eighth Ave.
- Shon 45 Liquors • 840 Eighth Ave.
- Turin Wines & Liquors Inc. • 609 Columbus Ave.
- US Wines & Liquor • 486 Ninth Ave.
- Vintage Wine Warehouse • 665 Eleventh Ave.
- West 57th St. Wine & Spirit • 340 W. 57th St.
- Westley Liquor • 921 Eighth Ave.

Movie Theatres

- Cineplex Odeon: Encore Worldwide • 340 W. 50th St.
- Common Basis Theater • 750 Eighth Ave.
- Show World • 675 Eighth Ave.
- Zanzibar • 645 Ninth Ave.

Pet Stores

- Animal Acts • 233 W. 54th St.
- Animal House 2 • 315 W. 57th St.
- Canine Castle Ltd. • 410 W. 56th St.
- Metropets • 594 Ninth Ave.
- Petland Discounts • 734 Ninth Ave.
- Spoiled Brats • 340 W. 49th St.

Video Rentals

- 57th St. Video & Photo • 332 W. 57th St.
- 691 Video Center Corp • 691 Eighth Ave.
- 763 Video Store • 763 Eighth Ave.
- Blockbuster Video • 588 Ninth Ave.
- Liman Video Rentals • 614 W. 49th St.
- Rec Video • 301 W. 46th St.

The Lincoln Tunnel jams this area up during the day. (If you're coming from downtown, try taking the Tenth Avenue approach. If you're coming from uptown, you're screwed). The mishmash of Columbus Circle also doesn't help matters. Parking is usually terrible because of the Theater District and the Javits Convention Center. This is also where the West Side "Highway" begins to have traffic lights and becomes a parking lot for most of the day (try taking Eleventh Avenue downtown if you can).

Subways

1 9 A C B D .... Columbus Circle
C E .... 50th St. at Eighth Ave.
42nd St. at Eighth Ave.
A C E .... (Port Authority Bus terminal)

Bus Lines

10 .... 7th Ave./8th Ave./Central Park West
11 .... 9th Ave./10th Ave.
16 34 .... 34th St. Crosstown
16 .... 49/50th St. Crosstown
23 .... 23rd St. Crosstown
42 .... 42nd St. Crosstown
50 .... 49/50th St. Crosstown
57 .... 57th St. Crosstown
104 .... Broadway

⦿ Car Rentals

- AAA Access Auto Rental • 542 W. 49th St.
- All State Auto Rental • 541 W. 43rd St.
- Arrow-U-Drive Inc. • 505 W. 57th St.
- Autorent Car Rental • 415 W. 45th St.
- Avis Rent-A-Car • 460 W. 42nd St.
  (also Dockside Service)
- Budget • 304 W. 49th St.
- Enterprise Rent-A-Car • 653-659 Eleventh Ave.
- Ford Rent-A-Car • 787 11th Ave. & 54th St.
- United Car Rental • 501 W. 55th St.

🌢 Car Wash

- Kenny Car Wash System Inc. • 625 Eleventh Ave.

P Gas Stations

- Gaseteria • 59th St. & Eleventh Ave.
- Sunoco • 639 Eleventh Ave.
- Mobil • 718 Eleventh Ave.

P Parking

- 333 W. 46th St. Si. • 333 W. 46th St.
- 59th St Public Parking • 641 W. 59th St.
- 888 Parking LLC • 888 Eighth Ave.
- Albatross Parking • 346 W. 37th St.
- B S K Parking • 408 W. 57th St.
- Begg's Garage • 515 W. 43rd St.
- Bright Management • 305 W. 48th St.
- Central Parking System • 235 W. 56th St.
- Central Parking Systems • 380 W. 50th St.
- Central Parking Systems • 350 W. 50th St.
- Cherry Parking • 350 W. 40th St.
- Eagle 56 Parking • 841 Tenth Ave.
- Edison Parking • 640 W. 42nd St.
- Effective Parking • 435 W. 57th St.
- Garage Management • 622 W. 57th St.
- Garage Management • 257 W. 47th St.
- Jabba Management • 343 W. 42nd St.
- Jody Parking • 430 W. 41st St.
- Katz Parking System • 325 W. 58th St.
- Kinney System • 345 W. 58th St.
- Kinney System • 264 W. 42nd St.
- Midtown Auto Care Service • 415 W. 45th St.
- Park Right • 605 W. 45th St.
- Rapid Park Industries • 411 W. 55th St.
- S & N Parking • 423 W. 53rd St.
- SLL West 44th St. • 322 W. 44th St.
- Square Plus Operating • 427 W. 42nd St.
- Square Plus Operating • 306 W. 44th St.
- Square Plus Operating • 332 W. 44th St.
- Square Plus Operating • 618 W. 49th St.
- Zenith Parking Garage • 301 W. 51st St.

Midtown ESSENTIALS

For all intents and purposes, this is the heart of New York. However, Times Square, the Theater District, and Rockefeller Center are all areas that many New Yorkers avoid, preferring instead the beautifully reconstructed Bryant Park, the classy Oak Bar at the Plaza Hotel, and Phillipe Starck's utterly cool Royalton Hotel.

💲 ATMs

- 1. Amalgamated • 1710 Broadway
- 2. Apple Bank For Savings • 1320 Ave. of the Americas
- 3. Bank Leumi • 579 Fifth Ave.
- 4. Bank Leumi • 1400 Broadway
- 5. Bank of New York • 51 W. 51st St.
- 6. Bank of New York • 530 Fifth Ave.
- 7. Bank of New York • 260 Madison Ave.
- 8. Bank of New York • 575 Madison Ave.
- 9. Bank of Tokyo • 360 Madison Ave.
- 10. Bank of Tokyo • 1251 Ave. of the Americas
- 11. Chase Manhattan • 1411 Broadway
- 12. Chase Manhattan • 100 W. 57th Street
- 13. Chase Manhattan • 11 W. 51st St.
- 14. Chase Manhattan • 1251 Ave. of the Americas
- 15. Chase Manhattan • 1501 Broadway
- 16. Chase Manhattan • 510 Fifth Avenue
- 17. Chase Manhattan • 821 Eighth Ave.
- 18. Chase Manhattan • 969 Eighth Ave.
- 19. Chase Manhattan • 401 Madison Ave.
- 20. Chase Manhattan • 488 Madison Ave.
- 21. Chase Manhattan • 98 Madison Ave.
- 22. Citibank • 1430 Broadway
- 23. Citibank • 40 W. 57th St.
- 24. Citibank • 640 Fifth Ave.
- 25. Citibank • 1155 Ave. of the Americas
- 26. Citibank • 1748 Broadway
- 27. Citibank • 330 Madison Ave.
- 28. Citibank • 411 Fifth Ave.
- 29. Commercial • 1407 Broadway
- 30. Commercial • 404 Fifth Avenue
- 31. Dime Savings • 589 Fifth Avenue
- 32. Dime Savings • 1700 Broadway
- 33. Emigrant Savings • 335 Madison Ave.
- 34. EAB • 1440 Broadway
- 35. EAB • 1 Rockefeller Plaza
- 36. EAB • 1345 Ave. of the Americas
- 37. Fleet • 1633 Broadway
- 38. Fleet • 1675 Broadway
- 39. Fleet • 592 Fifth Ave.
- 40. Fleet • Port Authority, Eighth Ave.
- 41. Fleet • 515 Seventh Ave.
- 42. Greenpoint • 1200 Ave. Of The Americas
- 43. Marine Midland (HBSC) • 550 Seventh Ave.
- 44. Marine Midland (HBSC) • 1271 Ave. of the Americas
- 45. Marine Midland (HBSC) • 41 Rockefeller Plaza
- 46. Marine Midland (HBSC) • 1095 Ave. of the Americas
- 47. Marine Midland (HBSC) • 666 Fifth Ave.
- 48. Marine Midland (HBSC) • 437 Madison Ave.
- 49. Marine Midland (HBSC) • 555 Madison Avenue
- 50. North Fork • 1001 Ave. of The Americas
- 51. Republic National • 452 Fifth Ave.
- 52. Republic National • 1185 Sixth Ave.
- 53. Republic National • 661 Fifth Ave.
- 54. Republic National • 1790 Broadway

🥯 Bagels

- B & Y Edibles, Inc. • 36 W. 48th St.
- Bagel House • 308 W. 50th St.
- Bagel-N-Bean • 828 Seventh Ave.
- Bagels & Co. • 243 W. 38th St.
- Bagels Off Fifth • 4 E. 38th St.
- Bruegger's Bagels • 1115 Ave. of the Americas
- Le Bon Bagel • 980 Ave. of the Americas
- Moms Bagels & Tables, Inc. • 15 W. 45th St.
- New World Coffee • 342 Madison Ave.
- Pick "A" Bagel On 57th • 200 W. 57th St.

🏥 Hospitals

- American Friends of Laniado Hospital • 18 W. 45th St.
- National Jewish Center For Immunology & Respiratory Medicine • 535 Fifth Ave.
- St Clare's Family Health Center • 350 W. 51st St.

★ Landmarks

- Carnegie Hall • 154 W. 57th St.
- Museum of Modern Art (MoMA) • 11 W. 53rd St.
- New York Public Library • Fifth Ave. and 42nd St.
- Plaza Hotel • 768 Fifth Ave.
- Rockefeller Center • 47th-50th Sts.
- Royalton Hotel • 44th St. between Fifth and Sixth Aves.
- St. Patrick's Cathedral • Fifth Ave. and 50th St.
- Times Square • 42nd St-Times Sq.

📖 Libraries

- Donnell Library Center • 20 W. 53rd St.
- Mid-Manhattan Library • 455 Fifth Ave.

℞ 24 Hour Pharmacies

- Buckingham Chemists, Inc. • 1405 Sixth Ave.
- Duane Reade • 224 W. 57th St. at Broadway
- Duane Reade • Port Authority, Eighth Ave.

✉ Post Offices

- Appraisers Stores • 580 Fifth Ave. Suite 407
- Bryant • 23 W. 43rd St.
- Midtown • 223 38th St.
- Rockefeller Center • 610 Fifth Ave.

🎓 Schools

- Alfred Adler Institute • 1780 Broadway
- Berkeley College • 3 E. 43rd St.
- Circle In The Square Theater School • 1633 Broadway
- City University Of New York • 33 W. 42nd St.
- Institute Of Allied Medical Professionals • 23D 106 Central Park South
- Laboratory Institute Of Merchandising • 12 E. 53rd St.
- New York Academy of Comedic Arts • 1626 Broadway
- New York School Of Astrology • 545 Eighth Ave.
- Practicing Law Institute • 810 Seventh Ave.
- Spanish American Institute • 215 W. 43rd St.
- Wood Tobe-Coburn School • 8 E. 40th St.

Columbus
Circle

Central Park South

GRAND ARMY
PLAZA

E 59th St

W 58th St   E 58th St

W 57th St   E 57th St

W 56th St   E 56th St

W 55th St   E 55th St

W 54th St   E 54th St

W 53rd St   E 53rd St

W 52nd St   E 52nd St

W 51st St   E 51st St

ROCKEFELLER
CENTER

W 50th St   E 50th St

W 49th St   E 49th St

W 48th St   E 48th St

W 47th St   E 47th St

W 46th St   E 46th St

THEATER

W 45th St   E 45th St

DISTRICT

W 44th St   E 44th St

W 43rd St   E 43rd St

TIMES SQUARE

W 42nd St   E 42nd St

PORT AUTHORITY
BUS TERMINAL

W 41st St   E 41st St

BRYANT
PARK

PUBLIC
LIBRARY

W 40th St   E 40th St

W 39th St   E 39th St

W 38th St   E 38th St

W 37th St   E 37th St

Eighth Ave

Broadway

Seventh Ave

Sixth Ave (Ave. of the Americas)

Rock. Plaza

Fifth Ave

Madison Ave

Midtown has three of the best places to see a movie in town—the huge Ziegfeld, the classy Paris, and outdoors at Bryant Park. And don't forget Show World.

24-Hour Copy Centers

- ADS Copying • 29 W. 38th St
- Kinko's • 16 E. 52nd St
- Kinko's • 1211 Ave. of the Americas
- Kinko's • 233 W. 54th St
- National Reproductions • 25 W. 45th St.
- The Village Copier • 25 W. 43rd St.

Gyms

- Apex Fitness • 244 W. 49th St.
- Art Of Fitness • 39 W. 56th St.
- Athletic and Swim Club at Equitable Center • 787 Seventh Ave.
- Bally Total Fitness • E. 53rd St. & Fifth Ave.
- Bally Total Fitness • 667 Fifth Ave.
- Body By Boris • 29 W. 57th St.
- Body Sculpt • 300 W. 40th St.
- Callanetics Studios of Manh. • 154 W. 57th St.
- Club La Raquette • 119 W. 56th St.
- Crunch Fitness • 38th & Broadway
- Definitions • 712 Fifth Ave.
- Drago's Gymnasium, Inc. • 50 W. 57th St.
- Estee Lauder, Inc. • 767 Fifth Ave.
- Exude Fitness, Inc. • 16 E. 52nd St.
- Fitness By Design • 41 W. 57th St.
- Fitness Center at the New York Palace • 455 Madison Ave.
- Gupta Mahesh K • 608 Fifth Ave.
- Insite • 150 W. 56th St.
- Mid-City Gym • 244 W. 49th St.
- New York Health & Racquet Club • 110 W. 56th St.
- New York Health & Racquet Club • 20 E. 50th St.
- New York Sports Clubs • 1601 Broadway
- New York Sports Clubs • 380 Madison Ave.
- Peninsula Spa • 2 W. 55th St.
- Prescriptive Fitness • 250 W. 54th St.
- Radu's Physical Culture Studio, Inc. • 24 W. 57th St.
- Ritz Plaza Health Club • 235 W. 48th St.
- Sheraton New York & Manhattan Health Clubs • 811 Seventh Ave.
- Town Sports International • 888 Seventh Ave.
- Ultimate Image • 532 Madison Ave.

Hardware Stores

- A A A Locksmiths • 44 W. 46th St.
- Barson Hardware Co., Inc. • 35 W. 44th St.
- Central Hardware & Elec. Corp. • 1055 Ave. of the Americas
- Friedlander Enterprises, Inc. • 250 W. 54th St.
- Garden Hardware & Supply Co. • 785 Eighth Ave.
- M J Hardware & Electric Corp. • 520 Eighth Ave.
- New Hippodrome Hardware, Inc. • 23 W. 45th St.
- Scheman & Grant, Inc. • 575 Eighth Ave.
- Silver & Sons Hardware Corp. • 711 Eighth Ave.

Laundromats

- Handy Laundry & Cleaners • 204 W. 55th St.
- Sister Fisher, Ltd. • 730 Fifth Ave.

Liquor Stores

- Acorn Wine & Liquor Co. • 268 W. 46th St.
- Athens Wine & Liquor • 302 W. 40th St.
- Cambridge Wine & Liquor, Inc. • 594 Eighth Ave.
- Carnegie Spirits & Wine, Ltd. • 849 Seventh Ave.
- Fifty-Fifth Street Liquor Store • 40 W. 55th St.
- Midtown Wine & Liquor Shop • 44 E. 50th St.
- Morrell & Company • 14 W. 49th St.
- Morrell & Co. Wine & Spirits Merchants • 535 Madison Ave.
- O'Ryan Package Store, Inc • 1424 Ave. of the Americas
- Park Av Liquor Shop • 292 Madison Ave.
- Reidy Wine & Liquor, Inc • 768 Eighth Ave.
- Royal Bee, Inc. • 1119 Ave. of the Americas
- Schumer's Wine & Liquors • 59 E. 54th St.
- Shon 45 Liquors • 840 Eighth Ave.
- Westley Liquor • 921 Eighth Ave.

Movie Theatres

- Bryant Park Summer Film Festival (outdoors) • Bryant Park, between 40th and 42nd Sts.
- Cineplex Odeon: Ziegfeld • 141 W. 54th St.
- Circle In The Square/ Civita Colonia Artistica • 1633 Broadway
- Clearview's 59th St. East • 239 E. 59th St.
- Common Basis Theater • 750 Eighth Ave.
- Crown Theatres • 712 Fifth Ave.
- D.G.A. Theater • 110 W. 57th St.
- Embassy 1,2,3 • 701 Seventh Ave
- Guild 50th • 33 W. 50th St at Rockefeller Plaza
- Loews Astor Plaza • 44th St. between Broadway & Eighth Ave.
- Loews State • 1540 Broadway
- Museum of Modern Art • 11 W. 53rd St.
- New Manhattan Repertory, Inc. • 1650 Broadway
- New York Public Library-Donnell Library Center • 20 W. 53rd St.
- Paris Theatre • 4 W. 58th St.
- Show World • 675 Eighth Ave.
- United Artists: Criterion • 1514 Broadway

Pet Store

- Animal House 2 • 315 W. 57th St.

Video Rentals

- 691 Video Center Corp. • 691 Eighth Ave.
- 763 Video Store • 763 Eighth Ave
- High Quality Video, Inc. • 21 W. 45th, 2nd fl.
- International Express Video • 219 Madison
- Rec Video • 301 W. 46th St.
- Video 54th Street • 231 W. 54th St.

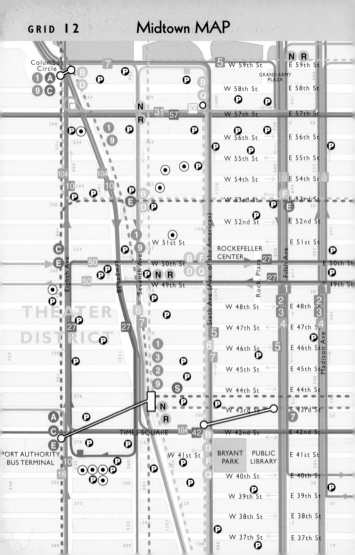

During the day, forget driving, forget parking, At night, however, 57th Street is one of the quickest cross-town routes in Manhattan. Times Square is a mess 24 hours a day.

Subways

Ⓐ Ⓒ Ⓑ Ⓓ ① ⑨	Columbus Circle
Ⓐ Ⓒ Ⓔ	42nd St. at 8th Ave. (Port Authority Bus Terminal)
Ⓑ Ⓓ Ⓔ	53rd St. at 7th Ave.
Ⓑ Ⓓ Ⓕ Ⓠ	42nd St. at 6th Ave.
Ⓑ Ⓓ Ⓕ Ⓠ	50th St. at 6th Ave. (Rockefeller Ctr.)
Ⓑ Ⓠ	57th St. at 6th Ave.
Ⓒ Ⓔ	50th St. at 8th Ave.
Ⓔ Ⓕ	53rd St. at 5th Ave.
Ⓝ Ⓡ	59th St. at 5th Ave.
Ⓝ Ⓡ	57th St. at 7th Ave.
Ⓝ Ⓡ	49th St. at 7th Ave.
Ⓝ Ⓡ Ⓢ ① ⑨ ② ③ ⑦	42nd St. at Broadway (Times Square)
① ⑨	50th St. at Broadway
⑦	42nd St. at 5th Ave.

Bus Lines

① ② ③ ④	5th Ave./Madison Ave.
⑤	5th Ave./Ave. of the Americas/Riverside Dr.
⑥	7th Ave./Broadway/Ave. of the Americas Columbus Ave./Amsterdam Ave./Lenox
⑦	6th Ave./7th Ave./Broadway 7th Ave./8th Ave. (Central Park West)/
⑩	Frederick Douglass Blvd.
⑯	34th St. Crosstown
㉗	49th St./50th St. Crosstown
㉚	57th St./72nd St. Crosstown
㊷	42nd St. Crosstown
㊲	57th St. Crosstown
⑩④	Broadway/42nd St.
⑯⑧	Penn Station-Jackson Heights, Queens

⊙ Car Rentals

- Avis Rent-A-Car • 153 W. 54th St.
- Budget • 304 W. 49th St.
- Dollar Rent-A-Car • 156 W. 54th St.
- Dollar Rent-A-Car • 235 W. 56th St.
- Hertz Car Rental • 126 W. 55th St.
- Hertz Truck & Van Rental (trucks & vans) • 126 W. 55th St.
- Manhattan Rent-A-Car • 1330 Ave. of the Americas
- NRC Rent-A-Car • 251 W. 40th St.
- National Car Rental • 241 W. 40th St.

- Nationwide Rent-A-Car • 241 W. 40th St.
- New York Rent-A-Car • 151 E. 51st St.

Ⓟ Parking

- 250 W. 43rd Parking Garage • 250 W. 43rd St.
- 888 Parking LLC • 888 Eighth Ave.
- Affiliated Parking • 261 Madison Ave.
- Allied 58th St. • 58 W. 58th St.
- Bright Management • 305 W. 48th St.
- Burlington House Garage • 100 W. 55th St.
- Central Parking • 25 W. 39th St.
- Central Parking • 235 W. 56th St.
- Champion Parking • 545 Madison Ave.
- Champion Parking • 31 W. 37th St.
- Circle Parking • 209 W. 51st St.
- Edison Park Fast Station No. 41 • 136 W. 40th St.
- Edison Park Fast Station No. 73 • 9 W. 57th St.
- Edison Parking • 1120 Ave. of the Americas
- Edison Parking • 745 Seventh Ave.
- Edison Parking • 13-15 W. 56th St.
- Garage Management • 257 W. 47th St.
- Garage Management • 148 W. 48th St.
- Garage Management • 225 W. 49th St.
- Garage Management • 218 W. 50th St.
- Garage Management • 200 Central Park South
- Global Parking • 143 W. 40th St.
- Gotham 55th Street Parking • 23 W. 55th St.
- Kinney System • 888 Seventh Ave.
- Kinney System • 264 W. 42nd St.
- Kinney System • 38 W. 46th St.
- Kinney System • 155 W. 48th St.
- Kinney System • 252 W. 40th St.
- Kinney System • 125 W. 58th St.
- Kinney System • 251 W. 40th St.
- Kinney System • 455 Madison
- Kinney System • 109 W. 56th St.
- Manhattan Parking 1350 • 1350 Sixth Ave.
- Manhattan Parking Madison • 437 Madison Ave.
- Manhattan Parking System • 120 W. 45th St.
- Manhattan Parking System • 137 W. 45th St.
- Meyer Parking System • 141 W. 43rd St.
- Meyers Parking System • 380 Madison Ave.
- Meyers Parking System • 31 W. 52nd St.
- New York Parking St. • 65 W. 56th St.
- Pace Parking • 990 Sixth Ave.
- Park-Serv • 140-166 W. 53rd St.
- Quik Park Garage • 586 Seventh Ave.
- Rapid Park Industries • 225 W. 58th St.
- Real Park • 239 W. 53rd St.
- S & M Parking • 666 Fifth Ave.
- Show Biz Parking • 251 W. 45th St.
- Square Plus Operating • 810 Seventh Ave.
- Times Square Garage • 220 W. 41st St.
- Trams Parking • 223 W. 46th St.
- Ultra Parking Systems & Garage Management Svces • 120 W. 41st St.

East Midtown MAP

E 60th St

QUEENSBORO BRIDGE

E 59th St

E 58th St

E 57th St

E 56th St

E 55th St

E 54th St

E 53rd St

E 52nd St

E 51St St

E 50th St

Mitchell Pl

E 49th St

E 48th St

E 47th St

E 46th St

E 45th St

E 44th St (Archbishop Fulton J.Sheen Pl)

E 43rd St

E 42nd St

E 41St St

E 40th St

E 39th St

E 38th St

E 37th St

Madison Av

Park Av

Lexington Av

Vanderbilt Av

Depew Pl

Third Av

Second Av

First Av

Sutton Pl

Beekman Pl

FDR DRIVE

United Nations Plaza

GEN. D. MACARTHUR PLZ

UNITED NATIONS

GRAND CENTRAL TERMINAL

TUDOR CITY

Tudor City Pl

Exit St

Entrance St

ROBERT MOSES PLGD

East River

FDR DRIVE

This is a busy and diverse part of town, packed with consulates, hotels, Grand Central Terminal, the United Nations, the Queensboro Bridge, and two exclusive housing enclaves—Tudor City and Sutton Place. Park Avenue between 40th and 60th Streets contains some of the finest examples of every major architectural style from the past 100 years.

💲 ATMs

- 1. AmEx Travel Related Services • 375 Park Ave.
- 2. Apple • 666 Third Ave.
- 3. Apple • 277 Park Ave.
- 4. Bank of NY • 100 E. 42nd St.
- 5. Bank of NY • 1006 First Ave.
- 6. Bank of NY • 360 Park Ave.
- 7. Bank of NY • 277 Park Ave.
- 8. Bank of NY • 260 Madison Ave.
- 9. Bank of NY • 575 Madison Ave.
- 10. Bank of NY • 979 Third Ave.
- 11. Bank of Tokyo • 360 Madison Ave.
- 12. Chase Manhattan • 221 Park Ave.
- 13. Chase Manhattan • Grand Central Lobby
- 14. Chase Manhattan • 1 Dag Ham. Plaza
- 15. Chase Manhattan • 241 E. 42nd St.
- 16. Chase Manhattan • 60 E. 42nd St.
- 17. Chase Manhattan • 633 Third Ave.
- 18. Chase Manhattan • 825 UN Plaza
- 19. Chase Manhattan • 200 E. 57th St.
- 20. Chase Manhattan • 410 Park Ave.
- 21. Chase Manhattan • 850 Third Ave.
- 22. Chase Manhattan • 405 Lexington Ave.
- 23. Chase Manhattan • 401 Madison Ave.
- 24. Chase Manhattan • 488 Madison Ave.
- 25. Chase Manhattan • 598 Madison Ave.
- 26. Chase Manhattan • 770 Lexington Ave.
- 27. Citibank • 734 Third Ave.
- 28. Citibank • 460 Park Ave.
- 29. Citibank • 135 E. 53rd St.
- 30. Citibank • 200 Park Ave.
- 31. Citibank • 230 Park Ave.
- 32. Citibank • 330 Madison Ave.
- 33. Citibank • 1044 First Ave.
- 34. Citibank • 985 Third Ave.
- 35. Commercial Bank • 750 Third Ave.
- 36. Commercial Bank • 845 Third Ave.
- 37. Emigrant Savings • 115 E. 56th St.
- 38. Emigrant Savings • 335 Madison Ave.
- 39. EAB • 90 Park Ave.
- 40. EAB • 866 UN Plaza
- 41. EAB • 800 Third Ave.
- 42. Fleet • 280 Park Ave.
- 43. Fleet • 345 Park Ave.
- 44. Greenpoint • 109 E. 42nd St.
- 45. Greenpoint • 641 Lexington Ave.
- 46. Greenpoint • 1010 Third Ave.
- 47. Marine Midland HBSC • 250 Park Ave.
- 48. Marine Midland HBSC • 441 Madison Ave.
- 49. Marine Midland HBSC • 777 Third Ave.
- 50. Marine Midland HBSC • 919 Third Ave.
- 51. Marine Midland HBSC • 437 Madison Ave.
- 52. Marine Midland HBSC • 555 Madison Ave.
- 53. Republic National • 605 Third Ave.
- 54. Republic National • 950 Third Ave.

🅞 Bagels

- B & Y Edibles Inc. • 36 W. 48 St.
- Daniel's Bagel Corp. • 569 Third Ave.
- Ess-A-Bagel • 831 Third Ave.
- Jumbo Bagels & Bialys • 1070 Second Ave.
- New World Coffee • 342 Madison Ave.
- Tal Bagels Inc. • 979 First Ave.
- The Bagel • 875 Third Ave.

★ Landmarks

- Chrysler Building • 405 Lexington Ave.
- Citicorp Center • 153 E. 53rd St.
- Grand Central Station • 42nd St.
- Seagram Building • 375 Park Ave.
- The United Nations • First Ave.
- The Waldorf-Astoria • 301 Park Ave.

📖 Libraries

- 58th St. • 127 E. 58th St.
- Terence Cardinal Cooke-Cathedral • 560 Lexington Ave.

🅡 24 Hour Pharmacies

- Duane Reade • 485 Lexington Ave.
- Kaufman Pharmacy • Lexington Ave. and 50th St.

🅟 Police Precinct

- 17th Precinct • 167 E. 51st St.

✉ Post Offices

- Dag Hammarskjol • 884 Second Ave.
- Franklin D. Roosevelt • 909 Third Ave.
- Grand Central Station • 450 Lexington Ave.
- Tudor City • 5 Tudor City Pl.
- United Nations • 405 E. 42nd St.

🅢 Schools

- High School of Art & Des • 1075 Second Ave.
- Neighborhood Playhouse School • 340 E. 54th St.
- 59 Beekman Hill School • 228 E. 57th St.
- SCS Business & Tech School • 575 Lexington Ave.
- The Sonia Moore Studio • 900 Third Ave.

QUEENSBORO BRIDGE

E 60th St

E 59th St

E 58th St

E 57th St

E 56th St

E 55th St

E 54th St

E 53rd St

E 52nd St

E 51St St

E 50th St

E 49th St

E 48th St

E 47th St

E 46th St

E 45th St

E 44th St(Archbishop Fulton J.Sheen Pl)

E 43rd St

E 42nd St

E 41St St

E 40th St

E 39th St

E 38th St

E 37th St

Madison Av

Park Av

Lexington Av

Third Av

Second Av

First Av

Sutton Pl

FDR DRIVE

Vanderbilt Av

Depew Pl

GRAND CENTRAL TERMINAL

Exit St

Entrance St

Tudor City Pl

United Nations Plaza

UNITED NATIONS

Beekman Pl

Mitchell Pl

GEN. D. MACARTHUR PLZ.

ROBERT MOSES PLGD

TUDOR CITY

East River

FDR DRIVE

C 24-Hour Copy Centers
- The Village Copier • 420 Lexington Ave.
- Kinko's • 305 E. 46th St.
- Kinko's • 600 Third Ave.
- Kinko's • 153 E. 53rd St.
- Copycats • 216 E. 45th St.
- Metro Copy and Duplicating • 222 E. 45th St.

24-Hour Diners
- Gemini Restaurant • 641 Second Ave.
- Sarge's Deli • 548 Third Ave.

Gyms
- Absolute Fitness • 343 Lexington Ave.
- Aline Fitness • 226 E. 53rd St.
- Away Spa-Gym At W New York • 541 Lexington Ave.
- Aquatic Recreational Management • 245 E. 40th St.
- Bally Sports Club • 335 E. 43rd St.
- Bally Total Fitness • E. 55th St.
- Crunch Fitness • 1109 Second Ave.
- Dag Hammarskjold Tower • 240 E. 47th St.
- Dolphin Fitness Club • 330 E. 59th St.
- Equinox Fitness Clubs • 250 E. 54th St.
- Excelsior Athletic Club • 301 E. 57th St.
- Fitness Center • 455 Madison Ave.
- Guest Passes • 301 E. 38th St.
- Huma Sports Training Center • 400 E. 51st St.
- Lift Gym • 139 E. 57th St.
- Manhattan Place Condominium Health Club • 630 First Ave.
- Midtown Karate Dojo • 465 Lexington Ave.
- NY Health & Racquet Club • 132 E. 45th St.
- NY Health & Racquet Club • 20 E. 50th St.
- NY Health & Racquet Club (Spa) • 115 E. 57th St.
- New York Sports Club • 633 Third Ave.
- New York Sports Club • 575 Lexington Ave.
- New York Sports Club • 380 Madison Ave.
- Plus One Fitness Clinic • 301 Park Ave.
- Spa 227 • 227 E. 56th St.
- Sparta Strength and Conditioning • 133 E. 55th St.
- Sports Training Institute • 575 Lexington Ave.
- U.S. Athletic Training Center • 515 Madison Ave.
- Ultimate Training Center • 532 Madison Ave.
- Upper Body • 343 Lexington Ave.
- Vanderbilt Health Club • 240 E. 41st St.
- YMCA • 224 E. 47th St.
- YWCA • 610 Lexington Ave.

T Hardware Stores
- 55th St. Hardware • 155 E. 55th St.
- Always Quick Service • 346 E. 59th St.
- Brass Center • 248 E. 58th St.
- Economy Buying Group • 211 E. 43rd St.
- Gasnick Supply Company True Value • 992 Second Ave.
- Kramer's • 952 Second Ave.
- Lumber Boys • 698 Second Ave.
- Midtown Hardware • 155 E. 45th St.
- Sherle Wagner International • 60 E. 57th St.

Laundromats
- 351 & 1/2 Corp. • 351 1/2 E. 54th St.
- C & Z Evergreen • 238 E. 58th St.
- Cen Long Su Laundry • 953 First Ave.
- Dry Cleaner • 211 E. 51 St.
- East 51st St. Launderette • 305 E. 51st St.
- Eastern Chinese Hnd. Lndry • 127 E. 39th St.
- Eastgate Cleaners • 944 First Ave.
- Expert Laundromat • 330 E. 53rd St.
- Gold Star Laundry • 249 E. 45th St.
- Laundercoin • 311 E. 37th St.
- Lee Wing • 1059 First Ave.
- Lee's Laundry • 137 E. 56th St.
- National Laundries • 505 Park Ave.
- New Turtle Bay Cleaners Corp. • 305 E. 45th St.
- Premiere Laundromat • 1028 Second Ave.
- Yu's Lucky Laundry • 956 First Ave.

Liquor Stores
- Ambassador Wines & Spirits • 1020 Second Ave.
- American First Liquors • 1059 First Ave.
- Beekman Liquors • 500 Lexington Ave.
- Biltmore Wine & Liquor Store • 1020 Second Ave.
- Diplomat Wine & Spirits • 939 Second Ave.
- D'Vine Wines • 764 Third Ave.
- Jeffrey Wine & Liquors • 939 First Ave.
- Grand Harvest Wines • 107 E. 42nd St.
- Maison De Vins • 883 First Ave.
- Schumer's Wine & Liquors • 59 E. 54th St.
- Sussex Liquor Store • 300 E. 41st St.
- Sutton Wine Shop • 403 E. 57th St.
- Turtle Bay Liquors Inc. • 855 Second Ave.
- You & Me Wines & Liquors • 1020 Second Ave.

Movie Theatres
- Cineplex Odeon: Coronet Cinemas • 993 Third Ave.
- City Cinemas: Eastside Playhouse • 919 Third Ave.
- City Cinemas: Sutton 1 & 2 • 205 E. 57th St.
- Crown Gotham Cinema • 969 Third Ave.
- Folksbiene Theatre • 123 E. 55th St.
- French Institute • Florence Gould Hall, 55 E. 59th St.
- Instituto Cervantes • 122 E. 42nd St.
- Japan Society • 333 E. 47th St.
- Manhattan Twin • 220 E. 59th St.
- Reading Entertainment • 950 Third Ave.
- YWCA • 610 Lexington Ave.

Pet Stores
- Beekman Pet Emporium • 900 First Ave.
- Furry Paws • 1039 Second Ave.
- International Kennel Club •1032 Second Ave.
- Petland Discounts • 976 Second Ave.
- Video Couch & Pet Supplies • 715 Second Ave.

Video Rentals
- Intl. Express Video • 219 Madison Ave.
- Intl. Film & Video Center • 989 First Ave.
- Khan Video • 59 E. 54th St.
- Lion's Den • 230 E. 53rd St.
- New York Video • 949 First Ave.
- Quick Photo • 962 Second Ave.
- Video Couch & Pet Supplies • 715 Second Ave.

Other than the quirky ramps running around Grand Central and the snarl around the Queensboro Bridge, traffic in this area could be far worse than it is. For instance, Park Avenue is a surprisingly excellent way to head downtown at rush hour. The best route to the Queensboro from downtown is First Avenue to 57th Street. However, it's always wise to pay attention for when the President or some other major dignitary is at the U.N., because you'll want to use mass transit that day. Street parking will always remain a dream.

Subways

6 **6** **6**	51 St. at Lexington Ave.
S **4** **5** **6** **7**	42 St. at Lexington Ave.
6 **F**	53rd St. at 5th Ave.
7	42 St. at 5th Ave.
N **R**	59 St. at Lexington Ave.

Bus Lines

1 **2** **3**	5th Ave./Madison Ave.
101 **102** **103**	3rd Ave./Lexington Ave.
104	Broadway
15	1st Ave./2nd Ave.
27 **50**	49th St./50th St. Crosstown
30	72nd St./57th St. Crosstown
31	York Ave./57th St.
42	42nd St. Crosstown
57	57th St. Crosstown
57	Washington Heights/Midtown Limited
32	Queens-to-Midtown

⊙ Car Rentals

- Avis • 217 E. 43rd St.
- Avis • 240 E. 54th St.
- Budget • 225 E. 43rd St.
- Hertz • 222 E. 40th St.
- Hertz • 310 E. 48th St.
- National • 138 E. 50th St.
- New York Rent A Car • 151 E. 51st St.
- Renault USA Inc • 650 First Ave.

◆ Car Washes

- Kenny Car Wash System Inc. • 625 Eleventh Ave.
- Westside Highway Car Wash • 638 W. 47th St.

⊞ Gas Station

- East 53rd St. Garage • 411 E. 53rd St.

P Parking

- Affiliated Parking • 261 Madison Ave.
- Apple Parking • 501 E. 59th St.
- Basic Parking • 225 E. 46th St.
- Beekman Garage • 420 E. 51st St.
- Carole Storage • 777 Third Ave.
- Champion Parking • 545 Madison Ave.
- Chelnik Parking • 575 Lexington Ave.
- Chelnik Parking • 425 Park Ave.
- Connaught Towers Car Park • 300 E. 54th St.
- Continental Garage • 300 E. 59th St.
- Distinctive Parking • 569-13 Lexington Ave.
- Edison 52nd St. Management • 400 E. 54th St.

- Edison • 711 Third Ave.
- Edison • 1113 York Ave.
- Elco Parking Systems • 312 E. 46th St.
- Enterprise Parking 45th • 333 E. 45th St.
- Ezey • 131 E. 55th St.
- Ezey Parking Systems • 155 E. 55th St.
- Garage Management • 400 E. 56th St.
- Garage Management • 229 E. 55th St.
- Garage Management • 435 E. 55th St.
- Garage Management • 420 E. 53rd St.
- Garage Management • 420 E. 51st St.
- Garage Management • 443 E. 49th St.
- Garage Management • 320 E. 48th St.
- Garage Management • 2 UN Plaza
- Garage Management • 3 UN Plaza
- Gemini Garage • 50 Sutton Pl. S.
- Gemini Parking • 222 E. 40th St.
- Harridge Garage • 222 E. 58th St.
- Kaufco Management • 450 E. 53rd St.
- Kinney System • 53 E. 53rd St.
- Kinney System • 333 E. 46th St.
- Kinney System • 455 Madison Ave.
- Kinney System • 315 E. 40th St.
- Lex & 58th Parking • 150 E. 58th St.
- MHM Parking • 300 E. 46th St.
- Manhattan Parking Park Ave • 277 Park Ave.
- Marlborough Garage • 242 E. 41st St.
- Midtown Parking • 575 Lexington Ave.
- New York Parking 51st St. • 251 E. 51st St.
- Nine One Nine Garage • 229 E. 59th St.
- Noble Parking • 310 E. 40th St.
- Noble Parking • 300 E. 40th St.
- Oxford Parking • 325 E. 49th St.
- Parklex Garage • 345 Park Ave.
- Professional Parking • 140 E. 56th St.
- Quik Park Garage • 240 E. 41st St.
- Rapid Park Industries • 340 E. 59th St.
- Realpro Parking • 330 E. 39th St.
- Regal Parking • 260 Madison Ave.
- River Edge Sutton Garden Garage • 425 E. 54th St.
- River Tower Parking • 420 E. 54th St.
- Saxon Garage • 230 E. 44th St.
- Select Parking • 301 E. 57th St.
- Sovereign Car Park • 425 E. 58th St.
- Square Plus • 135 E. 47th St.
- Sylvan • 231 E. 43rd St.
- Sylvan • 357 E. 57th St.
- 12 Beekman Pl. Garage •
  12 Beekman Pl.
- UND Unique Garage •
  1 U.N. Plaza
- Valor Parking • 235 E. 45th St.
- Wolf Lawrence Paul • 211 E. 43rd St.
- 205 E. 38th St. Parking • 207 E. 38th St.
- 211 E. 43rd St. Parking • 214 E. 44th St.
- 60 Sutton Pl. South Garage • 60 Sutton Pl.

The presence of Lincoln Center and the Museum of Natural History gives the southern half of the Upper West Side more than its share of the major cultural hotspots in Manhattan, and the presence of several truly remarkable apartment buildings (the Ansonia, the Apthorp, the Dorilton, the Dakota, the Majestic, and the San Remo) gives it the illusion that it would actually be a nice place to live.

💲 ATMs

- 1. ABC Employees Federal •
  30 W. 66th St., 1st Fl.
- 2. ABC Employees Federal • 77 W. 66th St., Lobby
- 3. Apple Bank For Savings • 2100 Broadway
- 4. Bank of New York • 47 W. 62nd St.
- 5. Chase Manhattan •1934 Broadway
- 6. Chase Manhattan • 2099 Broadway
- 7. Chase Manhattan • 260 Columbus Ave.
- 8. Chase Manhattan • 2219 Broadway
- 9. Chase Manhattan • 969 Eighth Ave.
- 10. Chase Manhattan • 124 W. 60th St.
- 11. Citibank • 162 Amsterdam Ave.
- 12. Citibank • 175 W. 72nd St.
- 13. Commercial • 2025 Broadway
- 14. Jamaica Savings • 1995 Broadway
- 15. Republic National • 1790 Broadway

🥯 Bagels

- B-J's Bagels • 130 W. 72nd St.
- H & H Bagels • 2239 Broadway
- Hot & Tasty Bakery • 2079 Broadway
- New World Coffee • 2151 Broadway
- New World Coffee • 159 Columbus Ave.
- New York City Bagels • 164 Amsterdam Ave.

🏵 Community Gardens

- W. 82nd St. Community Gardens (SOS) •
  103-5 W. 82nd St.
- MLK Jr. H.S. • 122 Amsterdam Ave.

★ Landmarks

- Ansonia Hotel • Broadway at 73rd St.
- The Dakota • Central Park West at 72nd St.
- The Dorilton • Broadway at 71st St.
- Lincoln Center • Broadway at 64th St.
- The Majestic • Broadway at 71st St.
- Museum of Natural History •
  Central Park West at 79th St.
- The San Remo • Central Park West at 74th St.

📖 Libraries

- New York Public Library for the Performing Arts •
  40 Lincoln Center Plaza
- Riverside • 127 Amsterdam Ave.
- St. Agnes • 444 Amsterdam Ave.

Ⓡ 24 Hour Pharmacy

- Rite Aid • 200 W. 70th St.

🅿 Police Precinct

- 20th Precinct • 120 W. 82nd St.

✉ Post Offices

- Ansonia Station • 211 W. 61st St.
- Columbus Circle • 27 W. 60th St.
- Planetarium • 131 W. 83rd St.

Ⓢ Schools

- Alvin Ailey American Dance Center •
  211 W. 61st St.
- American Musical and Drama Academy •
  2109 Broadway
- Beacon High School • 227 W. 61st St.
- The Calhouse School • 81st St. & West End Ave.
- Fiorello H. LaGuardia High School •
  108 Amsterdam Ave.
- Fordham University • 113 W. 60th St.
- IS 044 William J O'Shea School • 100 W. 77th St.
- Louis D. Brandeis High School • 145 W. 84th St.
- Mannes College Of Music • 150 W. 85th St.
- Metropolitan Center •1855 Broadway
- New York Institute of Tech • 1855 Broadway
- PS 009 Renaissance School • 100 W. 84th St.
- PS 087 William Sherman • 160 W. 78th St.
- PS 191 Amsterdam School • 210 W. 61st St.
- PS 199 Jesse Straus School •
  270 W. 70th St.
- PS 252 • 20 West End Ave.

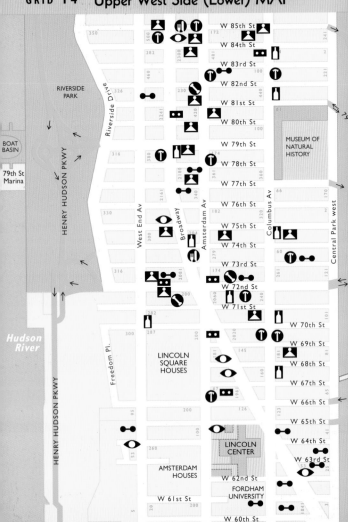

Home to the famous Zabar's, several amusing watering holes (such as the Dublin House and the All-State Café), and the viciously tasty and unhealthy Big Nick's Burger Joint (at 2175 Broadway), this part of the Upper West Side has more character than people suspect at first glance.

24-Hour Diners

- French Roast • 2340 Broadway
- Gray's Papaya • 2090 Broadway

Gyms

- Alfred Condominium Health Club • 161 W. 61st St.
- All Star Fitness Center • 75 West End Ave.
- BodyHeat Fitness • 49 W. 73rd St.
- Circle Club Inc. • 17 W. 60th St.
- Club 30 • 30 W. 63rd St.
- Crunch Fitness • 160 W. 83rd St.
- Equinox Fitness Club • 344 Amsterdam Ave.
- Extravertical Climbing Center • 61 W. 62nd St.
- New York Sports • 2162 Broadway
- Nickolaus Exercise Center • 237 W. 72nd St.
- Patricia Ripley's Fitness Studio • 131 W. 72nd St.
- West River Racquet Ball • 424 West End Ave.
- World Gym • 1926 Broadway
- YMCA of Greater NY: Westside • 5 W. 63rd St.

Hardware Stores

- Absolute Locksmith & Hardware • 207 Columbus Ave.
- Amsterdam Hardware • 147 Amsterdam Ave.
- Beacon Paint & Wallpaper Co. Inc. • 371 Amsterdam Ave.
- Gartner's Hardware Inc. • 134 W. 72nd St.
- Klosty Hardware • 471 Amsterdam Ave.
- Ronnie's Hardware • 208 Columbus Ave.
- Roxy Hardware and Paint Co. • 469 Columbus Ave.
- Mike's Lumber Store Inc. • 520 Amsterdam Ave.
- Riverside Houseware Inc. • 2315 Broadway
- Supreme Hardware & Supply Co. Inc. • 65 W. 73rd St.

Laundromats

- 102 West Laundromat • 102 W. 71st St.
- 85th Laundromat, Inc. • 251 W. 85th St.
- B.C. Laundry Corp. • 216 W. 85th St.
- Columbus Valet Service • 61 W. 74th St.
- CU Launderette, Inc. • 244 W. 72nd St.
- Ecowash • 72 W. 69th St.
- Immaculate Hand Laundry & Dry Cleaning • 271 W. 72nd St.
- Laundromat 77 • 221 W. 77th St.
- M&S Chinese Laundry & Dry Cleaning • 76 W. 85th St.
- P&K Laundromat • 432 Amsterdam Ave.
- Park West Laundromat • 101 W. 84th St.
- Prestige Laundry • 409 Amsterdam Ave.
- S&D Launderette • 200 W. 80th St.
- US Laundry & Cleaner • 200 W. 84th St.
- Wash N Dry • 228 W. 75th St.
- West 79 St. Laundromat • 218 W. 79th St.
- Westside Laundromat Corp. • 165 W. 74th St.

Liquor Stores

- 67 Wine & Spirits Inc. • 179 Columbus Ave.
- 79th Street Wine & Spirits Corp. • 230 W. 79th St.
- Acker Merrall • 160 W. 72nd St.
- Beacon Wines & Spirits • 2120 Broadway
- Central Wine & Liquor Store • 227 Columbus Ave.
- Nancy's Wines • 313 Columbus Ave.
- Rose Wine & Liquor Corp • 449 Columbus Ave.
- West End Wine Inc. • 204 West End Ave.
- West Side Wine & Spirits Shop • 481 Columbus Ave.

Movie Theatres

- American Museum of Natural History • Central Park West at 79th St.
- Cineplex Odeon: Regency • 1987 Broadway
- Clearview's 62nd & Broadway • 1871 Broadway
- Lincoln Plaza Cinemas • 30 Lincoln Plaza at Broadway & 62nd St.
- Loew's 84th St. • 2310 Broadway
- New York Society for Ethical Culture • 2 W. 64th St.
- Sony 84th St. • 2310 Broadway
- Sony Lincoln Square & IMAX Theatre • 1992 Broadway
- Walter Reade Theater • 70 Lincoln Center Plaza
- Women's Projects & Productions • 55 West End Ave.

Pet Stores

- Pet Bowl • 440 Amsterdam Ave.
- The Pet Market • 210 W. 72nd St.
- Petland Discounts • 137 W. 72nd St.

Video Rentals

- Blockbuster Video • 199 Amsterdam Ave.
- Channel Video • 472 Columbus Ave.
- Flik's Video 2 Go • 175 W. 72nd St.
- Kozmo Inc. • 251 W. 72nd St.
- Tower Records-Video-Books • 1961 Broadway
- The Video Connection • 2240 Broadway

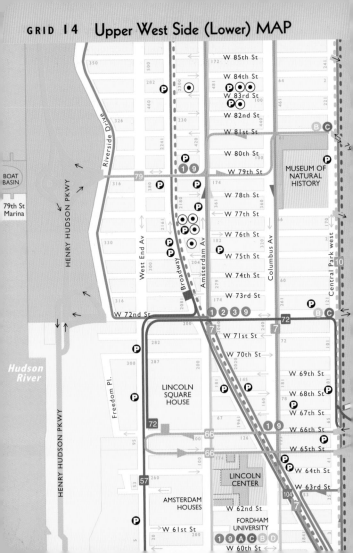

Upper West Side (Lower) TRANSPORTATION

Parking and driving are both actually do-able in this area, with most of the available spots on or near Riverside Drive. We recommend the 79th Street Transverse for crossing Central Park to go to the east side. The Lincoln Center area is by far the messiest traffic problem here—you can avoid it by taking West End Avenue.

Subways

1 9 ....79th St. at Broadway
B C ....81th St. at Central Park West
B C ....72nd St. at Central Park West
1 2 3 9 ....72nd St. at Broadway
1 9 A C B D ....Columbus Circle

Bus Lines

5 .... 5th Ave./
Ave. of the Americas/Riverside Dr.
Columbus Ave./Amsterdam Ave./
7 ....Lenox Ave./6th Ave./Broadway
10 ....7th Ave./8th Ave./Douglass Blvd.
11 ....9th Ave./10th Ave.
57 ....57th St. Crosstown
66 ....66th St./67th St. Crosstown
72 ....72nd St. Crosstown
79 .... 79th St. Crosstown
104 ....Broadway/42nd St.

Car Rentals

- Avis Rent-A-Car • 216 W. 76th St.
- Budget • 207 W. 76th St.
- Enterprise Rent- A-Car • 147 W. 83rd St.
- Hertz Car Rental • 210 W. 77th St.
- Hertz Truck & Van Rental • 210 W. 77th St.
- Manhattan Rent- A-Car • 143 W. 83rd St.
- National Car Rental • 219 W. 77th St.
- New York Rent- A-Car • 146 W. 83rd St.

P Parking

- 79th St. Garage • 200 W. 79th St.
- 80 Central Park West Garage • 80 Central Park West
- Amsterdam Parking • 350 Amsterdam Ave.
- Beacon Garage • 210 W. 76th St.
- Bew Parking • 254 W. 79th St.
- Carousel Parking • 201 W. 75th St.
- Continental 10th W. Garage • 10 W. 66th St.
- Copely Garage • 2000 Broadway
- Edison Park Fast Garages • 1916 Broadway
- Edison Park Fast Station No. 235 • 214 W. 80th St.
- Edison Parking • 214 W 80th St.
- Garage Management • 2000 Broadway
- Gemini 165 West End Parking • 165 West End Ave.
- Kinney System • 147 W. 83rd St.
- Kinney System • 150 W. 83rd St.
- Lincoln Towers Garage No. 5 • 150 West End Ave.
- MHM Parking • 225 W. 83rd St.
- New York Parking 56th St. • 65 W. 66th St.
- Omni Parking • 155 W. 68th St.
- RT Parking • 207 W. 76th St.
- Rapid Park Industries • 15 W. 72nd St.
- Square Plus Operating • 15 West End Ave.
- TPC Ansonia • 2109 Broadway
- Two Hundred Central Park South Garage • 200 Central Park South

E 86th St

E 85th St

E 84th St

E 83rd St

E 82nd St

E 81st St

E 80th St

E 79th St

E 78th St

E 77th St

E 76th St

E 75th St

E 74th St

E 73rd St

E 72nd St

E 71st St

E 70th St

E 69th St

E 68th St

E 67th St

E 66th St

E 65th St

E 64th St

E 63rd St

E 62nd St

E 61st St

E 60th St

Fifth Ave

Madison Ave

Park Ave

Lexington Ave

Third Ave

Second Ave

First Ave

York Ave

East End Ave

CARL SCHURZ PARK

JOHN JAY PARK

ROCKEFELLER UNIVERSITY

FDR Drive

East River

ROOSEVELT ISLAND TRAMWAY

QUEENSBORO BRIDGE

The southern half of the Upper East Side is a hotbed of culture, research, and education, containing one of the world's top museums (the Metropolitan Museum of Art); several top schools, including Cornell University Medical Center and Rockefeller University; and perhaps the foremost cancer hospital in the world, Memorial Sloan-Kettering Cancer Center.

$ ATMs

- 1. Apple Bank For Savings • 1555 First Ave.
- 2. Bank of New York • 1100 Third Ave.
- 3. Bank of New York • 706 Madison Ave.
- 4. Chase Manhattan • 1003 Lexington Ave.
- 5. Chase Manhattan • 1025 Madison Ave.
- 6. Chase Manhattan • 201 E. 79th St.
- 7. Chase Manhattan • 300 E. 64th St.
- 8. Chase Manhattan • 360 E. 72nd St.
- 9. Chase Manhattan • 501 E. 79th St.
- 10. Chase Manhattan • 515 E. 72nd St.
- 11. Chase Manhattan • 940 Madison Ave.
- 12. Citibank • 1078 Third Ave.
- 13. Citibank • 1266 First Ave.
- 14. Citibank • 1285 First Ave.
- 15. Citibank • 1510-12 First Ave.
- 16. Citibank • 171 E. 72nd St.
- 17. Citibank • 757 Madison Ave.
- 18. Citibank • 976 Madison Ave.
- 19. Commercial Bank of New York • 1180 Third Ave.
- 20. Commercial Bank of New York • 1258 Second Ave.
- 21. Dime Savings • 510 Park Ave.
- 22. Dime Savings • 1520 York Ave.
- 23. Fleet • 1143 Lexington Ave.
- 24. Fourth Federal Savings • 1355 First Ave.
- 25. Marine Midland HBSC • 1165 Third Ave.
- 26. Marine Midland HBSC • 1340 Third Ave.
- 27. Republic National Bank • 1002 Madison Ave.

O Bagels

- 1101 Bagel Corp • 1101 Lexington Ave.
- Amir Ram Bagels Inc. • 333 E. 86th St.
- Bagle & Co. • York Ave. & 76th St.
- Bagelry • 1228 Lexington Ave.
- Bagelworks • 1229 First Ave.
- The Bread Factory Cafe • 785 Lexington Ave.
- Café Group of New York • 1228 Second Ave.
- Eastside Bagel • 1496 Second Ave.
- Einstein Bros. Bagels • 1336 First Ave.
- Elaine's Bagel Ltd. • 941 Park Ave.
- H & H Bagels East • 1551 Second Ave.
- New World Coffee • 1246 Lexington Ave.
- Pick A Bagel On Second • 1473 Second Ave.

H Hospitals

- Gracie Square Hospital • 420 E. 76th St.
- Hospital For Special Surgery • 535 E. 70th St.
- Lenox Hill Hospital • 100 E. 77th St.
- Manhattan Eye, Ear & Throat Hospital •
  210 E. 64th St.
- Memorial Sloan-Kettering Cancer Center •
  1275 York Ave.
- New York Hospital-Cornell Medical Center •
  525 E. 68th St.

★ Landmarks

- Abigail Adams Smith Museum • 421 E. 61st St.
- Asia Society • 725 Park Ave.
- Frick Collection • 1 E. 70th St.
- Metropolitan Museum of Art • 1000 Fifth Ave.
- Temple Emanu-El • 1 E. 65th St.
- Whitney Museum of American Art • 945 Madison Ave.

📖 Libraries

- 67th Street • 328 E. 68th St.
- Webster • 1465 York Ave.
- Yorkville • 222 E. 79th St.

R 24-Hour Pharmacies

- CVS Pharmacy • 1400 Second Ave.
- Duane Reade • 1279 Third Ave.
- Genovese • Second Ave. at 68th St.
- Rite Aid • 144 E. 86th St.

P Police Precinct

- 19th Precinct • 153 W. 67th St.

✉ Post Offices

- Ansonia Finance • 40 W. 66th St.
- Cherokee • 1539 First Ave.
- Gracie • 229 E. 85th St.
- Lenox Hill • 221 E. 70th St.

S Schools

- Brandeis University • 12 E. 77th St.
- City University of New York • 535 E. 80th St.
- Cornell University Medical College • 445 E. 69th St.
- Evening School • 317 E. 67th St.
- Hunter College • 695 Park Ave.
- JHS 167 Robert F. Wagner School • 220 E. 76th St.
- Julia Richman High School • Second Ave. & 67th St.
- Manhattan International High School • 317 E. 67th St.
- Martha Graham School • 316 E. 63rd St.
- Marymount Manhattan College •
  221 E. 71st St.
- New York School Of Interior Design •
  170 E. 70th St.
- PS 006 Lillie D. Blake School • 45 E. 81st St.
- PS 158 Bayard Taylor School • 1458 York Ave.
- PS 183 R. L. Stevenson School •
  419 E. 66th St.
- PS 190 New School • 311 E. 82nd St.
- Sotheby's Educational Studies •
  1334 York Ave.
- Rockefeller University • 1230 York Ave.
- Vanguard High School • 317 E. 67th St.

The Upper East Side has itself covered pretty well here, and it also has another of New York's classic movie theaters, the Beekman.

◉ 24-Hour Copy Centers

- Copycats • 1646 Second Ave.
- Copycats • 968 Lexington Ave.
- Kinko's • 1122 Lexington Ave.

🍴 24-Hour Diners

- Doaba Diner • 1133 First Ave.
- Viand • 300 E. 86th St.
- Viand • 1011 Madison Ave.
- Viand • 673 Madison Ave.

● Gyms

- Belaire Health Club • 524 E. 72nd St.
- Casa Fitness Club • 48 E. 73rd St.
- Definitions • 39 E. 78th St.
- Eastside Sports Physical Therapy • 244 E. 84th St.
- Elissa's Personal Best Gym • 334 E. 79th St.
- Equinox Fitness Club • 140 E. 63rd St. & Lexington Ave.
- Equinox Fitness Club • 205 E. 85th St. & Third Ave.
- Hampton House Health Club • 404 E. 79th St.
- Lauder Estee Inc • 767 Fifth Ave.
- Lenox Hill Neighborhood House • 331 E. 70th St.
- Med Fitness • 12 E. 86th St.
- New York Health & Racquet Club • 1433 York Ave.
- New York Sports Clubs • 349 E. 76th St.
- New York Sports Clubs • 502 Park Ave.
- Pavilion Personal Fitness Center • 500 E. 77th St.
- Promenade Health Club • 530 E. 76th St.
- Savoy Spa • 200 E. 61st St.
- Strathmore Swim & Health Club • 400 E. 84th St.
- Synergy USA Inc • 1438 Third Ave.
- The Training Floor • 428 E. 75th St.
- Vertical Club • 330 E. 61st St.

🔧 Hardware Stores

- 72 Street Hardware • 1398 Second Ave.
- ATB Locksmith & Hardware Inc • 1603 York Ave.
- Gracious Home • 1220 Third Ave.
- Kraft Hardware Inc • 306 E. 61st St.
- Lexington Hardware & Electric Co. • 797 Lexington Ave.
- New York Paint & Hardware • 1593 Second Ave.
- Queensboro Hardware Co. • 1157 Second Ave.
- Rainbow Ace Hardware • 1449 First Ave.
- S & V General Supply Co. • 1450 First Ave.
- Sutton Hardware & Home Center • 1153 First Ave.
- Thaico Maintenance Supply Co. • 1462 Second Ave.
- Third Ave Supl Co. • 1301 Third Ave.

🧺 Laundromats

- 417 Cleaners • 417 E. 65th St.
- 64 St. Laundromat & Dry Cleaner • 412 E. 64th St.
- 77 Laundromat • 1481 First Ave.
- 79 Street Laundromat • 448 E. 79th St.
- 83rd St. Laundromat • 228 E. 83rd St.
- All Washed Up • 1217 Lexington Ave.
- All Washed Up • 1457 York Ave.
- All Washed Up • 1605 Second Ave.
- All Washed Up • 444 E. 81st St.
- Asia Laundromat • 1415 Second Ave.
- Best Cleaners • 172 E. 61st St.
- Chen Feng Ping • 1224 Lexington Ave.
- Chin Lee Laundry • 454 E. 84th St.
- Complete Laundromat • 1593 First Ave.
- Eddy's Laundry & Cleaners • 1067 First Ave.
- Engle Frank • 952 Lexington Ave.
- Ever Clean Laundry Service • 343 E. 66th St.
- Ever Clean Laundry • 400 E. 74th St.
- Excellent Laundry • 350 E. 67th St.
- Fine Laundromat • 147 E. 85th St.
- First Reliable Laundry & Cleaners • 506 E. 82nd St.
- Gentle Panda Laundry • 1341/2 E. 62nd St.
- Haric Laundry • 335 E. 65th St.
- Horng Ming, Inc. • 303 E. 80th St.
- Jack's Laundry & Dry Cleaning • 220 E. 78th St.
- Jim Lee's • 212 E. 67th St.
- Joe's Laundry • 400 E. 80th St.
- Laundry & Cleaners • 301 E. 85th St.
- Lee Wing • 1059 First Ave.
- Lee's Laundry • 308 E. 71st St.
- Lee's Laundry • 319 E. 75th St.
- Lok's Laundry • 500 E. 84th St.
- Lok's Laundry • 354 E. 81st St.
- M&I Launderama • 402 E. 78th St.

- Mekong Wash & Dry • 1612 York Ave.
- Millionaire Laundermat • 324 E. 73rd St.
- National Launders • 505 Park Ave.
- Nick & Nee Corp. • 328 E. 78th St.
- One Stop Do All Laundromat • 318 E 70th St.
- Our Laundry • 220 E. 82nd St.
- Royal Sutton Laundromat • 1138 First Ave.
- Simanese Laundromat, Inc. • 342 E. 71st St.
- Smart Cleaners & Laundry • 217 E. 84th St.
- Sunrise Laundry • 203 E.75th St.
- Susany Laundromat • 305 E. 84th St.
- Sylvia Gray Private Hand Laundry • 1293 Third Ave.
- TJ Laundromat • 1142 Second Ave.
- Tony's Hand Laundry • 242 E. 71st St.
- Waterworks • 357 E.68th St.
- York Launderette • 1554 York Ave.

🍾 Liquor Stores

- 76 Liquors • 1473 First Ave.
- Big Apple Wine & Spirits Inc. • 1408 Second Ave.
- Carlyle Wines Ltd. • 997 Madison Ave.
- Cork And Bottle Liquor Store • 1158 First Ave.
- East River Liquors • 1364 York Ave.
- Embassy Liquors Inc. • 796 Lexington Ave.
- Garnet Wines & Liquors Inc. • 929 Lexington Ave.
- Headington Wine & Liquors • 1135 Lexington Ave.
- Kris & Bill Wine & Liquor • 1587 Second Ave.
- Lumers Fine Wines & Spirits • 1479 Third Ave.
- McCabe's Liquor Store • 1347 Third Ave.
- Milli Liquors Inc. • 300 E. 78th St.
- Monro Wines & Liquors Inc. • 68 East End Ave.
- Sherry-Lehman Co. Inc. • 679 Madison Ave.
- Viski Wines Inc. • 1050 Lexington Ave.
- Waldorf Liquor Shop • 1495 York Ave.
- Wellington Wines & Spirits Inc. • 1043 Third Ave.
- Windsor Wine Shop • 1114 First Ave.
- The Wine Cart • 235 E 69th St.
- The Wine Shop, Inc. • 1585 First Ave.
- York Wines & Spirits • 1291 First Ave.

◯ Movie Theatres

- Asia Society • 725 Park Ave.
- Cineplex Odeon: Beekman • 1254 Second Ave.
- Cineplex Odeon: Coronet Cinemas • 993 Third Ave.
- City Cinemas 1, 2, 3 • 1001 Third Ave.
- Clearview's First & 62nd St. • 400 E. 62nd St.
- Czech Center • 109 Madison Ave.
- French Institute • 55 E. 59th St.
- Goethe Institute • 1014 Fifth Ave.
- Loews New York Twin • 1271 Second Ave.
- Loews Tower East • 1230 Third Ave.
- Metropolitan Museum of Art • 1000 Fifth Ave.
- New York Comedy Film Festival • 899 Lexington Ave.
- United Artists: 64th and 2nd Ave. • 1210 Second Ave.
- United Artists: E. 85th St. • 1629 First Ave.
- Whitney Museum • 945 Madison Ave.

🐾 Pet Stores

- American Kennels • 798 Lexington Ave.
- Calling All Pets • 301 E. 76th St.
- Calling All Pets • 1590 York Ave.
- Canine Styles • 830 Lexington Ave.
- DM Eleven • 343 E. 66th St.
- Dogs Cats & Co • 208 E. 82nd St.
- Karen's For People Plus Pets • 1195 Lexington Ave.
- Le Chien Pet Salon • 1044 Third Ave.
- Lolly's Pet Salon • 228 E. 80th St.
- Not Just Dogs • 244 E. 60th St.
- Peters Emporium For Pets • 1449 Second Ave.
- Pet Party • 1431A York Ave.
- Pet Necessities • 236 E. 75th St.
- Pets on Lex • 1271 Lexington Ave.
- Sutton Dog Parlour Kennel & Daycare Center • 311 E. 60th St.

📼 Video Rentals

- Blockbuster Video • 1251 Lexington Ave.
- Blockbuster Video • 1646 First Ave.
- Blockbuster Video • 1526 Second Ave.
- Couch Potato Video • 1456 Second Ave.
- Express Video • 421 E. 73rd St.
- Fifth Dimension Video Corp • 1427 York Ave.
- First Run Video • 1147 1/2 Second Ave.
- Video Vogue • 976 Lexington Ave.
- Videoroom • 1487 Third Ave.
- York Video Inc • 1472 York Ave.
- Zitomer Department Store & Electronics • 969 Madison Ave.

E 86th St
E 85th St
E 84th St
E 83rd St
E 82nd St
E 81st St
E 80th St
E 79th St
E 78th St
E 77th St
E 76th St
E 75th St
E 74th St
E 73rd St
E 72nd St
E 71st St
E 70th St
E 69th St
E 68th St
E 67th St
E 66th St
E 65th St
E 64th St
E 63rd St
E 62nd St
E 61st St
E 60th St

Fifth Ave
Madison Ave
Park Ave
Lexington Ave
Third Ave
Second Ave
First Ave
York Ave
East End Ave

JOHN JAY PARK

ROCKEFELLER UNIVERSITY

FDR Drive

East River

ROOSEVELT IS TRAMWA

QUEENSBORO BR

Parking is extremely difficult during the day due to the number of schools in this area. It gets a bit better (but not much) at night, especially in the upper 70s and lower 80s near the FDR (you'll never find legal street parking near Bloomingdale's, however). Park Ave. is the best street to travel on during rush hour.

Subways

4 5 6 .... 86th St. at Lexington Ave.

6 .... 77th St. at Lexington Ave.

6 .... 68th St. at Lexington Ave.

4 5 6 N R .... 60th St. at Lexington Ave.

N R .... 5th Ave. at 60th St.

Bus Lines

1 2 3 .... 5th Ave./Madison Ave.

4 .... 5th Ave./Madison Ave./Broadway

14 .... 14th St. Crosstown

15 .... 1st/2nd Aves.

30 .... 72nd St./57th St. Crosstown

31 .... York Ave./57th St. Crosstown

66 .... 67th St./68th St. Crosstown

72 .... 72nd St. Crosstown

79 .... 79th St. Crosstown

98 .... Washington Heights/Midtown

101 102 103 .... 3rd Ave./Lexington Ave.

Car Rentals

- Autorent Car Rental • 434 E. 77th St.
- Autorent Car Rental Corp • 433 E. 76th St.
- Avis Rent A Car • 310 E. 64th St.
- Dollar Rent A Car • 157 E. 84th St.
- Enterprise Rent A Car • 425 E. 61st St.
- Hertz Car Rental • 327 E. 64th St.
- Hertz Car Rental • 355 E. 76th St.
- Limousine By Mr Peck • 1521 Third Ave.
- National Car Rental • 305 E. 80th St.

Gas Station

- Mobil • York Ave. and 61st St.

Parking

- 157 E. 84th St. Parking • 157 E. 84th St.
- 200 E 61st St Garage • 202 E. 61st St.
- 222East 69th Garage • 222 E. 69th St.
- 301 East 62nd St Garage • 301 E. 62nd St.
- 336 Spar Park • 336 E. 61st St.
- 510 Garage • 510 E. 80th St.
- 530 Garage • 530 E. 72nd St.
- 67 St & Second Av Garage • 254 E. 68th St.
- 71 St Garden Garage • 211 E. 70th St.
- 73rd St Parking • 524 E. 73rd St.
- 79th St Parking • 900 Park Ave.
- 799 Park Ave Garage • 799 Park Ave.
- 80 East End Garage • 80 East End Ave.
- Alpha Parking • 200 E. 70th St.
- Apple Parking • 501 E. 59th St.
- Baron Parking • 1081 Third Ave.
- Bergers Parking Garage • 196 E. 75th St.
- Cam Garage • 35 E. 85th St.
- Celebrity Parking • 166 E. 67th St.
- Champion Parking 83rd St • 301 E. 83rd St.
- Champion Parking East 79 • 505 E. 79th St.
- Chelnik Parking • 700 Park Ave.
- Chelnik Parking • 880 Fifth Ave.
- Chelnik Parking • 1 E. 72nd St.
- Chelnik Parking • 425 E. 79th St.
- City Wide Parking • 245 E. 63rd St.
- Distinctive Parking • 35-53 E. 61st St.
- Edison Park Fast Garages • 250 E. 67th St.
- Edison Park Fast Sta No 110 • 5th Ave. and 80th St.
- Edison Park Fast Sta No 19 • 222 E. 67th St.
- Edison Parking • 1113 York Ave.

- F & F E 70 St • 10 E. 70th St.
- Fairmont Garage • 300 E. 75th St.
- Fifth Ave Garage • 5 E. 79th St.
- Four East 76th St Garage • 4 E. 76th St.
- Gallery Garage Management • 160 E. 62nd St.
- Garage Management • 113 E. 84th St.
- Garage Management • 167 E. 84th St.
- Garage Management • 351 E. 84th St.
- Garage Management • 8 E. 83rd St.
- Garage Management • 127 E. 83rd St.
- Garage Management • 75 East End Ave.
- Garage Management • 111 E. 82nd St.
- Garage Management • 121 E. 80th St.
- Garage Management • 305 E. 80th St.
- Garage Management • 301 E. 79th St.
- Garage Management • 332 E. 76th St.
- Garage Management • 115 E. 75th St.
- Garage Management • 177 E. 73rd St.
- Garage Management • 181 E. 73rd St.
- Garage Management • 135 E. 71st St.
- Garage Management • 191 E. 71st St.
- Garage Management • 203 E. 71st St.
- Garage Management • 400 E. 70th St.
- Garage Management • 30 E. 65th St.
- Garage Management • 189 E. 64th St.
- Garage Management • 337 E. 64th St.
- Garage Management • 124 E. 63rd St.
- Garage Management • 407 E. 61st St.
- Guardian Second Ave #225 • 200 E. 65th St.
- Harley 78 St Garage • 404 E. 79th St.
- Hollywood Parking • 234 E. 85th St.
- Hope Parking • 400 E. 84th St.
- Imperial House Parking • 155 E. 68th St.
- Julian Garage • 315 E. 70th St.
- Justin Parking • 340 E. 74th St.
- Kingdom Garages • 200 E. 69th St.
- Kinney System • 450 E. 63rd St.
- Kinney System • 155 E. 76th St.
- Kinney System • 301 E. 66th St.
- Kinney System • 202 E. 73rd St.
- L P S Management • 220 E. 63rd St.
- Lenox Club Garage • 439 E. 77th St.
- LPS Management • 2 E. 60th St.
- M H M Parking • 429 E. 74th St.
- Manhattan Parking • 923 Fifth Ave
- Manhattan Parking • 202 E. 67th St.
- Manhattan Parking E 72nd St • 520 E. 72nd St.
- Manhattan Parking E 69 St • 219 E. 69th St.
- Meyers Parking • 204 E. 80th St.
- Mutual Parking • 135 E. 71st St.
- Mutual Parking • 605 E. 82nd St.
- N & S Garage • 176 E. 77th St.
- Narragansett Garage • 124 E. 63rd St.
- New Systems Garage • 337 E. 64th St.
- Newport Garages • 370 E. 76th St.
- NYC Parking • 213 E. 80th St.
- Parkanlex Garage • 115 E. 75th St.
- Phoenix Garage • 189 E. 64th St.
- Prevost Garage • 420 E. 72nd St.
- Rapid Park Industries • 441 E. 78th St.
- Rapid Park Industries • 165 E. 77th St.
- Regency Garage • 239 E. 63rd St.
- Regent Garage • 181 E. 73rd St.
- Ropark Garage • 25 E. 75th St.
- SAS Parking • 182 E. 73rd St.
- Somerset Garage • 1365 York Ave.
- Square Plus Operating • 45 East End Ave.
- Tamir Parking • 401 E. 74th St.
- Ten Twenty Five Garage • 1025 Fifth Ave
- The M H M Parking • 315 E. 72nd St.
- Tower East Garage • 191 E. 71st St.
- Townhouse Garage • 177 E. 73rd St.
- Transalpha • 301 E. 64th St.
- Triple E Parking • 525 E. 80th St.
- Trito Parking • 225 E. 63rd St.
- Vassallo Joe • 445 E. 80th St.
- Vassallo Joe • 444 E. 82nd St.
- Waterview Garage • 10 East End Ave.
- Wayne Garage • 111 E. 82nd St.
- Windsor Garage • 340 E. 76th St.

💰 ATMs

- 1. Banco Popular • 799 Amsterdam Ave.
- 2. Chase Manhattan • 59 W. 86th St.
- 3. Chase Manhattan • 2460 Broadway
- 4. Chase Manhattan • 2760 Broadway
- 5. Chase Manhattan • 90 W. 96th St.
- 6. Citibank • 2350 Broadway
- 7. Citibank • 2560 Broadway
- 8. Dime Savings • 2438 Broadway
- 9. Marine Midland HBSC • 2401 Broadway
- 10. Marine Midland HBSC • 172 W. 96th St.
- 11. Republic National • 2520 Broadway

⭕ Bagels

- Absolute Bagels • 2788 Broadway
- Cooper's Bagels • 2415 Broadway
- Hot & Crusty Bagel Café • 2387 Broadway

❇️ Community Gardens

- Corner Community Garden •
  215-217 Manhattan Ave.
- La Perla Garden • 76 W. 105th St.
- Mobilization for Change • 955 Columbus Ave.
- NW Central Park Multiblock Assoc. •
  14-18 W 104 St.

★ Landmarks

- Pomander Walk • 261-7 W. 94th St.
- Soldiers and Sailors Monument • Riverside Drive and 89th St.

📖 Library

- Bloomingdale • 150 W. 100th St.

℞ 24-Hour Pharmacies

- Duane Reade • 2465 Broadway
- Rite Aid • 2833 Broadway

🅿️ Police Precinct

- 24th Precinct • 151 W. 100th St.

✉️ Post Offices

- Cathedral • 215 W.104th St.
- Park West • 693 Columbus Ave.

🅂 Schools

- JHS 054 B. Washington School • 103 W. 107th St.
- PS 075 Emily Dickinson School •
  735 West End Ave.
- PS 084 Lillian Weber School • 32 W. 92nd St.
- PS 145 Bloomingdale School • 150 W. 105th St.
- PS 163 Alfred E. Smith School • 163 W. 97th St.
- PS 165 Robert E. Simon School • 234 W. 109th St.
- PS 166 Arts & Sciences School • 132 W. 89th St.
- Mannes College Of Music • 150 W. 85th St.

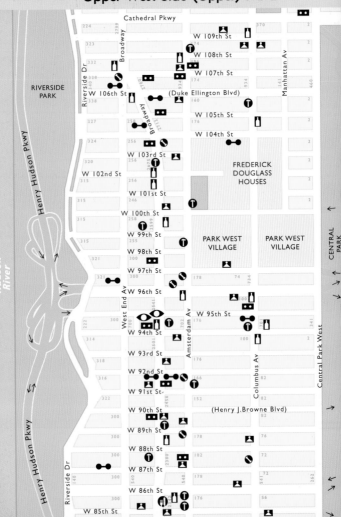

Gyms

- Aquatic Recreational Management Inc • 341 W. 87th St.
- Body Strength Fitness • 250 W. 106th St.
- Dolphin Fitness Clubs • 700 Columbus Ave.
- The Episode • 929 West End Ave.
- Equinox Fitness Club • 2465 Broadway & 92nd St.
- Invigorate International Inc • 83 W. 104th St.
- Lucille Roberts Health Club • 2700 Broadway
- Paris Health Club • 752 West End Ave.
- Peggy Levine Inc • 212 W. 92th St.

Hardware Stores

- AJO Lumber & Woodworking Co Inc. • 817 Amsterdam Ave.
- Altman Hardware Inc. • 641 Amsterdam Ave.
- Aquarius Hardware & Houseware • 601 Amsterdam Ave.
- Broadway Home Center Inc. • 2672 Broadway
- C&S Hardware • 788 Amsterdam Ave.
- Cohen B & Son • 969 Amsterdam Ave.
- Columbus Distributors Inc. • 687 Columbus Ave.
- Grand Metro Home Centers Inc. • 2524 Broadway
- Jimmy's Hardware • 914 Columbus Ave.
- Mike's Lumber Store Inc. • 254 W. 88th St.
- Mike's Lumber Store Inc. • 520 Amsterdam Ave.
- Quintessentials • 532 Amsterdam Ave.
- World Houseware • 2617 Broadway

Laundromats

- 2418 Broadway Laundry Corp. • 2418 Broadway
- 85th Laundromat, Inc. • 251 W. 85th St.
- 971 Columbus Laundromat, Inc. • 971 Columbus Ave.
- 98 Laundromat • 2612 Broadway
- B C Laundry Corp. • 216 W. 85th St.
- Chi Laundry • 2484 Broadway
- Jew Wun Gon • 104 W. 96th St.
- Kevin & Father Laundromat • 203 E. 109th St.
- Larry's Laundromat • 590 Amsterdam Ave.
- Lu Chinese Laundry • 201 W. 86th St.
- M&S Chinese Laundry & Dry Clng. • 76 W. 85th St.
- Maison Ciline, Inc. • 580 Columbus Ave.
- P&P Laundromat • 216 W. 103rd St.
- Phelina's Sudds • 984 Columbus Ave.
- Polano Laundrymat • 944 Amsterdam Ave.
- Sam Hop Laundry • 251 W. 91st St.
- Shu Sanglee Laundry • 107 W. 86th St.
- Syroz Inc. • 932 Amsterdam Ave.
- Westgate Wash & Fold • 120 W. 97th St.
- Zim Washcakamat Laundry & Clng. • 210 W. 94th St.

Liquor Stores

- Academy Liquor Store • 2648 Broadway
- Adel Wine & Liquor • 925 Columbus Ave.
- Columbus Wine & Spirits • 730 Columbus Ave.
- Gotham Wines And Liquors • 2519 Broadway
- H & H Broadway Wine Center Ltd. • 2669 Broadway
- Hong Liquor Store Inc • 2616 Broadway
- M E R Liquor • 998 Columbus Ave.
- Martin Brothers Liquor Store • 2781 Broadway
- Mitchell's Wine & Liquor Store • 200 W. 86th St.
- Polanco Liquor Store • 948 Amsterdam Ave.
- Riverside Liquor Co • 2746 Broadway
- Roma Discount Wine & Liquor • Amsterdam Ave. at 90th St.
- Westlane Wines & Liquor • 689 Columbus Ave.
- The Wine Place • 2406 Broadway

Movie Theatres

- Clearview's Metro Twin • 2626 Broadway
- Clearview's Olympia Twin • 2770 Broadway
- Symphony Space • 2537 Broadway
- Thalia • 250 W. 95th St.

Pet Stores

- Amsterdam Aquarium & Pet Shop • 652 Amsterdam Ave.
- Amsterdog Groomers • 586 Amsterdam Ave.
- Creature Comforts • 2778 Broadway
- Little Creatures • 770 Amsterdam Ave.
- Petland Discounts • 2708 Broadway
- Pet Shed • 209 W. 96th St.
- Pet Stop • 564 Columbus Ave.

Video Rentals

- 934 Amsterdam Ave Video • 934 Amsterdam Ave.
- Arthfoto Corp. • 2474 Broadway
- Blockbuster Video • 552 Amsterdam Ave.
- Blockbuster Video • 2689 Broadway
- Blockbuster Video • 726 Columbus Ave.
- Bus Stop Video • 9 W. 110th St.
- Khan Video Entertainment Center Inc • 2768 Broadway
- Movie Place • 237 W. 105th St.
- Paperback Discount-Film Fest Video • 2517 Broadway
- Solis's Video • 965 Amsterdam Ave.
- Video To Go • 2409 Broadway

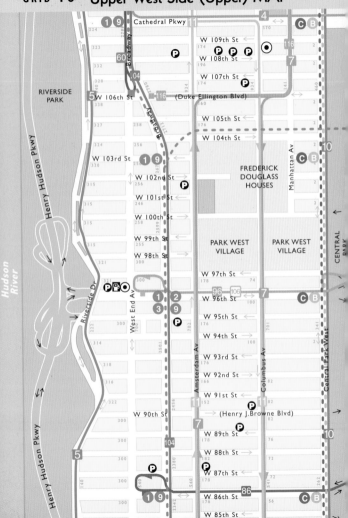

RIVERSIDE
PARK

Hudson River

Henry Hudson Pkwy

Riverside Dr

West End Av

Broadway

Amsterdam Av

Columbus Av

Manhattan Av

CENTRAL PARK WEST

CENTRAL PARK

Cathedral Pkwy

W 109th St
W 108th St
W 107th St

W 106th St

(Duke Ellington Blvd)

W 105th St
W 104th St
W 103rd St
W 102nd St
W 101st St
W 100th St
W 99th St
W 98th St

FREDERICK
DOUGLASS
HOUSES

PARK WEST
VILLAGE

PARK WEST
VILLAGE

W 97th St
W 96th St
W 95th St
W 94th St
W 93rd St
W 92nd St
W 91st St

(Henry J. Browne Blvd)

W 90th St
W 89th St
W 88th St
W 87th St
W 86th St
W 85th St

The 96th Street Transverse is by far the best way to cross Central Park. And isn't it nice that the Upper West Side has two separate subway lines?

Subways

1 **9**	110th St. at Broadway
1 **9**	103rd St. at Broadway
1 **9**	86th St. at Broadway
1 **2** **3** **9**	96th St. at Broadway
B **C**	110th St. at St. Nicholas Ave.
B **C**	103rd St. at Central Park West
B **C**	96th St. at Central Park West
B **C**	86th St. at Central Park West

Bus Lines

4	5th Ave./Madison Ave.
5	5th Ave./6th Ave./Riverside Dr.
7	Columbus Ave./Amsterdam Ave.
10	7th Ave./Central Park West
11	Columbus Ave./Amsterdam Ave.
60	LaGuardia Airport
104	Broadway
86	86th St. Crosstown
96	96th St. Crosstown
08	106th St. Crosstown
16	116th St. Crosstown

⊙ Car Rentals
- A A AMCAR • 303 W. 96th St.
- New York Rent A Car • 963 Columbus Ave.

🅿 Gas Station
- Exxon • 303 W. 96th St.

🅿 Parking
- Ca-Li Auto • 103 W. 108th St.
- Columbus W. 90 Garage • 101 W. 90th St.
- E & B Operating • 137 W. 108th St.
- Garage Management • 271 W. 87th St.
- Garsch Garage • 175 W. 87th St.
- Monterey Garage • 137 W. 89th St.
- Oliantha Garage • 102 W. 107th St.
- PAO Parking • 214 W. 95th St.
- Rapid W. 102 • 204 W. 102nd St.
- Stratford Garage • 323 W. 96th St.
- W. 108 St Parking Garage • 234 W. 108th St.
- Yorkshire Garage • 151 W. 108th St.

If you were unsure as to whether or not New York had enough cultural institutions, Museum Mile should convince you. The Guggenheim is perhaps the greatest architectural tour de force in Manhattan, notwithstanding its rapaciously high admission fees. Note the strange icon displacement between everything north of 96th Street and everything south of 96th Street.

💲 ATMs

- 1. Chase Manhattan • 126 E. 86th St.
- 2. Chase Manhattan • 255 E. 86th St.
- 3. Chase Manhattan • 453 E. 86th St.
- 4. Chase Manhattan • 2065 Second Ave.
- 5. Chase Manhattan • 1121 Madison Ave.
- 6. Citibank • 123 E. 86th St.
- 7. Citibank • 1275 Madison Ave.
- 8. Citibank • 446 E. 86th St.
- 9. Citibank • 1625-31 York Ave.
- 10. City and Suburban FSB • 345 E. 86th St.
- 11. Dime Savings • 1221 Madison Ave.
- 12. Emigrant Savings • 1270 Lexington Ave.
- 13. Fourth Federal Savings • 1751 Second Ave.
- 14. Marine Midland HBSC • 1220 Madison Ave.

⭕ Bagels

- Amir Ram Bagels, Inc. • 333 E. 86th St.
- Bagelry • 1324 Lexington Ave.
- Bagelry, Inc. • 1380 Madison Ave.
- Bagels Bob's On York • 1638 York Ave.
- Bagels Express of 2nd Ave. • 1804 Second Ave.
- David Bagel • 1651 Second Ave.
- Fanbro Bagel, Inc. • 1700 First Ave.
- New World Coffee • 1595 Third Ave.

❇️ Community Gardens

- Ebenezer Wesleyan Methodist Church • 1574 Lexington Ave.
- El Barrio's Operation Fightback • 184-188 E. 101st St.
- Hamacao Community Garden • 335 E. 108th St.
- SFDS Development Corp. • 123 E. 100th St.
- Union Settlement Association • 203, 208-10 E. 104th St.
- Jirasol Assoc • 75-77 E. 110th St.
- Nueva Esperanza Jardin • 4 E. 110th St.
- Catano Garden • 169 E. 110th St.

🏥 Hospitals

- Beth Israel Medical Center: North Division • 170 East End Ave.
- Mt. Sinai Hospital • Fifth Ave. at 100th St.
- Metropolitan Hospital • 1901 First Ave.

★ Landmarks

- Gracie Mansion • Carl Schulz Park at 88th St.
- St. Nicholas Russian Orthodox Cathedral • 15 E. 97th St.
- Cooper-Hewitt Museum • 2 E. 91st St.

- Guggenheim Museum • 1071 Fifth Ave.
- International Center of Photography • 1130 Fifth Ave.
- Jewish Museum • 1109 Fifth Ave.
- Museo Del Barrio • Fifth Ave. and 104th St.
- Museum of the City of New York • Fifth Ave. and 103rd St.

📖 Libraries

- 96th Street • 112 E. 96th St.
- Aguilar • 174 E. 110th St.

℞ 24-Hour Pharmacy

- Rite Aid • 144 E. 86th St.

🅿️ Police Precinct

- 23rd Precinct • 162 E. 102nd St.

✉️ Post Offices

- Gracie • 229 E. 85th St.
- Hell Gate • 153 E. 110th St.
- Yorkville • 1619 Third Ave.

🅢 Schools

- Central Park East Secondary School • 1573 Madison Ave.
- JHS 099 Julio De Burgos School • 410 E. 100th St.
- JHS 117 Jefferson Park School • 240 E. 109th St.
- National Academy School of Fine Arts • 5 E. 89th St.
- Park East High School • 234 E. 105th St.
- PS 050 Vito Marcantonio School • 433 E. 100th St.
- PS 072 • 131 E. 104th St.
- PS 083 Luis Munoz Rivera School • 219 E. 109th St.
- PS 108 Peter Minuit School • 1615 Madison Ave.
- PS 109 Century School • 215 E. 99th St.
- PS 121 Galileo School • 232 E. 103rd St.
- PS 146 Anna M. Short School • 421 E. 106th St.
- PS 151 Eleanore Roosevelt School • 1763 First Ave.
- PS 169 Robert F. Kennedy School • 110 E. 88th St.
- PS 171 Patrick Henry School • 19 E. 103rd St.
- PS 198 Isidor-Ida Straus School • 1700 Third Ave.
- Richard Green High School • 421 E. 88th St.
- School Of Cooperative Technical Education • 321 E. 96th St.

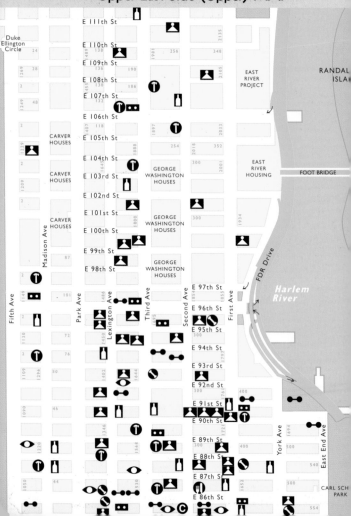

It's amazing how just as many people live north as south of 96th Street, yet there are so many fewer services.

24-Hour Copy Center
- Copycats • 1646 Second Ave.

24-Hour Diner
- Viand • 300 E. 86th St.

Gyms
- Asphalt Green, Inc. • 555 E. 90th St.
- Bally Total Fitness • 144 E. 86th St.
- Carnegie Park Swim & Health Club • 200 E. 94th St.
- Dolphin Fitness Clubs • 1781 Second Ave.
- Eastside Body Builders/Pumping Iron Gym • 403 E. 91st St.
- Equinox Fitness Club • 205 E. 85th St. & Third Ave.
- Med Fitness • 12 E. 86th St.
- Monterey Sports Club • 175 E. 96th St.
- Myrna Health Spa and Hair Stylist, Inc. • 326 E. 86th St.
- New York Sports Clubs • 151 E. 86th St.
- YM-YWHA 92nd St. Y • 1395 Lexington Ave.

Hardware Stores
- 86th St. Locksmith • 201 E. 86th St.
- Bean Housewares, Inc. • 1190 Madison Ave.
- El Barrio Hardware • 1876 Third Ave.
- Johnny's Hardware • 151 E. 106th St.
- K & G Hardware & Supply • 401 E. 90th St.
- M & E Madison Hardware, Inc. • 1396 Madison Ave.
- Morales Brothers Hardware, Inc. • 1959 Third Ave.
- Pinsky J Hardware Company, Inc. • 2035 Second Ave.
- S Feldman Housewares • 1304 Madison Ave.
- Service Hardware Corp. • 1338 Lexington Ave.
- Wankel's Hardware & Paint • 1573 Third Ave.

Laundromats
- 104 Laundromat • 29 E. 104th St.
- 108th Laundromat • 339 E. 108th St.
- 95 Laundromat • 313 E. 95th St.
- All Clean • 1515 Lexington Ave.
- Asia 94 • 1442 Lexington Ave.
- Commodore Fine Hand Laundromat • 1730 Second Ave.
- East Side Laundry Service • 1689 First Ave.
- East Side Wash & Dry • 218 E. 89th St.
- Fine Laundromat • 147 E. 85th St.
- Five Star Laundry • 1396 Lexington Ave.
- Great Wall Laundromat • 2141 Second Ave.
- Happy Laundering & Dry Cleaning • 324 E. 91st St.
- Ju Albert • 1466 Lexington Ave.
- Kat Laundry • 300 E. 88th St.
- Kin Chu Ching • 301 E. 90th St.
- Laundry & Cleaners • 301 E. 85th St.
- Laundry Boy • 1829 Second Ave.
- Laundry Com. • 1665 First Ave.
- Lee Peter Laundry • 1336 Lexington Ave.
- Linsu Self-Service Laundromat • 1950 Second Ave.
- Mard Management Corp. • 1751 Lexington Ave.
- The Mat Fresh Scent • 1717 First Ave.
- Mekong Wash & Dry • 1612 York Ave.
- Mona Laundromat • 1790 Third Ave.
- Mrs. Olan's Stevens Laundry & Cleaners • 1906 First Ave.
- Mrs. Roles Private Laundry • 1674 Third Ave.
- Ruppert Wash & Dry • 1670 Third Ave.
- Super Rich • 1741 First Ave.
- Tony C Laundromat • 303 E. 92nd St.
- Upper Yorkville Cleaners • 173 E. 99th St.
- Vikrams Laundromat & Dry Cleaning • 1814 Third Ave.
- Wook One Stop Cleaners • 159 E. 92nd St.
- Y Y Laundromat • 1468 Lexington Ave.
- Youme Cleaners • 210 E. 87th St.

Liquor Stores
- Edwin's Wines & Liquors • 176 E. 103rd St.
- Harmony Liquors, Inc. • 2073 Second Ave.
- K & D Wines & Spirits • 1366 Madison Ave.
- Luria-Colony Wine & Spirits, Inc. • 1217 Madison Ave.
- Maxwell Wines & Spirits • 1657 First Ave.
- Mister Wright, Inc. • 1593 Third Ave.
- Park East Liquors • 1657 York Ave.
- Third Avenue Liquor Corp • 2030 Third Ave.
- Uptown Wine Shop Inc. • 1361 Lexington Ave.
- Van Keith Liquors • 1743 First Ave.
- West Coast Wine & Liquor, Inc. • 1440 Lexington Ave.
- Wine Traders • 1693 Second Ave.
- Yorkshire Wines & Spirits • 1646 First Ave.

Movie Theatres
- 92nd St. Y • Lexington Ave. at 92nd St.
- City Cinemas: East 86th St. • 210 E. 86th St.
- Clearview's Park & 86th St. Twin • 125 E. 86th St.
- Guggenheim Museum • 1071 Fifth Ave.
- Loews Orpheum • 1538 Third Ave.
- United Artists: E. 85th St. • 1629 First Ave.

Pet Stores
- Calling All Pets • 1590 York Ave.
- Crystal Aquarium • 1659 Third Ave.
- Aquarium Environments • 305 E. 95th St.
- PETCO • 147 E. 86th St.
- Pets on Lex • 1271 Lexington Ave.
- Pet Shop • 1572 Third Ave.
- Shaggy Dog • 400 E. 88th St.

Video Rentals
- Blockbuster Video • Third Ave. & 106th St.
- Blockbuster Video • 205 E. 95th St.
- Blockbuster Video • 1251 Lexington Ave.
- Blockbuster Video • 1646 First Ave.
- Encore Entertainment • 175 E. 96th St.
- Express Video • 1577 Third Ave.
- TV Video Traders of Manhattan • 1756 First Ave.
- Video 96, Inc. • 1378 Madison Ave.

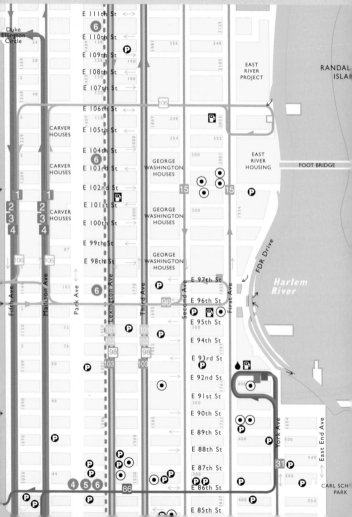

How anyone ever thought that one subway was enough for the Upper East Side is beyond us. It isn't. However, parking is about the best here as it's going to ever get in Manhattan. The 96th Street entrance to the FDR is jammed most of the day, usually with really, really bad drivers. A popular portal for the bridge and tunnel crowd?

Subways

④⑤⑥	E. 86th St. at Lexington Ave.
⑥	E. 96th St. at Lexington Ave.
⑥	E. 103rd St. at Lexington Ave.
⑥	E. 110th St. at Lexington Ave.

Bus Lines

①②③	5th Ave./Madison Ave.
④	5th Ave./Madison Ave./Broadway
⑮	1st Ave./2nd Ave.
㉛	York Ave./57th St.
⑧⑥	86th St. Crosstown
⑨⑥	96th St. Crosstown
⑨⑧	Washington Heights/Midtown
⑩①	3rd Ave./Lexington Ave.
⑩②	3rd Ave./Lexington Ave.
⑩③	3rd Ave./Lexington Ave.
⑩⑥	96th St./106th St. Crosstown

● Car Rentals

- 1995 1st Ave. Station, Inc. • 1995 First Ave.
- Apollo Auto Rental, Inc. • 335 E. 102nd St.
- A-Value Rent-A-Car, Inc. • 1989 First Ave.
- Avis Rent-A-Car • 424 E. 90th St.
- Budget • 234 E. 85th St.
- Enterprise Rent-A-Car • 1833 First Ave.
- Farrell's Limousine Service • 428 E. 92nd St.
- Hertz Car, Truck & Van Rental • 412 E. 90th St.
- Limousine By Mr. Peck • 1521 Third Ave.
- Marquis Auto Rental Inc • 337 E. 102nd St.
- Manhattan Rent-A-Car • 154 E. 87th St.
- Manhattan Rent-A-Car • 165 E. 87th St.
- New York Rent-A-Car • 240 E. 92nd St.

● Car Wash

- Eastside Car Wash, Inc. • 1770 First Ave.

⛽ Gas Stations

- Amoco • 96th St. & First Ave.
- Amoco • 1599 Lexington Ave.
- BP • 1770 First Ave.
- Getty • 348 E. 106th St.

℗ Parking

- 1065 Park Ave. Garage • 1065 Park Ave.
- 305 E. 86th Parking • 305 E. 86th St.
- 401 E. 86th Garage • 401 E. 86th St.
- 9495 Parking Garage • 1832 Second Ave.
- A & L Administrator • 177 E. 109th St.
- Arwin 88 Garage • 1675 York Ave.
- Cam Garage • 35 E. 85th St.
- Chelnik Parking • 535 E. 86th St.
- Croyden Garage • 12 E. 86th St.
- East 86th St Garage • 444 E. 86th St.
- Edison Park Fast Sta No. 169 • 501 E. 87th St.
- Gallant Parking • 182 E. 95th St.
- Garage Management • 231 E. 94th St.
- Garage Management • 340 E. 93rd St.
- Garage Management • 50 E. 89th St.
- Garage Management • 118 E. 86th St.
- Gold Parking • 115 E. 87th St.
- Hollywood Parking • 234 E. 85th St.
- LPS Management • 401 E. 89th St.
- Metro North Garage • 440 E. 102nd St.
- Newbury Operating • 249 E. 86th St.
- Newbury Operating • 250 E. 87th St.
- Pak Garage • 120 E. 87th St.
- S C R Parking • 169 E. 87th St.
- Safeway Parking • 345 E. 86th St.
- Super Arrow Parking • 222 E. 97th St.
- Swift Parking Garage • 160 E. 88th St.

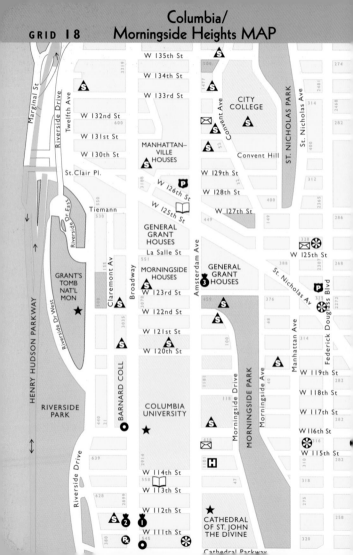

Marginal St

Riverside Drive

Twelfth Ave

3319

W 135th St

W 134th St

W 133rd St

500

1477

CITY COLLEGE

Convent Ave

St. Nicholas Ave

St. Clair Pl.

600

W 132nd St

W 131st St

W 130th St

314

2461

2460

282

52

ST. NICHOLAS PARK

274

3466

314

282

286

MANHATTAN–VILLE HOUSES

3188

Tiemann

530

Riverside Dr East

P

W 126th St

W 125th St

W 129th St

W 128th St

W 127th St

Convent Hill

400

312

2365

449

149

GENERAL GRANT HOUSES

GRANT'S TOMB NAT'L MON

Claremont Av

Broadway

La Salle St

551

MORNINGSIDE HOUSES

3078

W 123rd St

W 122nd St

W 121st St

W 120th St

Amsterdam Ave

459

GENERAL GRANT HOUSES

3

W 125th St

338

388

St. Nicholas Av

P

376

313

268

2272

2307

Frederick Douglass Blvd

68

100

Manhattan Ave

314

W 119th St

W 118th St

W 117th St

W 116th St

W 115th St

282

282

RIVERSIDE PARK

440

21

3035

BARNARD COLL

COLUMBIA UNIVERSITY

Morningside Drive

118

MORNINGSIDE PARK

Morningside Ave

40

316

282

HENRY HUDSON PARKWAY

Riverside Dr-West

639

3914

518

160

47

H

W 114th St

W 113th St

W 112th St

W 111th St

558

Riverside Drive

628

2890

380

545

S 2

Rx

1

CATHEDRAL OF ST. JOHN THE DIVINE

Cathedral Parkway

318

275

258

320

RIVERSIDE PARK

Columbia/
Morningside Heights ESSENTIALS

This is perhaps one of the most truly economically diverse parts of the city, with tons of Columbia students mixing with high-, middle-, and low-income professionals and families. The Cathedral of St. John the Divine is the most eclectic and astounding building in Manhattan, which is no easy thing to accomplish (the vertical tour is highly recommended). Grant's Tomb is the least visited tourist attraction in Manhattan, which is a shame because it's totally cool.

💲 ATMs
- 1. Banco Popular • 2852 Broadway
- 2. Citibank • 2861 Broadway
- 3. Citibank • 1310 Amsterdam Ave.

⭕ Bagels
- Columbia Bagels • 2836 Broadway
- New World Coffee • 2929 Broadway

✲ Community Gardens
- Garden of Eden • 202-204 W. 116th St.
- Green Thumb Garden Project •
  1036-53 Amsterdam Ave.
- Manhattan Ave Comm. Garden •
  318 W. 116th St.
- Project Harmony • 277-275 W. 122nd St.
- PBS's William B. Washington Memorial Garden •
  321-325 W. 126th St.

🏥 Hospital
- St. Luke's Hospital Center • 1111 Amsterdam Ave.

★ Landmarks
- Cathedral of St. John the Divine • 112th St. and
  Amsterdam Ave.
- Columbia University • 116th St. and Broadway
- Grant's Tomb • 122nd St. and Riverside Drive

📖 Libraries
- Columbia • 514 W. 113th St.
- George Bruce • 518 W. 125th St.

℞ 24-Hour Pharmacy
- Rite Aid • 2833 Broadway

🅟 Police Precincts
- 26th Precinct • 520 W. 126th St.
- 28th Precinct • 2271 Eighth Ave.
  (Frederick Douglass Blvd.)

✉ Post Offices
- Columbus University • 1123 Amsterdam Ave.
- Eastside Parcel Post • 500 E. 132nd St.
- Manhattanville • 365 W. 125th St.

🅢 Schools
- A. Philip Randolph Campus High School •
  Convent Ave. and W. 135th St.
- Bank Street College Of Education • 610 W. 112th St.
- Barnard College • 3009 Broadway
- City College • W. 135th St. & Convent Ave.
- Columbia University • 435 W. 116th St.
- IS 195 Roberto Clemente School • 625 W. 133rd St.
- Jewish Theological Seminary of America •
  3080 Broadway
- JHS 043 Adam C. Powell School • 509 W. 129th St.
- Manhattan School Of Music • 120 Claremont Ave.
- PS 036 Margaret Douglas School •
  123 Morningside Dr.
- PS 125 Ralph Bunche School • 425 W. 123rd St.
- PS 129 John H. Finley School • 425 W. 130th St.
- PS 161 Pedro A. Campos School • 499 W. 133rd St.
- PS 180 Hugo Newman School • 370 W. 120th St.
- PS-IS 223 Mott Hall School •
  W. 131st St. and Convent Ave.
- Teachers College, Columbia University •
  525 W. 120th St.

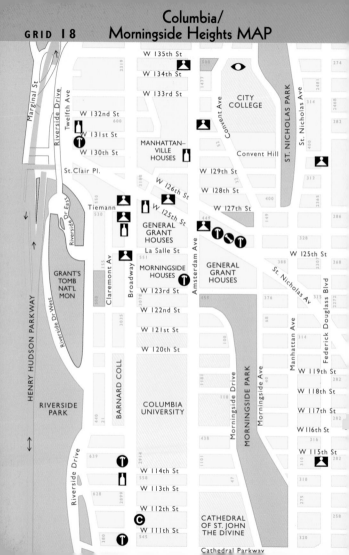

W 135th St

W 134th St

W 133rd St

W 132nd St

W 131st St

W 130th St

St. Clair Pl.

W 126th St

W 125th St

La Salle St

W 123rd St

W 122nd St

W 121st St

W 120th St

W 129th St

W 128th St

W 127th St

W 125th St

W 119th St

W 118th St

W 117th St

W 116th St

W 115th St

W 114th St

W 113th St

W 112th St

W 111th St

CITY
COLLEGE

Convent Hill

Convent Ave

ST. NICHOLAS PARK

St. Nicholas Ave

St. Nicholas Av

Frederick Douglass Blvd

Manhattan Ave

MANHATTAN-
VILLE
HOUSES

Tiemann

GENERAL
GRANT
HOUSES

MORNINGSIDE
HOUSES

GRANT'S
TOMB
NAT'L
MON

RIVERSIDE
PARK

BARNARD COLL

Claremont Av

Broadway

Amsterdam Ave

GENERAL
GRANT
HOUSES

COLUMBIA
UNIVERSITY

Morningside Drive

MORNINGSIDE PARK

Morningside Ave

CATHEDRAL
OF ST. JOHN
THE DIVINE

Cathedral Parkway

HENRY HUDSON PARKWAY

Riverside Dr West

Riverside Dr. or East

Riverside Drive

Twelfth Ave

Riverside Drive

Marginal St

A nice big multiplex on 125th Street would probably rake in millions.

24-Hour Copy Center
- Kinko's • 2872 Broadway

Hardware Stores
- Academy Hardware & Supply Co. Inc. • 2869 Broadway
- Clinton Supply Co. • 1262 Amsterdam Ave.
- Columbia Hardware Co. • 2905 Broadway
- Glick Philip Supply Co. • 421 W. 125th St.
- Pearl Green S & T Supply Corp. • 606 W. 131st St.
- TriBoro Hardware Co. • 433 W. 125th St.

Laundromats
- WIGL Corp. • 507 W. 125th St.
- 251 W. 116th St. Laundry Corp. • 251 W. 116th St.
- B Bubbles, Inc. • 3147 Broadway
- BJ Laundromat • 1496 Amsterdam Ave.
- Broadway Laundry • 3161 Broadway
- Harlem Laundry Center • 449 W. 125th St.
- Harlem Laundromat, Inc. • 2117 Eighth Ave. (Frederick Douglass Blvd.)
- Soft Touch Organization • 1411 Amsterdam Ave.
- Super Wash 4 • 2391 Eighth Ave. (Frederick Douglass Blvd.)
- Verybest Laundry • 557 W. 125th St.

Liquor Stores
- Alfarb Wine & Liquors • 574 W. 125th St.
- Amsterdam Liquor Mart • 1356 Amsterdam Ave.
- Campos Ernest F • 831 W. 131st St.
- International Wines and Spirits • 2903 Broadway
- Jimenez Ramon • 3139 Broadway

Movie Theatre
- Aaron Davis Hall • W. 135th St. and Convent Ave.

Pet Store
- NYC Pet Place • 431 W. 125th St.

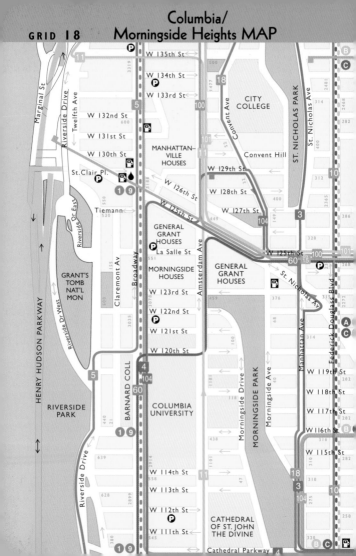

Driving and parking are both pretty decent around here, and the area is also served well by subway. We wish we could say that about the rest of the city.

Subways

① ⑨	..........125th St. at Broadway
	116th St. at Broadway
① ⑨	....................(Columbia University)
	110th St. at Broadway
① ⑨	....................(Cathedral Parkway)
Ⓑ Ⓒ	...............135th St. at St. Nicholas Ave.
Ⓐ Ⓑ Ⓒ Ⓓ	........125th St. at St. Nicholas Ave.
Ⓑ Ⓒ	...............116th St. at St. Nicholas Ave.
Ⓑ Ⓒ	...............110th St. at St. Nicholas Ave.

Bus Lines

③	........................5th Ave./Madison Ave.
④	................5th Ave./6th Ave./Riverside Dr.
⑤	..............Columbus Ave./Amsterdam Ave.
⑩	....................7th Ave./Central Park West
⑪	...............Columbus Ave./Amsterdam Ave.
⑱	....LaGuardia Airport
⑥⓪	....Broadway
⑩⓪	...................................86th St. Crosstown
⑩①	...................................96th St. Crosstown
⑩④	.................................106th St. Crosstown
⑯	...................................116th St. Crosstown

◆ Car Wash
• Interchange Services • 663 W. 125th St.

⛽ Gas Stations
• Amoco • 3233 Broadway
• BP • 125th St. & Broadway
• Exxon • 2040 Eighth Ave. (Frederick Douglass Blvd.)
• Matthews Service Station • 355 W. 124th St.
• Mobil • 3260 Broadway

Ⓟ Parking
• 512-520 W. 112th St Garage •
  512 W. 112th St.
• Garage Management • 532 W. 122nd St.
• HCCS Parking Lot • 325 W. 124th St.
• Edison Riverside • 3333 Broadway
• MTP 129th St. Parking • 627 W. 129th St.
• Morningside Garage • 3100 Broadway
• Y & H Garages • 526 W. 134th St.

W 135th St

W 134th St

W 133rd St

LENOX
TERRACE

W 132nd St

W 131st St

City College

St. Nicholas Park

Convent Ave

St. Nicholas Ave

Convent Hill

W 130th St

W 129th St

W 128th St

ST.
NICHOLAS
HOUSES

W 127th St

W 126th St

Frederick Douglass Blvd

Adam Clayton Powell Jr. Blvd

W 125th St

W 124th St

W 123rd St

Lenox Ave (Malcolm X Blvd)

MARCUS
GARVEY
PARK

Manhattan Ave

W 122nd St

W 121st St

Mt. Morris Pk. W.

Morningside Drive

Morningside Ave

MORNINGSIDE
PARK

St. Nicholas Ave

W 120th St

W 119th St

W 118th St

W 117th St

Fifth Ave

W 116th St

W 115th St

W 114th St

MARTIN
LUTHER
KING JR
TOWERS

W 113th St

W 112th St

W 111th St

CATHEDRAL
OF ST. JOHN
THE DIVINE

Duke
Ellington

Central Park North

Sylvia's really is as good as everyone says it is.

💰 ATMs
- 1. Banco Popular • 231 W. 125th St.
- 2. Carver Federal Savings • 75 W. 125th St.
- 3. Chase Manhattan • 55 W. 125th St.
- 4. Chase Manhattan • 2218 Fifth Ave.

✴ Community Gardens
- 129th St. Block Assoc. • 151-153 W. 129th St.
- 135-137-139 Tenants Assoc. • 132 W. 112th St.
- 206 W. 121st St. Tenants Assoc. • 263 W. 121th St.
- Ada Jane Scott Memorial Committee • 155-159 W. 133rd St.
- American Federation of Police Assoc. • 126-28 W. 129th St.
- Bishop House/Urban Gardens • 21-27 W. 128th St.
- Black United Fund of NY • 190 W. 134th St.
- CEP Community Garden • 2351 Eighth Ave & 303 W. 126th St.
- CS 154 (EIG) • 250 W. 127th St.
- Garden Eight • 2187-89 Eighth Ave. (Frederick Douglass Blvd.)
- Garden of Eden • 202-204 W. 116th St.
- Henry Rivera's Children's Garden • 142 W. 127th St.
- Manhattan Ave. Community Garden • 318 W. 116th St.
- Margaret Banks Memorial Committee • 126 W. 134th St.
- Minority Task Force on AIDS • N/S W. 115th St w/o Lenox Ave.
- New Chance Garden • 203-205 W. 119 St.
- PS 185/208M (EIG) • 20 W. 112th St.
- Project Harmony • 219 W. 122nd St.
- Project Harmony • 275-277 W. 122nd St.
- PS 207/149 • 34 W. 118th St.
- PS 76 • 203 W. 120th St.
- PS 76 Garden of Love • 213 W. 121st St.
- Rev. Linnette C. Williamson Memorial Pk Assn. • 53-55 W. 128th St.
- Rice HS Env. Club/Mother Hale's Garden • 22 W. 124th St.
- Striving Together • 129&123 W. 128th St.
- Success Gardens/PS 175 • 116-122 W. 134th St.
- The Five Star Block Assoc. • 250-252 W. 121st St.
- The Five Star Block Assoc. • 233 W. 121st St.
- The New 123rd St. Block Assoc. • 112-116 W. 123rd St.
- The Sowers • 33 W. 118th St.
- The W. 132nd St. Bl. Assoc. Inc. • 108-114 W. 132nd St.
- The W. 132nd St. Bl. Assoc. Inc. • 138-140 W. 132nd St.
- United Block Front Street Assoc. • 108-110-112 W. 128th St.
- Williamson Memorial Garden Assoc. • 65 W. 128th St.
- Flower Garden #1 • 1401 Fifth Ave.
- PBS's William B. Washington Memorial Garden • 321-325 W. 126th St.

🏥 Hospitals
- The Paul Robeson Family Medical Center • 140 W. 125th St.
- Renaissance Health Care Network • 215 W. 125th St.

★ Landmarks
- Apollo Theater • 253 W. 125th St.
- Duke Ellington Circle • 110th St. and Fifth Ave.
- Sylvia's • 328 Lenox Ave.

📖 Libraries
- 115th St. • 203 W. 115th St.
- Harlem • 9 W. 124th St.

Ⓟ Police Precinct
- 28th Precinct • 2271 Eighth Ave. (Frederick Douglass Blvd.)

✉ Post Offices
- Manhattanville • 365 W. 125th St.
- Morningside • 232 W. 116th St.

🅢 Schools
- City College • 135th St. & Convent Ave.
- PS 036 Margaret Douglas School • 123 Morningside Dr.
- PS 076 A. Philip Randolph School • 220 W. 121st St.
- PS 092 Mary M. Bethune School • 222 W. 134th St.
- PS 113 Whitehead Whaley School • 240 W. 113th St.
- PS 125 Ralph Bunche School • 425 W. 123rd St.
- PS 144 Hans C. Anderson School • 134 W. 122nd St.
- PS 149 Sojourner Truth School • 34 W. 118th St.
- PS 175-IS Henry Highland • 175 W. 134th St.
- PS 180 Hugo Newman School • 370 W. 120th St.
- PS 185 John M. Langston School • 20 W. 112th St.
- PS 207 Norbert Rillieux School • 41 W. 117th St.
- PS 208 Alain L. Locke School • 21 W. 111th St.
- PS 133 Fred R. Moore School • 2121 Fifth Ave.
- Wadleigh High School • 215 W. 114th St.

CITY
COLLEGE

Convent Ave

ST. NICHOLAS PARK

St. Nicholas Ave

Convent Hill

ST.
NICHOLAS
HOUSES

Frederick Douglass Blvd

Adam Clayton Powell Jr. Blvd

Lenox Ave (Malcolm X Blvd)

Mt. Morris Pk. W.

LENOX
TERRACE

MARCUS
GARVEY
PARK

Fifth Ave

Morningside Drive

MORNINGSIDE PARK

Manhattan Ave

Morningside Ave

St. Nicholas Ave

MARTIN
LUTHER
KING JR
TOWERS

CATHEDRAL
OF ST. JOHN
THE DIVINE

W 135th St
W 134th St
W 133rd St
W 132nd St
W 131st St
W 130th St
W 129th St
W 128th St
W 127th St
W 126th St
W 125th St
W 124th St
W 123rd St
W 122nd St
W 121st St
W 120th St
W 119th St
W 118th St
W 117th St
W 116th St
W 115th St
W 114th St
W 113th St
W 112th St
W 111th St

Central Park North

Duke
Ellington

Blockbuster finally moved in on 125th Street and everyone seemed pretty happy. Time for other people to start moving in, too…

●━● Gyms

- Becki's Health Salon • 174 St. Nicholas Ave.
- YMCA of Greater NY: Harlem • 180 W. 135th St.

🕕 Hardware Stores

- Bill's Hardware & Paints Inc • 1 W. 125th St.
- Citi General Hardware • 100 St. Nicholas Ave.
- Glick Philip Supply Co. • 421 W. 125th St.
- Harlem Locksmith •
  1846 Seventh Ave. (Adam Clayton Powell Jr. Blvd.)
- Manhattan Paint Fair Inc. • 17 W. 125th St.
- StaLoc Lock & Hardware Ltd •
  1958 Seventh Ave. (Adam Clayton Powell Jr. Blvd.)
- TriBoro Hardware Co. • 433 W. 125th St.
- Virgo Houseware & Hardware •
  188 Lenox Ave.

👝 Laundromats

- WIGL Corp. • 507 W. 125th St.
- 2248 7 Avenue Laundromat • 2248 Seventh Ave.
- 251 St. 116th St. Laundry Corp. • 251 W. 116th St.
- B Bubbles, Inc. • 3147 Broadway
- Broadway Laundry • 3161 Broadway
- Harlem Laundry Center • 449 W. 125th St.
- Harlem Laundromat Inc. •
  2117 8th Ave. (Frederick Douglass Blvd.)
- Laundry • 133rd St. & Lenox Ave.
- Super Wash 4 • 2391 Eighth Ave.
  (Frederick Douglass Blvd.)

🍾 Liquor Stores

- 115th St. Liquor Store Inc. • 5 E. 115th St.
- 458 Lenox Liquors Inc. • 458 Lenox Ave.
- A&D Liquor • 23 Lenox Ave.
- Conrad Spirits Ltd. • 178 Lenox Ave.
- Express Liquor • 312 Lenox Ave.
- Fred's Wine & Liquors • 77 Lenox Ave.
- Harlem Retail Wine & Liquor Store Inc. •
  1902 Seventh Ave. (Adam Clayton Powell Jr. Blvd.)
- Harlem USA Wine & Liquor Store •
  101 W. 132ndSt.
- Just In Liquors • 2178 Fifth Ave.
- Palace Liquors Inc. •
  2215 Seventh Ave. (Adam Clayton Powell Jr. Blvd.)

●● Video Rentals

- Blockbuster Video • 121 W. 125th St.
- Films & Games • 243 W. 125th St.
- Ndyndory Video • 365 Lenox Ave.
- TK Video Store • 35 W. 116th St.

Harlem (Lower) TRANSPORTATION

Driving across 110th Street should be good, but it's usually a pain. 116th Street is much better. Avoid 125th St. entirely. Parking is pretty good, even on the major avenues.

Subways

2 3 ....135th St. at Malcolm X Blvd.
2 3 ....125th St. at Malcolm X Blvd.
2 3 ....116th St. at Malcolm X Blvd.
2 3 ....110th St. at Malcolm X Blvd.
(Central Park North)
B C ....135th St. at St. Nicholas Ave.
A B C D ....125th St. at St. Nicholas Ave.
B C ....116th St. at St. Nicholas Ave.
B C ....110th St. at St. Nicholas Ave.
(Cathedral Parkway)

Bus Lines

1 .... 5th Ave./Madison Ave.
2 ....5th Ave./Madison Ave./Powell Ave.
3 .... 5th Ave./Madison Ave./St. Nicholas Blvd.
4 ....5th Ave./Madison Ave./Broadway
Columbus Ave./Amsterdam Ave.
7 ....Lenox Ave./6th Ave./7th Ave./Broadway
10 .... 7th Ave./8th Ave./Fred. Douglass Blvd.
18 ....Convent Ave.
60 ....LaGuardia Airport via 125th St.
100 ....Amsterdam Ave./Broadway/125th St.
101 ...3rd Ave./Lexington Ave./Amsterdam Ave.
102 ......3rd Ave./Lexington Ave./Malcolm X Blvd.
104 ....Broadway
116 ....116th St. Crosstown
15 ....125th St. Crosstown
33 ....135th St. Crosstown

Gas Stations

- Exxon • 2040 Frederick Douglass Blvd.
- Amoco • 355 W. 124th St.

Parking

- Central Park North Parking Systems •
  7 St. Nicholas Ave.
- Giselle Garage • 161 W. 132nd St.
- HCCS Parking Lot • 325 W. 124th St.
- Fifth Central Parking • 1330 Fifth Ave.
- NYC Harlem Parking • 506 Lenox Ave.

THE
BRONX

*Harlem
River*

E 135th St

ABRAHAM LINCOLN HOUSING

E 132nd St

Harlem River

E 131st St

THIRD AVE BRIDGE

E 130th St

E 129th St

E 128th St

E 127th St

E 126th St

Harlem River Drive

WILLIS AVE BRIDGE

E 125th St (Dr. Martin Luther King Jr Blvd)

TRIBOROUGH BRI

PALADINO AVE

E 124th St

E 123rd St

MARCUS GARVEY PARK

Ronald McNair Pl

E 122nd St

SEN. R. WAGNER. SR. HOUSES

E 121st St

Sylvan Pl

E 120th St

E 119th St

Fifth Ave

Madison Ave

Park Ave

Lexington Ave

Third Ave

Second Ave

First Ave

Pleasant Ave

E 118th St

E 117th St

E 116th St

E 115th St

SEN R. TAFT HOUSES

J.W. JOHNSON HOUSING

JEFFERSON HOUSES

JEFFERSON HOUSES

E 114th St

JEFFERSON PARK

FDR Drive

E 112nd St

E 111th St

Duke Ellington Circle

E 110th St

East Harlem ESSENTIALS

💰 ATMs

- 1. Apple • 124 E. 125th St.
- 2. Banco Popular • 164 East 116th St.
- 3. Chase Manhattan • Lexington Ave. & 125th St.
- 4. Chase Manhattan • 1 Lincoln Plaza
- 5. Chase Manhattan • 2218 Fifth Ave.
- 6. Citibank • 2261 First Ave.
- 7. Fleet • Third Ave. & 122nd St.

✳️ Community Gardens

- 110th St. Block Assoc. • 1651 Madison Ave.
- 111th St. Betterment Assoc. • 176 E. 111th St.
- 111th St. Children's Garden • 156 E. 111th St.
- 116th St. Block Assoc. •
  8 E. 116th St. east of Fifth Ave.
- 117th St. Community Garden • 172 E. 117th St.
- 117th St. Homeowners Assoc. • 170 E. 117th St.
- 119th St. • 332-340-42 E. 119th St.
- 500 E. 118th St. Block Assoc. •
  505-507 E. 118th St.
- Ana Rosa's Garden of Eden • 330-336 E. 120th St.
- Barrio Obrero's Garden • 1659 Madison Ave.
- Block and School Assoc. • 306-310 E. 118th St.
- Boricua Brothers • 204 E. 126th St.
- Boy's Club Swim Team • 431 E. 114th St.
- Carver • 236-242 E. 124th St.
- Catano Garden • 169 E. 110th St.
- Chenchitas' Group • 1691-93 Madison Ave.
- CoColon Garden • 64 E. 117th St.
- E. Harlem Council • 429-433 E. 117th St.
- El Gallo • 1891-1895 Lexington Ave.
- Flower Garden #1 • 1401 Fifth Ave.
- Fountain of Living Waters • 1816-1822 Madison Ave.
- Garden of Eden • 165 E. 111th St.
- Holy Rosary Garden • 433-439 E. 119th St.
- Jackie Robinson Tenant Assoc. • 103 E. 122nd St.
- Jirasol Assoc. • 75-77 E. 110th St.
- La Casita • 223 E. 119th St.
- La Cuevita • 71 E. 115th St.
- Los Amigos Garden • 326 Pleasant Ave.
- Lucky Neighborhood Group •
  1879 Madison Ave.
- McLoyrd Garden • 54-58 E. 117th St.
- Mini Barrio Gardeners • 1887 Lexington Ave.
- Neighborhood Assoc. • 4-8 E. 129th St.
- Nueva Esperanza Jardin • 4 E. 110th St.
- PAPO's Garden • 218-220 E. 119th St.
- Peaceful Valley • 50-52 E. 117th St.
- Perla del Sur Grupo Ponceno • 169 E. 111th St.
- Pinones Gardens • 228 E. 128th St.
- Pleasant Park Garden • 437-39 E. 114th St.
- Pleasant Village Comm Garden •
  342-352 Pleasant Ave./502 E.119th St.
- Primera Iglesia Bautista Garden • 207 E. 116th St.
- Sanidad Del Cielo • 1881-83 Lexington Ave.
- St. Mark's • 415-421 E. 117th St.
- The Children's Garden • 63-65 E. 117th St.
- The Friendly Garden • 95 E. 111th St.
- The Little Blue House • 1675 Madison Ave.

- The Magic Garden • 1665-71 Park Ave.
- The Tiny Thing Garden • 75 E. 117th St.
- United Block Assoc. • 54-50 E. 131st St.
- UPACA Senior Citizens & Handicapped Gdn. •
  127 E. 119th St.
- Villa Corozo • 1815-21 Madison Ave.
- Villa Santurce Jardineras • 74/70-72 E. 112th St.
- Yauco Ponce Group • 110-12 E. 118th St.
- Young Devils Inc. • 1753 Madison Ave.

🏥 Hospitals

- Manhattan Eye, Ear & Throat Hospital •
  55 E. 124th St.
- North General Hospital • 1879 Madison Ave.

★ Landmark

- Marcus Garvey Park •
  E. 120-124th Sts. at Madison Ave.

📖 Libraries

- 125th St. • 224 E 125th St.
- Aguilar • 174 E 110th St.

Ⓟ Police Precinct

- 25th Precinct • 120 E. 119th St.

✉️ Post Offices

- Hell Gate • 153 E. 110th St.
- Triborough • 167 E. 124th St.

💲 Schools

- Helene Fuld School of Nursing North •
  1879 Madison Ave.
- JHS 045 J. S. Roberts School • 2351 First Ave.
- JHS 101 Bridge School • 141 E. 111th St.
- NY College of Podiatric Medicine • 53 E. 124th St.
- PS 007 Samuel Stern School • 160 E. 120th St.
- PS 030 Hernandez-Hughes School • 144 E. 128th St.
- PS 057 James W. Johnson School • 176 E. 115th Ave.
- PS 079 Horan School • 55 E. 120th St.
- PS 096 Joseph Lanzetta School • 216 E. 120th St.
- PS 101 Draper School • 141 E. 111th St.
- PS 102 Cartier School • 315 E. 113th St.
- PS 112 Jose Celso Barbasa School • 535 E. 119th St.
- PS 133 Fred R. Moore School • 2121 Fifth Ave.
- PS 138 • 144 E. 128th St.
- PS 155 William Paca School • 319 E. 117th St.
- PS 206 Barbosa School • 508 E. 120th St.

East Harlem MAP

THE BRONX

E 135th St

ABRAHAM LINCOLN HOUSING

E 132nd St

E 131st St

E 130th St

E 129th St

E 128th St

E 127th St

E 126th St

Harlem River

THIRD AVE BRIDGE

Drive

Harlem River

WILLIS AVE BRIDGE

E 125th St (Dr. Martin Luther King Jr Blvd)

TRIBOROUGH BRIDGE

E 124th St

E 123rd St

MARCUS GARVEY PARK

E 122nd St

Ronald McNair Pl

Sylvan Pl

SEN. R. WAGNER. SR. HOUSES

Paladino Ave

E 121st St

E 120th St

E 119th St

E 118th St

Fifth Ave

Madison Ave

Park Ave

Lexington Ave

Third Ave

E 117th St

Second Ave

E 116th St

First Ave

Pleasant Ave

E 115th St

SEN R. TAFT HOUSES

J.W. JOHNSON HOUSING

JEFFERSON HOUSES

JEFFERSON HOUSES

E 114th St

JEFFERSON PARK

FDR Drive

E 112nd St

E 111st St

E 110th St

Duke Ellington Circle

Time for a Blockbuster! Time for a lot of other stuff, too…

Farmer's Market
• La Marqueta • E. 112-116th Sts. at Park Ave.

Gym
•Top Of The One Club & Spa • 1 Lincoln Plaza

Hardware Stores
• B & B Supply & Hardware • 2338 Second Ave.
• N & J Locksmith & Hardware Inc. •
  1637 Park Ave.
• Novelle • 218 E. 125th St.
• SM Hardware • 2139 Third Ave.
• Third Avenue Hardware • 2194 Third Ave.

Laundromats
• Bana Co. • 2037 Third Ave.
• Laundry • 110th St. & Second Ave.
• Laundry • 118th St. & First Ave.

Liquor Stores
• 115th Street Liquor Store, Inc. • 5 E. 115th St.
• Jebke Liquor Store, Inc. • 2010 Lexington Ave.
• JM Liquor • 1861 Lexington Ave.
• R A Landrau • 2334 Second Ave.
• Ramos Liquor Store • 1814 Madison Ave.
• Just In Liquors • 2178 Fifth Ave.
• Third Avenue Liquor Corp • 2030 Third Ave.
• Two Islands Wine & Liquor Store •
  2255 First Ave.

Pet Stores
• Harlem Pet Gallery • 1931 Madison Ave.
• Ideal Pet Warehouse, Ltd. • 356 E. 116th St.
• JB Pets • 111 E. 125th St.
• Julius Pet Shop • 122 E. 116th St.

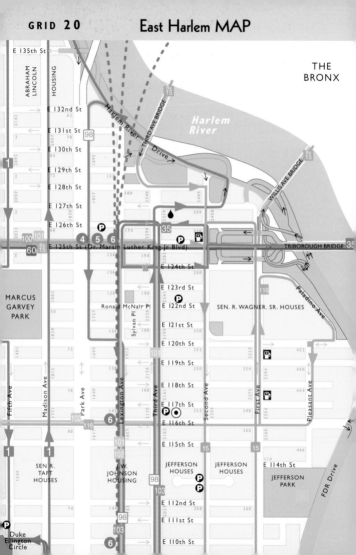

The best route to the Triborough is to go up Third Avenue and make a right on 124th Street, especially when the FDR is jammed. We feel for the folks who live over on Pleasant Ave and have to hike five miles to the nearest subway (or worse yet, wait for the bus).

Subways

4 5 6 ....125th St. & Lexington Ave.
6 ....116th St. & Lexington Ave.
6 ....110th St. & Lexington Ave.

Bus Lines

1 ....5th and Madison Aves.
15 ....1st/2nd Aves.
35 ....Randall's Island/Ward Island
60 ....LaGuardia Airport
98 ....Washington Heights/Midtown
101 ....3rd/Lexington/Amsterdam Aves.
102 ....3rd/Lexington Aves./Malcolm X. Blvd.
103 ....3rd/Lexington Aves.
116 ....116th St. Crosstown
15 ....125th St. Crosstown

Car Rental

• Alpha Auto Rental Inc •220 E. 117th St.

Car Wash

• JRP Carwash • 247 E. 127th St.

Gas Stations

• Amoco • 2276 First Ave.
• Amoco • 125th St. and Second Ave.
• Gaseteria • 119th St. & First Ave.

Parking

• East-End Parking • 227 E. 125th St.
• Guardian Water • 1 Lincoln Plaza
• JDL Garage • 221 E. 122nd St.
• Fifth Central • 1330 Fifth Ave.
• Performance Parking • 3 Lincoln Plaza
• PTM Garage • 228 E. 117th St.
• Willie's Parking • 128 E. 126th St.

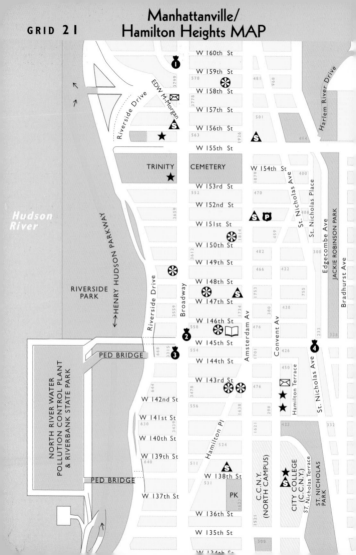

Manhattanville/
Hamilton Heights MAP

W 160th St
W 159th St
W 158th St
W 157th St
W 156th St
W 155th St
W 154th St

TRINITY   CEMETERY

W 153rd St
W 152nd St
W 151st St
W 150th St
W 149th St
W 148th St
W 147th St
W 146th St
W 145th St
W 144th St
W 143rd St
W 142nd St
W 141st St
W 140th St
W 139th St
W 138th St
W 137th St
W 136th St
W 135th St
W 134th St

EDW M Morgan

Riverside Drive

Hudson River

HENRY HUDSON PARKWAY

RIVERSIDE PARK

Riverside Drive

PED BRIDGE

NORTH RIVER WATER POLLUTION CONTROL PLANT & RIVERBANK STATE PARK

PED BRIDGE

Broadway

Amsterdam Av

Convent Av

Hamilton Pl

Hamilton Terrace

St. Nicholas Av

St. Nicholas Place

St. Nicholas Ave

Edgecombe Ave

JACKIE ROBINSON PARK

Bradhurst Ave

Harlem River Drive

PK

C.C.N.Y. (NORTH CAMPUS)

CITY COLLEGE (C.C.N.Y.) St. Nicholas Terrace

ST. NICHOLAS PARK

Riverbank State Park should be the dictionary definition of the phrase "only in New York"—a park built over a sewage treatment plant. Trinity Cemetery and Audubon Terrace are two completely overlooked Manhattan landmarks, and Hamilton Terrace is one of the prettiest streets in the city. We await gentrification.

💰 ATMs

- 1. Apple Bank For Savings • 3815 Broadway
- 2. Banco Popular • 3540 Broadway
- 3. Chase Manhattan • 3515 Broadway
- 4. Greenpoint • 700 St. Nicholas Ave

✹ Community Gardens

- 500 Block Association of 149th St. W. • 564 W. 149th St.
- Community Group of the 500 146th St. Block • 522 W. 146th St.
- Community League's Environmental Active Neighborhood Comm. • 513 W. 158th St.
- Frank White Neighborhood Service Center • 508 W. 143rd St.
- MO-PALS • 545 W. 147th St.
- W. 150th St. 500 Block Association • 499 W. 150th St.
- West Harlem Group Assistance Program • 1656 Amsterdam Ave.

★ Landmarks

- Audubon Terrace, including:
  - American Academy and Institute of Arts and Letters
  - American Numismatic Museum
  - Hispanic Society of America • W. 155th St.
- CUNY-City College • W. 138th St. and Convent Ave.
- Hamilton Grange National Memorial • 287 Convent Ave.
- Hamilton Heights Historic District • W. 141st- W. 145th Sts. and Convent Ave.
- Trinity Church Cemetery's Graveyard of Heroes • 153rd/155th Sts. and Broadway

📖 Library

- Hamilton Grange • 521 W. 146th St.

🅿 Police Precinct

- 30th Precinct • 451 W. 151st St.

✉ Post Office

- Hamilton Grange • 521 W. 146th St.

🛡 Schools

- Boricua College • 3755 Broadway
- CUNY-City College • Convent Ave. & 138th St.
- Dance Theatre Of Harlem Inc. • 466 W. 152nd St.
- PS 028 Wright Brothers School • 475 W. 155th St.
- PS 153 Adam C. Powell School • 1750 Amsterdam Ave.
- PS 192 Jacob H. Schiff School • 500 W. 138th St.

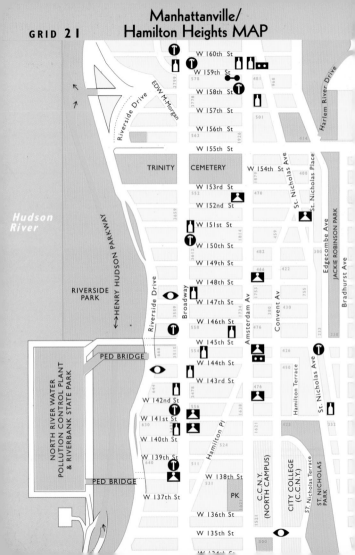

Manhattanville/
Hamilton Heights MAP

GRID 21

Hudson
River

TRINITY CEMETERY

RIVERSIDE PARK

NORTH RIVER WATER POLLUTION CONTROL PLANT & RIVERBANK STATE PARK

PED BRIDGE

PED BRIDGE

Riverside Drive

EDW M-Morgan

HENRY HUDSON PARKWAY

Riverside Drive

Broadway

Hamilton Pl

Amsterdam Av

Convent Av

Hamilton Terrace

St. Nicholas Av

St. Nicholas Place

St. Nicholas Av

Edgecombe Av

Bradhurst Av

JACKIE ROBINSON PARK

Harlem River Drive

ST. NICHOLAS PARK

C.C.N.Y. (NORTH CAMPUS)

CITY COLLEGE (C.C.N.Y.)

St. Nicholas Terrace

W 160th St
W 159th St
W 158th St
W 157th St
W 156th St
W 155th St
W 154th St
W 153rd St
W 152nd St
W 151st St
W 150th St
W 149th St
W 148th St
W 147th St
W 146th St
W 145th St
W 144th St
W 143rd St
W 142nd St
W 141st St
W 140th St
W 139th St
W 138th St
W 137th St
W 136th St
W 135th St
W 134th St

PK

Gym

- Elmo's Gym Co., Inc. • 552 W. 158th St.

Hardware Stores

- 3841 Hardware • 3841 Broadway
- All Star Hardware Distributors Inc. • 3547 Broadway
- Americana Hardware • 3628 Broadway
- Cohen & Cohen, Inc. • 1982 Amsterdam Ave.
- Concordia Electrical & Plumbing • 2297 Seventh Ave. (Adam Clayton Powell)
- Frame Hardware • 3806 Broadway
- Fred's Locksmith and Hardware • 708 St. Nicholas Ave.
- O&J Hardware Co. • 3405 Broadway
- Westside Home Center • 3447 Broadway

Laundromats

- 3440 Broadway Laundromat • 3440 Broadway
- Amsterdam Laundromat Corp. • 1701 Amsterdam Ave.
- Clean Action Laundromat Inc. • 3476 Broadway
- F&J Laundromat • 1773 Amsterdam Ave.
- Laundry • 151st St. & St. Nicholas Ave.
- MOH Corp. • 3403 Broadway
- Quezadad Laundromat • 1848 Amsterdam Ave.
- Raspberry's Cleaning Center Inc. • 1645 Amsterdam Ave.

Liquor Stores

- Augustine Wines & Liquor Inc. • 550 W. 145th St.
- Duran Liquor Store • 2001 Amsterdam Ave.
- H L K Liquors Inc. • 3375 Broadway
- In Good Spirits Corp. • 3819 Broadway
- JOCL Liquor Store • 561 W. 147th St.
- Jumasol Liquors Inc. • 1963 Amsterdam Ave.
- La Alta Gracia Liquor Store • 3435 Broadway
- Mc Liquor Store Inc. • 2208 Amsterdam Ave.
- New York Minority Beverages Inc. • 501 W. 145th St.
- South Nourth Inc. • 3490 Broadway
- Unity Liquors Inc. • 708 St. Nicholas Ave.
- Vasquez & Urena • 3658 Broadway

Movie Theatres

- Aaron Davis Hall • W. 135th St. and Convent Ave.
- Africa Arts Theatre Co. Inc • 660 Riverside Dr.
- Nova Cinema • 3589 Broadway

Video Rentals

- Hunter Video • 468 W. 159th St.
- Video Box • 1706 Amsterdam Ave.

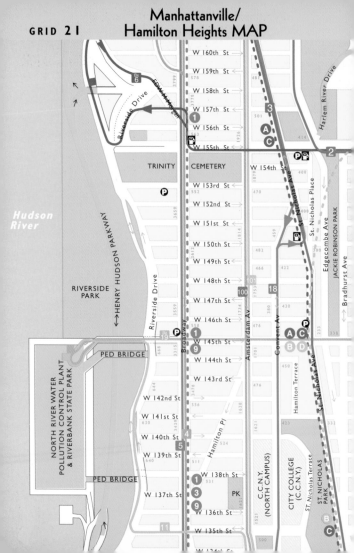

Hudson
River

Henry Hudson Parkway

Riverside Drive

RIVERSIDE
PARK

NORTH RIVER WATER
POLLUTION CONTROL PLANT
& RIVERBANK STATE PARK

PED BRIDGE

PED BRIDGE

Riverside Drive

Broadway

Hamilton Pl

Amsterdam Av

Convent Av

St. Nicholas Av

St. Nicholas Place

Edgecombe Av

JACKIE ROBINSON PARK

Bradhurst Av

Harlem River Drive

Hamilton Terrace

St. Nicholas Terrace

C.C.N.Y.
(NORTH CAMPUS)

CITY COLLEGE
(C.C.N.Y.)

ST. NICHOLAS
PARK

TRINITY   CEMETERY

W 160th St
W 159th St
W 158th St
W 157th St
W 156th St
W 155th St
W 154th St
W 153rd St
W 152nd St
W 151st St
W 150th St
W 149th St
W 148th St
W 147th St
W 146th St
W 145th St
W 144th St
W 143rd St
W 142nd St
W 141st St
W 140th St
W 139th St
W 138th St
W 137th St
W 136th St
W 135th St
W 134th St

PK

Riverside Drive can be an intriguing alternative to traffic on the Henry Hudson, which begins to get serious during rush hour as one moves closer to the George Washington Bridge. A great way to get to the Bronx (and Yankee Stadium) from the Upper West Side is to take Broadway up to 155th Street and cross the Harlem River at the Macombs Dam Bridge. You heard it here first.

Subways

①⑨	Broadway at 157th St.
①⑨	Broadway at 145th St.
①⑨③	137th St. at Broadway (City College)
Ⓐ Ⓑ Ⓒ Ⓓ	145th St. at St. Nicholas Ave.
Ⓐ Ⓒ	155th St. at St. Nicholas Ave.
Ⓑ Ⓒ	135th St. at St. Nicholas Ave.

Bus Lines

2	Fifth Ave./Madison Ave./Powell Blvd.
3	Fifth Ave./Madison Ave./St. Nicholas Blvd.
4	Fifth Ave./Madison Ave./Broadway
5	Fifth Ave./Ave. of the Americas/ Riverside Dr.
11	Ninth (Columbus Ave.)/Tenth (Amsterdam Ave)/Convent Ave..
18	Convent Ave.
10x	Amsterdam Ave./Broadway/125th St.
01	Third Ave./Lexington Ave./ Broadway/125th St.
8	E. 161st St./E 163rd St.
13	145th St. Crosstown

🅿 Gas Stations

- Getty • 119 W. 145th St.
- Mobil • 3740 Broadway
- Mobil • 150th St. & St. Nicholas Ave.

🅿 Parking

- Easyway Parking • 404 W. 155th St.
- Edison Riverside • 3333 Broadway
- FS & M Garage • 673 St. Nicholas Ave.
- Kinney System • 614 W. 153rd St.

Harlem (Upper) MAP

COLONIAL PARK HOUSES

Harlem River Drive

POLO GROUND HOUSES

W 155th St

THE BRONX

MACOMBS DAM BRIDGE

St. Nicholas Place

W 154th St

W 153rd St

W 152nd St

Macombs Place

W 151st St

Edgecombe Ave

JACKIE ROBINSON PARK

Bradhurst Ave

HARLEM RIVER HOUSES

W 150th St

W 149th St

Harlem River

W 148th St

ESPLANADE GARDENS

W 147th St

W 146th St

W 145th St

145th ST BRIDGE

St. Nicholas Ave

Pool

W 144th St

W 143rd St

Frederick Douglass Blvd

Adam Clayton Powell Jr. Blvd

W 142nd St

W 141st St

Lenox Ave (Malcolm X Blvd)

Chisum Pl

N. HARLEM HOUSES

W 140th St

W 139th St

ST. NICHOLAS PARK

W 138th St

W 137th St

W 136th St

MADISON

W 135th St

H HARLEM HOSPITAL CENTER

Fifth Ave

RIVERTON HOUSES

Madison Ave

W 134th St

P

As much as people who live in the Polo Grounds Houses need housing, we really wish the Polo Grounds itself was still there.

💰 ATMs

- 1. Chase Manhattan • 2218 Fifth Ave.
- 2. Chase Manhattan • 1421 St. Nicholas Ave.
- 3. Chase Manhattan • 135th St. & F. D. Blvd.
- 4. Greenpoint • 700 St. Nicholas Ave.

✴️ Community Gardens

- 153rd St. Harlemites-Garden Beautiful • 263-265 W. 153rd St.
- Bradhurst Ave. Tenants Association N/E/C • Bradhurst Ave. & W. 152nd St.
- Comm Leaders of W. 146th St. • 226-234 W. 146th St.
- CS 46 Tappan School • 2987 Frederick Douglass Blvd.
- Gholson Gardens • W. 152nd St.
- JAH Children's Association-Senior Intercessors • 207-209 W. 140th St.
- The Elizabeth Langley Memorial Garden • 121-123 W. 137th St.

🏥 Hospital

- Harlem Hospital Center • 506 Lenox Ave.

★ Landmarks

- Abyssinian Baptist Church • 132 W. 138th St.
- Harlem YMCA • 180 W. 135th St.
- St. Nicholas Historic District • 202-250 W. 138th St. & W. 139th St.

📖 Libraries

- Countee Cullen • 104 W. 136th St .
- Macomb's Bridge • 2650 Adam Clayton Powell Jr. Blvd.

🅿️ Police Precinct

- 32nd Precinct • 250 W. 135th St.

✉️ Post Offices

- College Station • 217 W. 140th St.
- Colonial Park • 99 Macombs Pl.
- Lincolnton • 2266 Fifth Ave.

🅰️ Schools

- Dance Theatre Of Harlem Inc. • 466 W. 152nd St.
- PS 046 Tappan School • 2987 Frederick Douglass Blvd.
- PS 123 Mahalia Jackson School • 301 W. 140th St.
- PS 194 Countee Cullen School • 242 W. 144th St.
- PS 197 John Russwurm School • 2230 Fifth Ave.
- PS 200 James Smith School • 2589 Adam Clayton Powell Jr. Blvd

COLO-
NIAL
PARK HOUSES

Harlem River Drive

POLO
GROUND
HOUSES

W 155th St

St. Nicholas Place

Edgecombe Ave

Jackie Robinson Park

Bradhurst Ave

Macombs Place

W 154th St

W 153rd St

W 152nd St

W 151st St

HARLEM
RIVER
HOUSES

W 150th St

W 149th St

W 148th St

W 147th St

W 146th St

Pool

W 145th St

W 144th St

Federick Douglass Blvd

W 143rd St

Adam Clayton Powell Jr. Blvd

W 142nd St

W 141st St

W 140th St

St. Nicholas Ave

W 139th St

ST. NICHOLAS PARK

W 138th St

W 137th St

W 136th St

W 135th St

W 134th St

MACOMBS DAM BRIDGE

THE
BRONX

*Harlem
River*

Harlem River Drive

ESPLANADE
GARDENS

145th ST BRIDGE

Lenox Ave (Malcolm X Blvd)

Chisum Pl

N. HARLEM
HOUSES

MADISON

HARLEM
HOSPITAL
CENTER

Fifth Ave

RIVERTON
HOUSES

Madison Ave

Gym

- Diamond Gym • 104 W. 145th St.

Hardware Stores

- B&E Hardware & Lockshop • 2647 Eighth Ave. (Frederick Douglass)
- B&J's Hardware • 2477 Seventh Ave. (Adam Clayton Powell)
- Concordia Electrical & Plumbing • 2297 Seventh Ave. (Adam Clayton Powell)
- Fred's Locksmith and Hardware • 708 St. Nicholas Ave.
- R&R Hardware And Houseware • 2824 Eighth Ave. (Frederick Douglass)
- St Nicholas Hardware • 1488 St. Nicholas Ave.

Laundromats

- All Season Laundry Corp. • 1506 St. Nicholas Ave.
- BR Wash & Dry • 2906 Eighth Ave. (Frederick Douglass Blvd.)
- CC Laundromat • 2394 Seventh Ave. (Adam Clayton Powell Jr. Blvd.)
- David Allen Service, Inc. • 2350 Fifth Ave.
- Eggen Private Laundry • 2350 Fifth Ave.
- Giselle Laundromat • 1644 St. Nicholas Ave.
- GrandView Laundry • 2350 Fifth Ave.
- Laundry • 135th St. & A.C.Powell Jr. Blvd.
- Laundry • 136th St. & A.C.Powell Jr. Blvd.
- Laundry • 147th St. & A.C.Powell Jr. Blvd.
- Service First Laundromat, Inc. • 2741 Eighth Ave. (Frederick Douglass Blvd.)
- Soap Opera 3 Corp. • 2815 Frederick Douglass Blvd.
- Swiss American Hand Laundry, Inc. • 2350 Fifth Ave.
- Sylvia Gray Laundry • 2350 Fifth Ave.
- Veva Laundromat • 203 W. 145th St.

Liquor Stores

- 249 E 155 Liquor • 249 E. 155th St.
- All-Rite Liquors Inc. • 2651 Eighth Ave. (Frederick Douglass Blvd.)
- Dorden Liquors Inc. • 555 Lenox Ave.
- Doyle's Liquor Shop • 2521 Seventh Ave. (Adam Clayton Powell Jr. Blvd)
- Friedland Wine & Liquor Store • 605 Lenox Ave.
- Luis Liquor Corp • 108 W. 145th St.
- Oz Liquors • 2610 Eighth Ave. (Frederick Douglass Blvd.)
- Stop One Wine & Liquor • 272 W. 154th St.
- Unity Liquors Inc. • 708 St. Nicholas Ave.

Movie Theatre

- Schomburg Center for Research in Black Culture • 515 Malcolm X Blvd.

Video Rental

- Mad Videos • 318 W. 142nd St.

Harlem (Upper) MAP

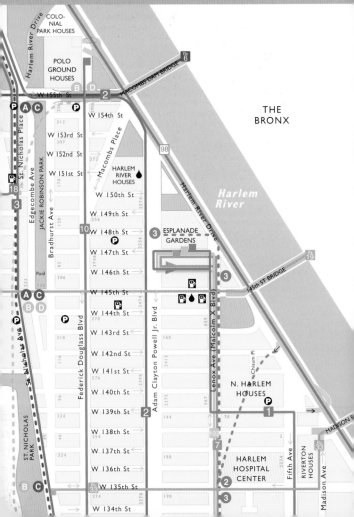

THE
BRONX

*Harlem
River*

COLO-
NIAL
PARK
HOUSES

POLO
GROUND
HOUSES

Harlem River Drive

Bx
6

Macombs Dam Bridge

W 155th St

98

Harlem River Drive

HARLEM
RIVER
HOUSES

Macombs Place

W 154th St

W 153rd St

W 152nd St

W 151st St

W 150th St

W 149th St

W 148th St

ESPLANADE
GARDENS

W 147th St

W 146th St

145th ST BRIDGE

W 145th St

W 144th St

W 143rd St

W 142nd St

W 141st St

W 140th St

N. HARLEM
HOUSES

Chisum Pl

W 139th St

W 138th St

HARLEM
HOSPITAL
CENTER

RIVERTON
HOUSES

W 137th St

W 136th St

W 135th St

W 134th St

St. Nicholas Place

Edgecombe Ave

JACKIE ROBINSON PARK

Bradhurst Ave

Frederick Douglass Blvd

Adam Clayton Powell Jr. Blvd

Lenox Ave (Malcolm X Blvd)

Fifth Ave

Madison Ave

MADISON

So. Nicholas Ave

ST.
NICHOLAS
PARK

Pool

18

10

3

2

7

1

33

Subways

Ⓐ Ⓒ ....St. Nicholas Ave. at 155th St.
Ⓐ Ⓑ Ⓒ Ⓓ ....St. Nicholas Ave. at 145th St.
Ⓑ Ⓒ ....135th St. at St. Nicholas Ave.
Ⓑ Ⓓ ....155th St. at Frederick Douglass Blvd.
② ③ ....Malcolm X Blvd. at 135th St.
................................Adam Clayton Powell Jr. Blvd.
③ ....at 148th St.
③ ....Malcolm X Blvd. at 145th St.

Bus Lines

1 ....5th Ave./Madison Ave.
2 ....5th Ave./Madison Ave./Powell Blvd.
3 ....5th Ave./Madison Ave./St. Nicholas Ave.
................................Columbus Ave./Amsterdam
7 ....Ave./6th Ave./7th Ave./Broadway
................7th Ave./8th Ave. (Central Park West)/
10 ....Frederick Douglass Blvd.
18 ....Convent Ave.
98 ....Washington Heights/Midtown
100 ......3rd Ave./Lexington Ave./Malcolm X Blvd.
6/8 ....E. 161st St./E 163rd St.
19 ....145th St. Crosstown
33 ....145th St. Crosstown

🔻 Car Washes
• Harlem Hand Car Wash • 2600 Seventh Ave.
  (Adam Clayton Powell Jr. Blvd.)
• Car Wash • 119 W. 145th St.

⛽ Gas Stations
• Amoco • 232 W. 145th St.
• Merit Gasoline Stations • 128 W. 145th St.
• Mobil • 150th St. & St. Nicholas Ave.
• Mobil • 126 W. 145th St.
• Getty • 119 W. 145th St.

🅿 Parking
• D S Trucking • 17 W. 139th St.
• Giselle Garage • 310 W. 144th St.
• Giselle Garage • 240 W. 148th St.
• J & L Parking • 280 W. 155th St.
• Easyway Parking • 404 W. 155th St.
• F S & M Garage • 673 St. Nicholas Ave.

Washington Heights MAP

Riverside Drive

Cabrini Blvd

W 183rd St

W 183rd St

Col. R. Magaw Pl

Bennett Ave

584
177
4280

W 182nd St

W 181st St

W 180th St

W 179th St

500

PLAZA LAFAYETTE

Pinehurst Ave

2414

WASHINGTON BRIDGE

ALEXANDER HAMILTON BRID

568
301
516

BUS TERMINAL

GEORGE WASHINGTON BRIDGE

Fort Washington Ave

Wadsworth Ave

W 178th St

W 177th St

W 176th St

W 175th St

598
500

219
650
611

596

Harle River

The Little Red Lighthouse

J.N. WRIGHT PARK

Haven Ave

W 174th St

W 173rd St

W 172nd St

W 171st St

W 170th St

W 169th St

W 168th St

600
500

266
4075

St. Nicholas Ave

1254
2240

Audubon Ave

109

570
565
57

500

HIGH BRIDGE (P

Pool

HIGH BRIDGE PARK

622
185

736
709
715

4

514
2218

Amsterdam Ave

Harlem River Drive

Jumel Pl

COLUMBIA PRESBYTERIAN MEDICAL CENTER

N.Y.S. PSYCHIATRIC INSTITUTE

WASHINGTON PARK

Riverside Drive

HENRY HUDSON PKWY

Hudson River

Fort Washington Ave

Broadway

W 167th St

201

500

H H

W 166th St

3

McKenna Sq

St. Nicholas Ave

P

Jumel Terr

2715
2006

W 165th St

W 164th St

W 163rd St

W 162nd St

W 161st St

W 160th St

W 159th St

3915
97
562
3878
580
578

301

2010

458
454
424
448

Edgecombe Ave

ROGER MORRIS PARK

Sylvan Terrace

644
1816
4811

COL PA HO

Sylvan Terrace is the most un-Manhattan-looking place in Manhattan. It's way cool.

💰 ATMs
- 1. Apple • 4251 Broadway
- 2. Banco Popular • 615 W. 181st St.
- 3. Chase • 3940 Broadway
- 4. Citibank • 4058 Broadway
- 5. Citibank • 4249 Broadway

❀ Community Gardens
- 181st St. Beautification • 814 W. 181st St.
- IS 143 • 511 & 516 W. 182nd St
- Morris-Jumel Eco Educational Garden • 455-457 W. 162nd St.

🏥 Hospitals
- Babies & Children's Hospital Of New York • 3959 Broadway
- Columbia-Presbyterian • 622 W. 168th St.

★ Landmarks
- George Washington Bridge • W. 178st St.
- The Little Red Lighthouse • under the George Washington Bridge
- Morris-Jumel Mansion • Edgecombe Ave. and 161st St.
- Sylvan Terrace • between Jumel Terrace & St. Nicholas Ave.

📖 Libraries
- Fort Washington • 535 W. 179th St.
- Washington Heights • 1000 Nicholas Ave.

🅿 Police Precinct
- 33rd Precinct • 2120 Amsterdam Ave.

✉ Post Offices
- Audubon • 515 W. 165th St.
- Washington Bridge • 555 W. 180th St.

🅢 Schools
- I S 143 Eleanor Roosevelt School • 511 W. 182nd St.
- I S 164 Edward W Stitt School • 401 W. 164th St.
- I S 90 • 21 Jumel Pl.
- P S 8 • 168th St. & Amsterdam Ave.
- P S 115 Humboldt School • 586 W. 177th St.
- P S 128 Audubon School • 560 W. 169th St.
- P S 132 Juan Pablo Duarte School • 185 Wadsworth Ave.
- P S 173 • 306 Fort Washington Ave.
- P S 528 Bea Fuller Rodgers School • 180 Wadsworth Ave.

Washington Heights MAP

W 183rd St

W 183rd Ave

W 182nd St

W 181st St

WASHINGTON BRIDGE

W 180th Ave

W 179th St

PLAZA
AFAYETTE

ALEXANDER HAMILTON BRIDGE

W 178th St

BUS
TERMINAL

GEORGE WASHINGTON BRIDGE

Harle
River

W 177th St

Wadsworth Ave

W 176th St

HIGH BRIDGE (PE

W 175th St

W 174th St

J.N. WRIGHT
PARK

W 173rd St

St. Nicholas Ave

Pool

W 172nd St

HIGH BRIDGE
PARK

W 171st St

Audubon Ave

W 170th St

Haven Ave

W 169th St

Harlem River Drive

Riverside Drive

W 168th St

Amsterdam Ave

COLUMBIA
PRESBYTERIAN
MEDICAL
CENTER

Jumel Pl

N.Y.S.
PSYCHIATRIC
INSTITUTE

WASHINGTON
PARK

W 167th St

Broadway

HENRY HUDSON PKWY

W 166th St

McKenna
Sq

W 165th St

Edgecombe Ave

Hudson
River

W 164th St

Fort Washington Ave

W 163rd St

W 162nd St

Jumel Terr

ROGER
MORRIS
PARK

W 161st St

Sylvan Terr

W 160th St

W 159th St

CO
NIA
PA
HO

Gyms

- Frank's Fitness Inc. • 4271 Broadway
- Urban Total Fitness Inc. • 1387 St Nicholas Ave.

Hardware Stores

- A H S Hardware • 2416 Amsterdam Ave.
- Chavin Hardware, Inc. • 1348 St. Nicholas Ave.
- Cohen & Cohen, Inc. • 1982 Amsterdam Ave.
- Cora Children Ware, Inc. • 4189 Broadway
- Ernesto's Hardware Store • 2180 Amsterdam Ave.
- Frame Hardware • 3806 Broadway
- Martinez Hardware • 1269 St. Nicholas Ave.
- Nunez Hardware • 4145 Broadway
- Washington Heights Hardware • 736 W. 181st St.

Laundromats

- 106 Audubon Ave. Laundromat • 106 Audubon Ave.
- Happy Laundry • 4092 Broadway
- Jocelyn Laundromat • 2057 Amsterdam Ave.
- Kleener King • 823 W. 181st St.
- Roland Laundromat • 188 Audubon Ave.
- Victor's Laundromat • 134 Audubon Ave.

Liquor Stores

- All-Star Spirits, Ltd. • 4189 Broadway
- Campos Ernest F • 831 W. 181st St.
- Duran Liquor Store • 2001 Amsterdam Ave.
- Galicia Liquors, Inc. • 3906 Broadway
- Guadalupe Barbara • 4084 Broadway
- Puma Wine & Liquor • 182 Audubon Ave.
- Vazac Frank J • 114 Audubon Ave.

 ## Movie Theatre

- Coliseum Theatre • Broadway at 181st St.

Pet Stores

- Feliciano Yvonne • 518 W. 181st St.
- Uptown Pets • 4232 Broadway

Video Rental

- Blockbuster Video • 4211 Broadway

Washington Heights MAP

W 183rd St

W 182nd St

W 181st St

WASHINGTON BRIDGE

W 180th St

W 179th St

BUS TERMINAL

W 178th St

W 177th St

ALEXANDER HAMILTON BRIDGE

W 176th St

Harle
River

W 175th St

W 174th St

HIGH BRIDGE (PE)

J.N. WRIGHT PARK

W 173rd St

W 172nd St

Pool

W 171st St

HIGH BRIDGE PARK

W 170th St

W 169th St

W 168th St

COLUMBIA PRESBYTERIAN MEDICAL CENTER

W 167th St

Jumel Pl

N.Y.S. PSYCHIATRIC INSTITUTE

W 166th St

McKenna Sq

W 165th St

W 164th St

W 163rd St

W 162nd St

W 161st St

Sylvan Terr

ROGER MORRIS PARK

W 160th St

Hudson River

W 159th St

Cabrini Blvd

Bennett Ave

Col. R Magaw Pl

Pinehurst Ave

Fort Washington Ave

Wadsworth Ave

Broadway

St Nicholas Ave

Audubon Ave

Amsterdam Ave

Edgecombe Ave

Jumel Terr

Harlem River Drive

GEORGE WASHINGTON BRIDGE

HENRY HUSON PKWY

WASHINGTON PARK

Riverside Drive

Haven Ave

The George Washington Bridge is slightly less of a nightmare than the other two Hudson River crossings, mainly because it can be reached independently from both the west and east sides and because it has several more lanes. If you have a choice, take the lower level going outbound, and always take the Harlem River Drive instead of the West Side Highway.

Subways

A ....Fort Washington Ave. & 175th St.

A ....Fort. Washington Ave. & 181st St.

A C ....Amsterdam Ave. & 163rd St.

A C 1 9 ....Broadway & 168th St.

1 9 ....St. Nicholas Ave. & 181st St.

Bus Lines

5th and Madison Aves.

2 ..../Adam Clayton Powell Jr. Blvd.

3 ....5th and Madison Aves./St. Nicholas Ave.

4 ....5th and Madison Aves./Broadway

5 ....5th Ave./Ave. of the Americas/Riverside Dr.

18 ....Convent Ave.

98 ....Washington Heights/Midtown

10X ....Amsterdam Ave./Broadway/125th St.

101 ....3rd/Lexington Aves./Malcolm X Blvd.

7 ....to Riverdale, 238th St.-Broadway

7 ....Riverdale Ave./Broadway

11 ....to Southern Blvd. via 170th St.

13 ....to Yankee Stadium via Ogden Ave.

14 ....to West Farms Rd. via 167th St.

36 ...to Olmstead Ave./Randall Ave. via 180th St.

⊙ Car Rental

• Aamcar: Uptown Car Rental • 506 181st St.

🅿 Gas Stations

• Shell • 2420 Amsterdam Ave.
• Shell • 2149 Amsterdam Ave.

🅿 Parking

• 284 Audubon Parking • 284 Audubon Ave.
• Garage Management • 120-200 Cabrini Blvd.
• M A North Parking • 528 W. 162nd St.
• MNS Parking • 554 W. 174th St.
• Tri County Parking • 506 W. 181st St.

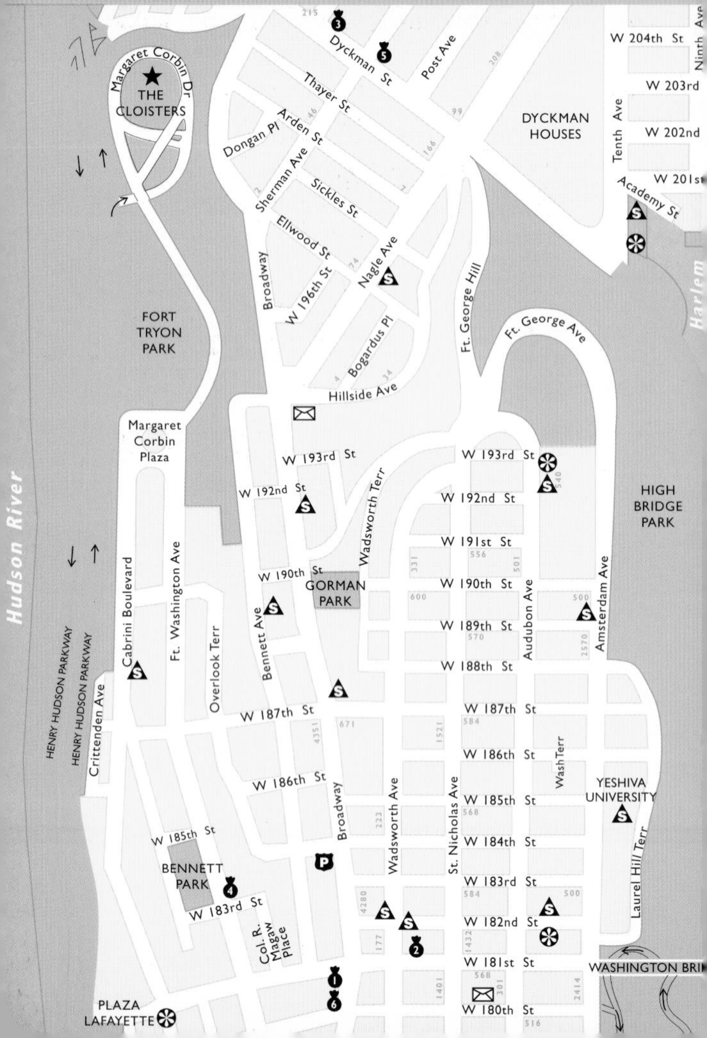
Dyckman St
Post Ave
Thayer St
Arden St
Dongan Pl
Sherman Ave
Sickles St
Ellwood St
Nagle Ave
Broadway
W 196th St
Bogardus Pl
Hillside Ave
Ft. George Hill
Ft. George Ave
DYCKMAN HOUSES
W 204th St
W 203rd
W 202nd
W 201st
Tenth Ave
Ninth Ave
Academy St
Harlem
Margaret Corbin Dr
THE CLOISTERS
FORT TRYON PARK
Margaret Corbin Plaza
Hudson River
HENRY HUDSON PARKWAY
HENRY HUDSON PARKWAY
Crittenden Ave
Cabrini Boulevard
Ft. Washington Ave
Overlook Terr
Bennett Ave
W 193rd St
W 192nd St
W 190th St
GORMAN PARK
Wadsworth Terr
W 193rd St
W 192nd St
W 191st St
W 190th St
W 189th St
W 188th St
Audubon Ave
Amsterdam Ave
HIGH BRIDGE PARK
W 187th St
W 187th St
W 186th St
W 186th St
Broadway
Wadsworth Ave
St. Nicholas Ave
Wash Terr
YESHIVA UNIVERSITY
W 185th St
W 185th St
W 184th St
BENNETT PARK
W 183rd St
W 183rd St
W 182nd St
Col. R. Magaw Place
W 181st St
W 180th St
Laurel Hill Terr
WASHINGTON BRI
PLAZA LAFAYETTE

The Cloisters and Fort Tryon Park are absolutely two of the quietest and most beautiful places in Manhattan.

💰 ATMs
- 1. Apple • 4251 Broadway
- 2. Banco Popular • 615 W. 181st St.
- 3. Banco Popular • 175 Dyckman
- 4. Chase Manhattan • 596 Fort Washington Ave.
- 5. Chase Manhattan • 161 Dyckman
- 6. Citibank • 4249 Broadway

❇️ Community Gardens
- George Washington High School • 549 Audubon Ave.
- IS 143 • 511 & 516 W. 182nd St.
- IS 218 Children Garden • Harlem River Dr./Dyckman St.
- 181st St. Beautification Project • 814 W. 181st St.

★ Landmark
- The Cloisters • Fort Tryon Park

🚔 Police Precinct
- 34th Precinct • 4295 Broadway

✉️ Post Offices
- Fort George • 4558 Broadway
- Washington Bridge • 555 W. 180th St.

🅢 Schools
- IS 143 Eleanor Roosevelt School • 511 W. 182nd St.
- IS 218 Salome Urena School • 4600 Broadway
- PS 005 Ellen Lurie School • 3703 Tenth Ave.
- PS 048 Officer Buczek School • 4360 Broadway
- PS 132 Juan Pablo Duarte School • 185 Wadsworth
- PS 152 Dyckman Valley School • 93 Nagle Ave.
- PS/IS 187 Hudson Cliffs School • 349 Cabrini Blvd.
- PS 189 • 2580 Amsterdam Ave.
- PS 528 Bea Fuller Rodgers School • 180 Wadsworth
- George Washington High School • 549 Audubon Ave.
- Beth Medrash Jeshurun • 220 Bennett Ave.
- Yeshiva University • 500 W. 185th St.

Fort George MAP

Dyckman St
Post Ave
W 204th St
Ninth
W 203rd
Thayer St
Tenth Ave
W 202nd
DYCKMAN HOUSES
W 201st
Academy St
THE CLOISTERS
Margaret Corbin Dr
Dongan Pl
Arden St
Sherman Ave
Sickles St
Ellwood St
Nagle Ave
Broadway
W 196th St
Bogardus Pl
Hillside Ave
Ft. George Hill
Ft. George Ave
Harlem
FORT TRYON PARK
Margaret Corbin Plaza
W 193rd St
W 193rd St
W 192nd St
W 192nd St
HIGH BRIDGE PARK
Wadsworth Terr
W 191st St
W 190th St
W 190th St
GORMAN PARK
W 189th St
Bennett Ave
Cabrini Boulevard
Ft. Washington Ave
Audubon Ave
Amsterdam Ave
W 188th St
Hudson River
Overlook Terr
W 187th St
W 187th St
Broadway
St. Nicholas Ave
Wash Terr
W 186th St
Henry Hudson Parkway
Henry Hudson Parkway
W 186th St
W 185th St
W 185th St
YESHIVA UNIVERSITY
Crittenden Ave
Wadsworth Ave
W 184th St
BENNETT PARK
W 183rd St
W 183rd St
Laurel Hill Terr
W 182nd St
Col. R. Magaw Place
W 181st St
WASHINGTON BRID
W 180th St
PLAZA LAFAYETTE

Gyms

- Frank's Fitness Inc. • 4271 Broadway
- Multi Fitness • 104 Sherman Ave.
- Urban Total Fitness Inc. • 1387 St. Nicholas Ave.

Hardware Stores

- 756 Hardware Inc. • 756 W. 181st St.
- AHS Hardware • 2416 Amsterdam Ave.
- Apex Supply Co. • 4580 Broadway
- Castro Heights Supply Co Inc. • 1539 St. Nicholas Ave.
- Century Maintenance • 4309 Broadway
- Geomart Hardware • 607 Fort Washington Ave.
- K & N Hardware • 4454 Broadway
- Nagle Hardware Store • 145 Nagle Ave.
- Papelin Hardware • 1488 St. Nicholas Ave.
- Tsigonia Industries Corp. • 568 W. 184th St.
- VNJ Hardware • 4476 Broadway
- Washington Heights Hardware • 736 W. 181st St.
- Win Mar Enterprises • 602 W. 184th St.

Laundromats

- Kleener King • 823 W. 181st St.
- Launderiffic • 812 W. 187th St.
- OK Laundry, Inc. • 4450 Broadway
- On Broadway Laundromat • 4401 Broadway
- Santo Domingo Super Laundromat • 400 Audubon Ave.

Liquor Stores

- 949 Liquor Store Inc. • 4329 Broadway
- Campos Ernest F • 831 W. 181st St.
- ECA Liquor Inc. • 55 Sherman Ave.
- Hou & Hou Liquors • 1492 St. Nicholas Ave.
- Las Vegas Wines • 154 Nagle Ave.
- Nunez Alex • 1598 St Nicholas Ave.
- Sanchez Liquors • 4500 Broadway
- Sherman Liquor Corp • 25 Sherman Ave.
- UR Liquor • 377 Audubon Ave.

Movie Theatre

- Coliseum Theatre • Broadway at 181st St.

Pet Stores

- Feliciano Yvonne • 518 W. 181st St.
- Uptown Pets • 4232 Broadway

Video Rentals

- Blockbuster Video • 161 Dyckman
- Blockbuster Video • 4211 Broadway
- Charlene Ebony Inc. • 58 Sherman Ave.
- M A Video Future • 4417 Broadway

Fort George MAP

Margaret Corbin Dr

THE CLOISTERS

Dyckman St
Post Ave
Thayer St
Arden Pl
Dongan Pl
Sherman Ave
Sickles St
Ellwood St
Nagle Ave
W 196th St
Bogardus Pl
Hillside Ave

DYCKMAN HOUSES

W 204th St
W 203r
Tenth Ave
W 202n
Academy St
W 201s

FORT TRYON PARK

Broadway

Ft. George Hill
Ft. George Ave

Margaret Corbin Plaza

W 193rd St
W 192nd St

Bennett Ave

W 190th St

GORMAN PARK

Wadsworth Terr

W 193rd St
W 192nd St
W 191st St
W 190th St
W 189th St
W 188th St

Audubon Ave
Amsterdam Ave

HIGH BRIDGE PARK

Cabrini Boulevard

Overlook Terr

Fr. Washington Ave

W 187th St

W 186th St

W 185th St

Wash Terr

YESHIVA UNIVERSITY

Wadsworth Ave

St. Nicholas Ave

W 187th St
W 186th St
W 185th St
W 184th St
W 183rd St
W 182nd St
W 181st St

Pinehurst Ave
Crittenden Ave

HENRY HUDSON PARKWAY

Hudson River

Harlem

W 185th St

BENNETT PARK

Col. R. Magaw Place

W 183rd St

Laurel Hill Terr

PLAZA LAFAYETTE

W 181st St
WASHINGTON BR

W 180th St

Fort George TRANSPORTATION

Pay close attention when you cross over into Manhattan from New Jersey on the George Washington Bridge, because if you miss the "Harlem River Drive-Last Exit in Manhattan" exit, you'll be crossing over into the Bronx and sitting in traffic on what is categorically the most miserable highway in all the world, the Cross Bronx Expressway.

Subways

Ⓐ	Fort Washington Ave.
Ⓐ	190th St.
❶	St. Nicholas Ave.
❶ ❾	181st St.

Bus Lines

3	ST. Nicholas Ave.
4	Ft. Washington Ave.
98	Ft. Washington Ave.
100	Broadway
101	Amsterdam Ave.
3	181st St
7	Broadway
11	181st St
18	181st St
13	181st St
36	181st St

⊙ Car Rental
- Aamcar: Uptown Car Rental • 506 W. 181st St.

◈ Car Wash
- Sunoco Ultra Car Wash • 4469 Broadway

🅿 Gas Stations
- Amoco • 4355 Broadway
- Gaseteria • 4519 Broadway
- Raamco Service Station • 4275 Broadway
- Shell • 201st St. and Tenth Ave.
- Shell • 2420 Amsterdam Ave.
- Snoco • 4469 Broadway

🅿 Parking
- 284 Audubon Parking • 284 Audubon Ave.
- Empire State Garage • 2479 Amsterdam Ave.
- Garage Management • 120-200 Cabrini Blvd.
- Manhattan Parking • 900 W. 190th St.
- Nagel Garage • 31 Nagle Ave.
- Nick's Parking • 400 W. 204th St.
- Pilot Garage • 2 Sherman Ave.
- Square Plus Parking • 140 Dyckman
- Tri County Parking • 506 W. 181st St.

Inwood MAP

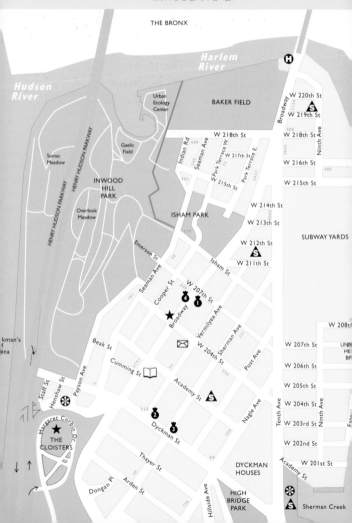

THE BRONX

Harlem River

H

Hudson River

Urban Ecology Center

BAKER FIELD

W 220th St

Broadway

W 219th St

S

W 218th St

W 218th St

Ninth Ave

Indian Rd

Seaman Ave

W Park Terrace W.

W 217th St

Park Terrace E.

W 216th St

Sumac Meadow

Gaelic Field

W 215th St

W 215th St

INWOOD HILL PARK

Overlook Meadow

ISHAM PARK

W 214th St

W 213th St

SUBWAY YARDS

Emerson St

Isham St

W 212th St

S

W 211th St

HENRY HUDSON PARKWAY

Seaman Ave

Cooper St

W 207th St

Vermilyea Ave

Sherman Ave

W 208th

4

1

Beak St

Broadway

W 207th St

UNIN HE BR

Post Ave

Cumming St

W 204th St

W 206th St

Academy St

W 205th St

Staff St

Henshaw St

Prayson Ave

Nagle Ave

W 204th St

Tenth Ave

Ninth Ave

S

2

W 203rd St

3

Dyckman St

W 202nd St

★ THE CLOISTERS

Margaret Corbin Dr.

Thayer St

DYCKMAN HOUSES

Academy St

W 201st St

Arden St

HIGH BRIDGE PARK

Dongan Pl

Hillside Ave

S

Sherman Creek

kman's f na

Inwood is definitely Manhattan's best-kept housing secret—the houses along Payson Avenue and Seaman Avenue are very nice. Inwood Hill Park is a shady, overgrown, semi-wild park with a killer view of The Cloisters and Fort Tryon Park. Inwood also contains Manhattan's oldest building, the Dyckman House (it looks it!)

💰 ATMs
• 1. Apple Bank For Savings • 4950 Broadway
• 2. Banco Popular • 175 Dyckman St.
• 3. Chase Manhattan • 161 Dyckman St.
• 4. Citibank • 4949 Broadway

✺ Community Gardens
• IS 218 Children's Garden •
  Harlem River Dr and Dyckman St.
• The Ring Garden • 1835 Riverside Dr.

🅷 Hospital
• Columbia-Presbyterian Allen Pavilion •
  5141 Broadway

★ Landmarks
• Dyckman House • 204th St. and Broadway
• The Cloisters • Fort Tryon Park

📖 Library
• Inwood • 4790 Broadway at Academy

✉ Post Office
• Inwood Post Office • 90 Vermilyea Ave.

🅢 Schools
• IS 052 Inwood School • 650 Academy St.
• PS 005 Ellen Lurie School • 3703 Tenth Ave.
• PS 018 • Ninth Ave. & 220th St.
• PS 098 Shorackappock School • 512 W. 212th St.

Inwood MAP

THE BRONX

Harlem River

Hudson River

Urban Ecology Center

BAKER FIELD

W 220th St

Broadway

W 219th St

W 218th St

Ninth Ave

W 218th St

Seaman Ave

Indian Rd

W Park Terrace W.

Park Terrace E.

W 217th St

W 216th St

Gaelic Field

W 215th St

W 215th St

Sumac Meadow

HENRY HUDSON PARKWAY

HENRY HUDSON PARKWAY

INWOOD HILL PARK

W 214th St

W 213th St

Overlook Meadow

ISHAM PARK

W 212th St

SUBWAY YARDS

Emerson St

Isham St

W 211th St

Seaman Ave

Cooper St

W 207th St

Broadway

Vermilyea Ave

Sherman Ave

W 208th

W 207th St

UNI
HE
BI

ckman's
of
rina

Payson Ave

Beak St

Cumming St

Post Ave

W 206th St

W 205th St

Academy St

Tenth Ave

Ninth Ave

W 204th St

Nagle Ave

W 203rd St

Staff St

Henshaw St

Dyckman St

W 202nd St

Margaret Corbin Dr.

THE CLOISTERS

Thayer St

Academy St

W 201st St

Dongan Pl

Arden St

Hillside Ave

DYCKMAN HOUSES

HIGH BRIDGE PARK

Sherman Creek

Gym

- Multi Fitness • 104 Sherman Ave.

Hardware Stores

- Burton Supply Co., Inc. • 519 W. 207th St.
- Inwood Paint & Hardware • 5085 Broadway
- J&A Hardware • 132 Vermilyea Ave.
- Nagle Hardware Store • 145 Nagle Ave.
- Sherman Hardware • 151 Sherman Ave.

Laundromats

- Duce Laundromat • 267 Dyckman St.
- Ecomat • 3867 Tenth Ave.
- Inwood Laundromat • 89 Cooper St.
- Jancer Laundromat • 217 Sherman Ave.
- Rita's Fluff and Fold • 271 Sherman Ave.

Liquor Stores

- Dyckman Liquors,Inc. • 121 Dyckman St.
- ECA Liquor,Inc. • 155 Sherman Ave.
- Las Vegas Wines • 154 Nagle Ave.
- PJ Liquor Warehouse • 4898 Broadway
- Q Royal, Inc. • 517 W. 207th St.
- Sherman Liquor Corp • 25 Sherman Ave.

Video Rentals

- Blockbuster Video • 161 Dyckman St.
- Charlene Ebony Inc. • 58 Sherman Ave.
- Gameover SA • 229 Dyckman St.
- Joel's Videos • 5008 Broadway

Inwood MAP

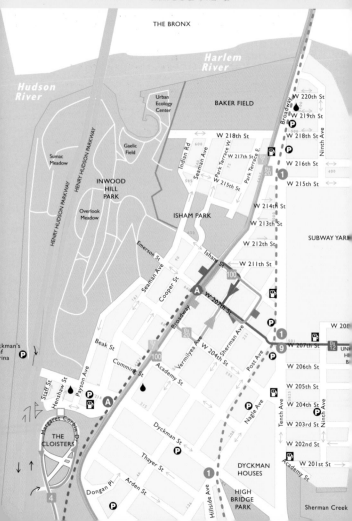

The stupid toll plaza at the tip of the Henry Hudson is only one of many reasons why driving in New York is nothing short of a nightmare. You might as well be getting your car washed at one of Inwood's many fine establishments. Parking is usually not too much of a problem, even close to Inwood Hill Park.

Subways

Ⓐ	............................207th St.
Ⓐ	.................Dyckman St. & Broadway
①	............................215th St.
①⑨	...........................207th St.
①	............................Dyckman St.

Bus Lines

4	...............5th and Madison Aves./Broadway
100	...........Amsterdam Ave./Broadway/125th St.
97	............................Riverdale Ave./Broadway
Bx 12	...........Riverdale/263rd St. via Riverdale Ave.
	Riverdale/246th St.
20	......................via Henry Hudson Parkway

🔴 Car Washes

• Broadway Bridge Car Wash • 5134 Broadway
• Broadway Hand Car Wash • 4778 Broadway
• J&S Management Property Inc. • 284 Dyckman St.

🅿 Gas Stations

• Amoco • Tenth Ave. & Sherman Ave.
• Gaseteria • 204th St. & Tenth Ave.
• Getty • Dyckman St. & Seaman Ave.
• Merit • 401 W. 207th St. & Ninth Ave.
• Shell • 201st St. and Tenth Ave.
• Sunoco • 3936 Tenth Ave.

🅿 Parking

• 10th Mari Al Parking • 3976 Tenth Ave.
• 3966 Parking • 3966 Tenth Ave.
• 5060 Auto Service • 5060 Broadway
• Auto Park • 228 Nagle Ave.
• Marina Garage • 270 Dyckman St.
• Nick's Parking • 400 W. 204th St.
• Pilot Garage • 2 Sherman Ave.
• Square Plus Operating • 141 Dyckman St.
• Universal Parking • 2 Sherman Ave.

PARKS & PLACES

Battery Park City

To some, Battery Park City is Manhattan's worst nightmare, a planned, controlled, and safe community devoid of any amount of character or soul. But as the saying goes, it's come a long way, baby. While Battery Park City may not be replacing the Lower East Side as a hipster paradise any time soon, attractions such as the Winter Garden, the Museum of Jewish Heritage (designed by Kevin Roche), the new Mercantile Exchange, and several acres' worth of beautiful waterfront parks (with sculptures by Louise Bourgeois, Tom Otterness, Martin Puryear, and Jim Dine) are now making many New Yorkers grudgingly admit that while they still wouldn't want to live there, it is an okay place to visit.

Battery Park City is a 92-acre landfill on Manhattan's southwest tip. It has gone through many stages of urban planning over the course of its history, but the latest plan—42% residential, 30% open space, 19% streets, and 9% commercial—does seem to include something for everyone. A total of 14,000 living units are planned, with a potential occupancy of 25,000 residents. Its network of parks—Robert F. Wagner, Jr., South Cove, Rector, North Cove, the Esplanade, and Governor Nelson A. Rockefeller—are swiftly becoming known for beautiful views, excellent outdoor sculptures, and as great places to just chill out. And the presence of Stuyvesant High School, Siah Armajani's Tribeca Bridge, Kevin Roche's Museum of Jewish Heritage, and Caesar Pelli's Winter Garden and World Financial Center make the architecture of Battery Park City nothing to sneeze at.

Where BPC still needs to improve is in the quality and quantity of its services. Basic necessities do exist, but unless you live there, it can be a pretty dull place at night. Yet as more residents pour in, this will doubtlessly change for the better—it's already many steps ahead of a similar planned, controlled, and safe community on Roosevelt Island. At least it's got a decent web site (www.batteryparkcity.org).

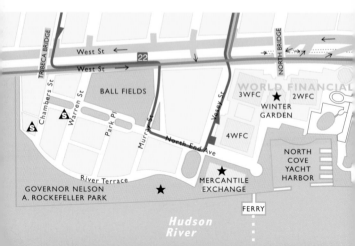

Battery Park City

💰 ATM
- Chase Manhattan • 331-337 South End Ave.
  (plus many in the World Financial Center)

★ Landmarks
- Museum of Jewish Heritage
- Winter Garden
- Mercantile Exchange
- Otterness Sculpture

🏫 Schools
- PS/IS 89 School • 201 Warren St.
- Stuyvesant High School • 345 Chambers St.

🏋 Gyms
- Battery Park Gym • 375 South End Ave.
- Plus One Fitness • 1 WFC

🧺 Laundromats
- Gateway Cleaners • 325 South End Ave.
- Liberty Cleaners • 225 South End Ave.

🍾 Liquor Store
- Bulls & Bears Winery • 309 South End Ave.

Bus Lines
9	....	Avenue B/East Broadway
10	....	7th & 8th Aves/Douglass Blvd.
22	....	Madison/Chambers Sts.

◉ Car Rental
- Avis Rent-A-Car • 345 South End Ave.

🅿 Parking
- Garage Management • 333 Rector Pl.
- Garage Management • 350 Albany St.
- Gateway Parking • 339 South End Ave.
- Jade Car Park • 2 South End Ave.

Other Transportation
- Ferry to Jersey City

PARKS & PLACES

Central Park

Central Park Conservancy: 310-6600
Shakespeare in the Park: 539-8750

Central Park, designed by Frederick Law Olmsted (with help from Calvert Vaux) in the 1850s, is an 843-acre haven to many New Yorkers. On a summer Saturday, one can walk through the park and see jugglers, magicians, disco roller-skater-bladers, Hungarian folk dancing, skateboarders, joggers, operas, rock concerts, ball players, Troilus and Cressida, boaters, art, turtles, frogs, birds, and…oh, yes, billions of people. However, the park is big enough so that there are many, many quiet spots (including official "quiet zones" such as the Shakespeare Gardens (17)) for reading, picnicking, and napping.

Practicalities
Central Park is easily accessible by subway, since the A, C, B, D, N, R, 1, 2, 3, 9 trains all ring the park (odd, though, that there are no stations within the park). Parking along Central Park West is usually pretty good. And if you go in the mornings, for instance, you'll have an even easier time of it since most New Yorkers are "late to bed, late to rise" types. Unless you're there for a big concert, a softball game, or for Shakespeare in the Park, walking around Central Park (especially alone!) at night is not recommended.

Attractions
Like the city itself, Central Park is an eclectic mix of many different types of attractions. Just when you think that Central Park is nothing more than an overcrowded noisy place crawling with roller bladers banging into each other, you'll stumble upon a quiet glade that houses a small sculpture and three people reading books.

Nature
Ironically, perhaps the attributes of Central Park least thought about by New Yorkers are its flora and fauna. There are an amazing number of both plant and animal species that inhabit the park (separate from the creatures housed in its two zoos (4)&(8)). A good source of information on all the flora and fauna is schoolteacher Leslie Day's web site, at http://www.nysite.com/nature/index.htm.

Architecture & Sculpture
Architecturally, Central Park is known for several structures. Calvert Vaux designed the beautiful Bethesda Fountain and Terrace (11) that has become the "center" of the park for many people. The view of Turtle Pond from Belvedere Castle (16) (home of the Central Park Learning Center) is also not to be missed. The Arsenal (5) is a wonderful ivy-clad building that houses several Parks Department offices. There are tons of sculptures in

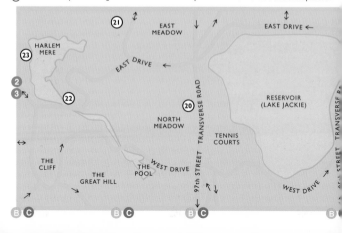

Central Park

the park, although two of the most notable are perhaps Alice in Wonderland (15) and the Obelisk (19). Oh...The Metropolitan Museum of Art also happens to be in the park.

Open Spaces

Perhaps the attractions most loved by New Yorkers are Central Park's "spaces." Space being at a premium in the average New Yorker's apartment probably has a lot to do with this, but nonetheless, places such as Strawberry Fields (10), The Great Lawn, The Ramble, and Sheep Meadow are prime hang-outs for many New Yorkers.

Performance

Central Park is a microcosm of the great cultural attractions New York has to offer. The Delacorte Theater (18) is the home of Shakespeare in the Park, a New York tradition begun by famous director Joseph Papp. Summerstage (9) is now an extremely popular summer concert venue for all types of music, including the occasional killer rock concert. Opera companies and classical philharmonics also show up in the park frequently, as does the odd mega-star (Garth Brooks, Diana Ross, etc.).

Sports

There are so many types of sport occurring in Central Park at any one time that it's pretty dizzying to contemplate. Roller blading is very popular (not just at the Roller Skating Rink (7)), as is jogging, especially around the Reservoir. The Great Lawn, since its reconstruction, has beautiful softball fields. There are also softball fields at Heckscher Playground. There are 30 tennis courts in Central Park (usually with a long waiting list). There is also volleyball, basketball, skateboarding, bicycling, and an infinite number of pick-up soccer, frisbee, football and kill-the-carrier games being played. Finally, Central Park is where the NYC Marathon ends each year, in case you're still not tired.

Landmarks of Central Park

1. Wollman Rink	10. Strawberry Fields	19. The Obelisk
2. Carousel	11. Bethesda Fountain	20. North Meadow Rec. Center
3. The Dairy	12. Bow Bridge	21. Conservatory Garden
4. The Zoo	13. Loeb Boathouse	22. Lasker Rink
5. The Arsenal	14. Model Boat Racing	23. Dana Discovery Center
6. Tavern on the Green	15. Alice in Wonderland	24. Metropolitan Museum of Art
7. Roller Skating Rink	16. Belvedere Castle	
8. Children's Zoo	17. Shakespeare Gardens	**Police Precinct**
9. Summerstage	18. Delacorte Theater	• Central Pk • 86th St. & Transverse Rd.

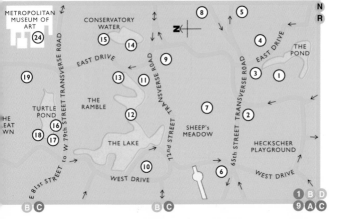

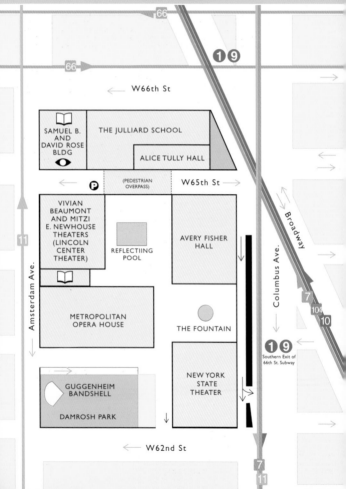

Lincoln Center

Lincoln Center is easily one of Manhattan's most vibrant and romantic spots. It's almost obscene how much culture is packed into this four-square-block area—Lincoln Center has one of the world's most famous opera houses, three beautiful theaters, an acoustically-designed music hall, an outdoor bandshell, a movie theater, a performing arts library, a ballet school, and an association with one of the best music schools in the country. Not bad for what was once a terrible, poverty-ridden section of New York. Even Robert Moses got some things right.

Lincoln Center, besides all its performance spaces, also boasts some of the city's signature art and architectural gems. Henry Moore's Reclining Figure is the centerpiece of the reflecting pool, and Mark Chagall's murals grace the foyer of the Metropolitan Opera House. Philip Johnson's plaza fountain holds the entire center together, creating an intimate space where New Yorkers can go to forget about their appallingly high rents and their unpaid parking tickets.

Who Lives Where

Lincoln Center is home to so many different companies, groups, and troupes that we figured we'd provide a chart on who is where. Perhaps the most confusing thing about Lincoln Center is that the "Lincoln Center Theater" is actually two theaters—the Vivian Beaumont and the Mitzi E. Newhouse Theaters. The newest building at Lincoln Center, the Samuel B. and David Rose Building, contains the Stanley Kaplan penthouse performance space, the School of American Ballet, the administrative offices of the Film Society and the Chamber Music Society, the Walter Reade Theater, dorms for the Julliard School, the Riverside Branch of the New York Public Library, and a fire house.

Company/Event/Space	Location
New York City Ballet	New York State Theater
New York City Opera	New York State Theater
Metropolitan Opera Company	Metropolitan Opera House
American Ballet Theater	Metropolitan Opera House
New York Philharmonic	Avery Fisher Hall
Mostly Mozart Festival	Avery Fisher Hall
Jazz at Lincoln Center	Avery Fisher Hall
Vivian Beaumont Theater	Lincoln Center Theater
Mitzi E. Newhouse Theater	Lincoln Center Theater
Chamber Music Society	Alice Tully Hall
Julliard Orchestra	Alice Tully Hall
Julliard Symphony	Alice Tully Hall
Film Society of Lincoln Center	Samuel B. and David Rose Building
School of American Ballet	Samuel B. and David Rose Building

Practical Information

Lincoln Center is right off Broadway and only a few blocks north of Columbus Circle, so getting there is pretty easy. The closest subway is the 66th St. 1 and 9 train, which has an exit right on the edge of the center. It's also only a five-minute walk from the plethora of trains that roll into Columbus Circle (1, 9, A, C, B, and D lines). There is a parking lot underneath Lincoln Center.

Phone Numbers

General Information:	875-5999
Alice Tully Hall:	875-5050
Avery Fisher Hall:	875-5030
The Chamber Music Society:	875-5888
Guided Tours:	875-5350
Jazz at Lincoln Center:	875-5299
The Julliard School:	769-7406
Lincoln Center Theater:	362-7600
The Metropolitan Opera House:	362-6000
New York State Theater:	870-5570
Walter Reade Theater:	875-5601
website:	www.lincolncenter.org

Ticket Purchase Phone Numbers

Center Charge,	
Alice Tully and Avery Fisher Halls:	721-6500
MovieFone, Walter Reade Theater:	777-FILM
TeleCharge, Lincoln Center Theater:	239-6200
Ticketmaster, New York State Theater:	307-4100

PARKS & PLACES

Roosevelt Island

Roosevelt Island could be one of the coolest places in New York—imagine, a 147-acre island in the middle of the East River, connected to Manhattan by tramway and subway, and connected to Queens by roadway and subway. Unfortunately, though, it's not one of the coolest places in New York. "Bland residential community" is Sidewalk.com's assessment, and we're forced to agree. All services are conveniently located on "Main St." (wherever did they come up with that name?!?), which makes the rest of the island feel deserted. Two hospitals, several abandoned buildings, and the lack of comforting city sights such as taxis, hot dog vendors, and crazy people make Roosevelt Island feel, well…creepy.

However, Roosevelt Island's creepiness is part of its charm. The ivy-covered remains of the Smallpox Hospital, the looming Octagon Tower (formerly the site of a 19th-century mental hospital), and the solitary house and church on West Rd. make a jaunt to Roosevelt Island interesting, to say the least. A trip to the island is best done on the Tramway (costing $1.50 and forever immortalized in the movie "Nighthawks"). Other attractions include the Chapel of the Good Shepherd, the Blackwell House, the western and eastern promenades, and the island's several parks. Perhaps the residential renovation of an abandoned factory near the subway station will add some grit and charm to this bland and creepy island. We certainly hope so.

Practical Information

Roosevelt Island can be reached via the B and Q subway lines, and by the extremely quick but not totally reliable tramway at 60th St. and Second Ave. in Manhattan. To get there by car, take the Queensboro Bridge and follow signs for the "21st St.-North" exit. Go north on 21st St. and make a left on 36th Ave. Go west on 36th Ave. and cross over the red Roosevelt Island Bridge. The only legal parking is at Motorgate Plaza at the end of the bridge, but it's more fun to drive around and harass the Roosevelt Island police by parking illegally and stopping in front of all the really creepy stuff. For more information, the Roosevelt Island Operating Corporation has a very informative website at www.rioc.com. This site discusses several interesting proposals for further development of the island, as well as providing practical information and demographics on the Roosevelt Island community.

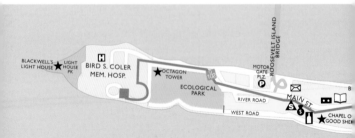

Roosevelt Island

 ATM
• Chase • 691 Main St.

H Hospitals
• Bird S. Coler Memorial Hospital
• Goldwater Memorial Hospital

★ Landmarks
• Blackwell House
• Blackwell's Lighthouse
• Chapel of the Good Shepherd
• Octagon Tower
• Smallpox Hospital
• Tramway

Library
• Roosevelt Island Library • 524 Main St.

✉ Post Office
• Roosevelt Island Post Office • 694 Main St.

School
• PS-IS 217 • 645 Main St.

●—● Gym
• Sportspark • Main St.

Liquor Store
• The Grog Shop • 544 Main St.

Video Rentals
• KIO Enterprise • 544 Main St.

Subway
B Q .... Roosevelt Island

Bus Line
.... Main St./East and West Rds.

P Parking
• Motorgate Plaza

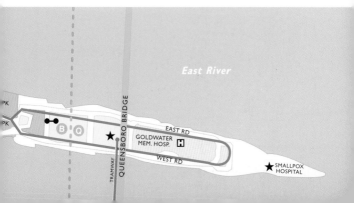

PARKS & PLACES

World Trade Center

General Information

Height of the Twin Towers: 1350 feet, tallest buildings in Manhattan

Observation Deck, 107th Floor, 2 WTC: 9:30 a.m.-9:30 p.m. (Sept.-May)
9:30 a.m.-11:30 p.m. (June-August)

Mall hours (individual stores may vary): 8:00 a.m.-7 p.m. Monday-Friday
10:00 a.m.-5 p.m. Saturday-Sunday

Website: www.panynj.gov/wtc/wtcfram.HTM

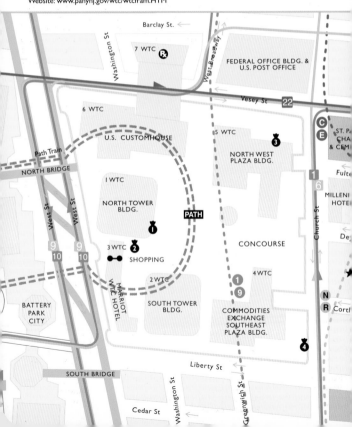

World Trade Center

The World Trade Center is one of Manhattan's best-known landmarks, but, as a famous architectural historian once said, would have been a complete monstrosity if the architects (Minoru Yamasaki and Emery Roth & Sons) had only built one tower instead of two. Apparently, the overkill of the twin towers is what makes it bearable. That's New York logic for you; if we're going to be ridiculous, then let's be really ridiculous.

The WTC has 10 million square feet of office space (seven times more than the Empire State Building!), a shopping mall with 70 stores, an observation deck, a newly-reconstructed outdoor plaza, a summer concert series, access to the 1, 9, C, E, N, R and PATH trains, and tourists galore. It also has a daily working population of 40,000 people (we're really not making these numbers up, we promise). The dirt from the excavation was used to create Battery Park City. Our favorite place in the complex is, of course, Krispy Kreme.

💰 ATMs

1. • Chase • 2 WTC
2. • Citibank • 3 WTC
3. • Marine Midland (HBSC) • 5 WTC
4. • Republic Bank • 5 WTC Concourse

★ Landmark

• Century 21 • Church and Cortlandt Sts.

℞ 24-Hour Pharmacy

• Duane Reade • 7 WTC

●━● Gym

• Executive Fitness Center • 3 WTC

Subways

1 **9**	..........................Vesey St. / WTC
C **E**	......................................WTC
N **R**	..........................Cortland St. / WTC

Bus Lines

22	....Vesey St.
1 **6**	..................................Church St.
9 **10**	........................West St. / Vesey St.

WTC Shops:

APPAREL
August Max
Baker's Shoes
Banana Republic
Casual Corner
The Children's Place
Coach Express
Gap
J. Crew
The Limited
Nine West
Strawberry
Structure
Tie Rack

BANKS/FINANCE
Charles Schwab
Chase
Citibank
HSBC
Republic Bank

ITEMS & SERVICES
Bath & Body Works
Bell Atlantic Mobile
The Body Shop
Borders Books
Claire's
Cosmetics Plus
Crabtree & Evelyn
Duane Reade
Flowers of the World

Golden Nugget
Hallmark
Kelly Film
Lechter's
Minas Shoe Repair
Natisse Hair Salon
Daniel Pehr
Locksmith
Perfumeria Milano
Radio Shack
Sam Goody
Sunglass Hut
Thirteen/WNET
Warner Bros. Studio
    Store
Watch World

FOOD
America's Coffee
Au Bon Pain
Ben & Jerry's
Cornucopia
Devon & Blakely
Ecce Panis
Salad Cafe
Fine & Schapiro
Gemelli
Godiva Chocolatier
Hale & Hearty Soups
Krispy Kreme
Pastabreak
Pretzel Time
Sbarro

Directory Assistance-ESSENTIALS

Address Locator

Streets	Riverside	West End	Broadway	Amsterdam	Columbus	C.P.W.	Central Park
110-116	370-440		2800-2950	995-1120			
102-110	290-370	850-920	2675-2800	856-995	850-1021	419-500	
96-102	240-290	737-850	2554-2675	733-856	740-850	360-419	
90-96	180-240	620-737	2440-2554	620-733	621-740	300-360	
84-90	120-180	500-619	2321-2439	500-619	501-620	241-295	
78-84	60-120	380-499	2201-2320	380-499	381-500	239-241	
72-78	1-60	262-379	2081-2200	261-379	261-380	121-239	
66-72		122-261	1961-2079	140-260	141-260	65-115	
58-66		2-121	1791-1960	1-139	2-140	0-65	

Streets	12th Ave.	11th Ave.	Broadway	10th Ave.	9th Ave.	8th Ave.	7th Ave.	6th Ave.
52-58	710-850	741-854	1674-1791	772-889	782-907	870-992	798-921	1301-1419
46-52	600-710	625-740	1551-1673	654-770	662-781	735-869	701-797	1180-1297
40-46	480-600	503-624	1440-1550	538-653	432-662	620-734	560-701	1061-1178
34-40	360-480	405-502	Macy's-1439	430-537	431-432	480-619	442-559	1060-1061
28-34	240-360	282-404	1178-1282	314-429	314-431	362-479	322-442	815-1060
22-28	0-240	162-281	940-1177	210-313	198-313	236-361	210-321	696-814
14-22		26-161	842-940	58-209	91-197	80-235	64-209	5520-695
8-14			748-842	0-58	0-44	0-80	2-64	420-520
Houston-8			610-748					244-402

The address locator below is formatted north-south, from 116th Street to Houston Street. For east-west adreesses, simply remember that Fifth Ave. is the dividing line–2 E. 54th would be right off of Fifth, while 200 E. 54th would be around Third Ave.

5th Ave.	Madison	Park	Lexington	3rd Ave.	2nd Ave.	1st Ave.	York	Streets
1280-1400	1630-1770	1489-1617	1766-1857	1981-2103	2109-2241	2175-2238		110-116
1209-1280	1500-1630	1350-1489	1612-1766	1820-1981	1880-2109	1975-2175		102-110
1148-1209	1379-1500	1236-1350	1486-1612	1709-1820	1854-1880	1855-1975		96-102
1090-1148	1254-1379	1120-1236	1361-1486	1601-1709	1736-1854	1740-1855	1700-end	90-96
1030-1089	1130-1250	1000-1114	1248-1355	1490-1602	1624-1739	1618-1735	1560-1700	84-90
970-1028	1012-1128	878-993	1120-1248	1374-1489	1498-1623	1495-1617	1477-1560	78-84
910-969	896-1006	760-877	1004-1116	1250-1373	1389-1497	1344-1494	1353-1477	72-78
850-907	772-872	640-755	900-993	1130-1249	1260-1363	1222-1343	1212-1353	66-72
755-849	621-771	476-639	722-886	972-1129	1101-1260	1063-1222	1100-1212	58-66

5th Ave.	Madison	Park	Lexington	3rd Ave.	2nd Ave.	1st Ave.	Avenue A	Streets
656-754	500-611	360-475	596-721	856-968	984-1101	945-1063		52-58
562-655	377-488	240-350	476-593	741-855	862-983	827-944		46-52
460-561	284-375	99-240	354-475	622-735	746-860	701-827		40-46
352-459	188-283	5-99	240-353	508-621	622-747	599-701		34-40
250-351	79-184	4-404	120-239	394-507	500-621	478-598		28-34
172-249	1-78	286-403	9-119	282-393	382-499	390-478		22-28
69-170	University	0-285	1-8	126-281	230-381	240-389		14-22
9-69	0-120			59-126	138-230	134-240	129-210	8-14
0-9				1-59	0-138	0-134	0-129	Houston-8

Directory Assistance-ESSENTIALS

Bike & Skate Information

General Information

Department of City Planning website: www.ci.nyc.ny.us/html/dcp/html/bikenet.html
Transportation Alternatives website: www.transalt.org
Phone: 212-629-8080

While not for the faint of heart, biking and skating around Manhattan can be one of the most efficient and exhilarating forms of transportation (insight into the abundance of bike messengers careening around town). The terrain of Manhattan is pretty flat (for the most part), and the fitness and environmental advantages of using people power are immense. However, there are also some downsides, including but not limited to: psychotic cab drivers, buses, traffic, pedestrians, pavement with potholes, glass, and debris, and poor air quality. In 1994 the Bicycle Network Development Program was created to increase bicycle usage in the NYC area. Since then, many bike lanes have been created on streets and in parks. These tend to be the safest places to ride (to get a listing, go to the web-sites listed above). Central Park is a great place to ride, as are the newly developed paths from Battery Park to Chelsea Piers that run along the Hudson River. You'll also find East River Park to be nice for recreational riding and skating – just not after dark!

An advantage of skating is that you can easily put your skates in a bag and carry them with you anywhere – subways, indoors, on buses – which also eliminates the possibility of theft. Bikes are less convenient, and are always at risk of being stolen (always lock them to immovable objects with the best lock you can afford), but can be a much faster, less demanding form of transport.

Words of Wisdom

- Always wear a helmet and protective gear (for skating)
- Beware of car doors
- Use hand signals
- Be careful at intersections
- Never ride against traffic
- Use lights at night

Bikes and Mass Transit

Surprisingly, you can take your bike on trains and some buses - just make sure it's not during rush hour and you are courteous to other passengers. The subway requires you to carry your bike down staircases, use the service gate instead of the turnstile, and board at the very front or back end of the train. The commuter railroads require you to purchase a bike permit.

Amtrak	New Jersey Transit	Staten Island Ferry
800-872-7245	201-762-5100	718-815-BOAT
train with baggage car required	Free Permit required	Enter at lower level
LIRR	Path	
718-558-8228	800-234-PATH	
$5 Permit required	No Permit required	
Metro-North	NY Waterway	
212-532-4900	800-53-FERRY	
$5 Permit required	$1 extra fee	

Call individual bus companies for restrictions and access information (page 209 of NFT).

Dog Runs

NYC is full of dog runs—both formal and informal—scattered throughout the city's parks and neighborhood community spaces. The city, while not actually administrating the runs, does provide space to community groups who then manage them. The runs are eager for help (volunteer time or financial contributions) and most post volunteer information on park bulletin boards. The formal runs are probably your safest bet, as most are enclosed and are maintained for cleanliness and order. When your dog is in a run, it is important to remove any choke or pronged collars, as they may get tangled with another dog's collar or a fence (both of which can severely injure your dog). Do leave your dog's flat collar and identification tag on. Most runs prohibit dogs in heat, aggressive dogs, and dogs without inoculations. Many do not allow toys, balls or Frisbees.

Resources

Currently, there are a few websites that provide some decent information about dog runs. The best is perhaps www.doglaw.com, written by a lawyer, Joel R. Zand. Another is the parks department website, www.nycparks.org, and a third is www.allny.com/pets.html. Additionally, there is an infrequently-published newsletter called "D.G.N.Y." that has a ton of information about owning pets in New York.

Grid #	Name • Address • Comments
Battery Park City	Battery Park City • West St. at West Thames St. • This long, narrow, concrete-surfaced enclosed run is located along the West Side Highway and offers a pleasant view of the river and some shade. It has been temporarily relocated during construction.
2	P.S. 234 300 • Greenwich St. at Chambers St.
3	Fish Bridge Park • Pearl and Dover Streets • Concrete surfaced run.
6	Washington Square Park • MacDougal St. at W. 4th St. • Located in the southwest corner of the park, this is a gravel-surfaced run with many spectators. This popular run gets very crowded but is well-maintained nonetheless.
6	LaGuardia Place • Mercer St. at Houston St. • This is a private run with a membership (and a waiting list.) The benefits to this run include running water and a plastic wading pool for your dog to splash in.
6	Union Square • Broadway at 16th St.
7	Tompkins Square Park • Ave. B at 10th St. • New York City's first dog run is quite large and has a wood chip surface. Toys, balls, frisbees, and dogs in heat are all prohibited. This community-centered run offers lots of shade, benches, and running water.
8	Thomas Smith Triangle • Eleventh Ave. at 23rd St. • Concrete surfaced run.
10	Madison Square Park • Madison Ave. at 25th St. • Medium-sized run with gravel surface and plenty of trees.
11	DeWitt Clinton Park • Eleventh Ave. at 52nd & 54th Sts. • Two small concrete-surfaced runs.
13	E. 60th Street Pavilion • 60th St. at the East River • Concrete surfaced run.
13	Peter Detmold Park • Beekman Pl. at 51st St. • Large well-maintained run with cement and dirt surfaces and many trees.
13	Robert Moses Park • First Ave. and 42nd St. • Temporarily closed due to reconstruction.
Riverside Park	Riverside Park • Riverside Dr. at 77th St.
15/17	Carl Shulz Park • East End Ave. at 85/86th Sts. • Medium-sized enclosed run with pebbled surface with separate space for small dogs. This run has benches, shady trees, and running water is available in the bathrooms.
Riverside Park	Riverside Park • Riverside Dr. at 87th St. • Medium-sized run with gravel surface.
Riverside Park	Riverside Park • Riverside Dr. at 105/106th Sts. • Medium-sized run with gravel surface.
21	Harlem • Riverside Dr. at 140th St.
23	J. Hood Wright Park • Haven Ave. at W. 173rd St. • An enclosed dirt-surfaced run.

Directory Assistance-ESSENTIALS

FedEx Locations

Name	Address	Zip Code	Pick-Up Time (M-F)	Grid #
Complete Mail Centers	28 Vesey St.	10007	6:30 p.m.	1
FedEx Drop Box	1 Broadway	10004	8:30 p.m.	1
FedEx Drop Box	1 State St. Plaza	10004	8:30 p.m.	1
FedEx Drop Box	17 Battery Pl.	10004	8:30 p.m.	1
FedEx Drop Box	26 Broadway	10004	8:30 p.m.	1
FedEx Drop Box	7 Hanover Sq.	10004	8:00 p.m.	1
FedEx Drop Box	90 Broad St.	10004	8:30 p.m.	1
FedEx Drop Box	14 Wall St.	10005	8:30 p.m.	1
FedEx Drop Box	40 Exchange Pl.	10005	8:30 p.m.	1
FedEx Drop Box	45 Wall St.	10005	7:00 p.m.	1
FedEx Drop Box	67 Wall St.	10005	8:30 p.m.	1
FedEx Drop Box	88 Pine St.	10005	8:30 p.m.	1
FedEx Drop Box	19 Rector St.	10006	8:30 p.m.	1
FedEx Drop Box	40 Rector St.	10006	8:30 p.m.	1
FedEx Drop Box	15 Gold St.	10038	8:00 p.m.	1
FedEx Drop Box	150 Broadway	10038	8:30 p.m.	1
FedEx Drop Box	33 Liberty St.	10045	7:00 p.m.	1
FedEx World Service Center	40 Broad St.	10004	9:15 p.m.	1
FedEx World Service Center	110 Wall St.	10005	9:00 p.m.	1
FedEx World Service Center	55 Broadway	10006	9:00 p.m.	1
FedEx World Service Center	100 William St.	10038	9:00 p.m.	1
FedEx World Service Center	175 Water St.	10038	9:00 p.m.	1
FedEx World Service Center	55 Water St.	10041	9:00 p.m.	1
FedEx World Service Center	2 WTC	10048	9:00 p.m.	1
Kinko's	100 Wall St.	10005	8:00 p.m.	1
Packaging Store	66 West St.	10006	4:30 p.m.	1
Parcel Plus	1 New York Plaza	10004	6:00 p.m.	1
Postnet	29 John St.	10038	6:00 p.m.	1
Staples	217 Broadway	10007	6:00 p.m.	1
Complete Mail Centers	28 Vesey St.	10007	6:30 p.m.	2
FedEx Drop Box	11 Park Pl.	10007	8:30 p.m.	2
FedEx Drop Box	158 Church St.	10007	6:00 p.m.	2
FedEx Drop Box	86 Warren St.	10007	8:30 p.m.	2
FedEx Drop Box	145 Hudson St.	10013	6:00 p.m.	2
FedEx Drop Box	315 Hudson St.	10013	8:30 p.m.	2
FedEx Drop Box	361 Broadway	10013	6:30 p.m.	2
FedEx Drop Box	401 Broadway	10013	8:30 p.m.	2
FedEx Drop Box	75 Varick St.	10013	7:00 p.m.	2
FedEx Drop Box	Grand St. & B'way	10013	8:00 p.m.	2
FedEx Drop Box	150 Broadway	10038	8:30 p.m.	2
FedEx World Service Center	4 Barclay St.	10007	9:00 p.m.	2
Kinko's	105 Duane St.	10007	8:00 p.m.	2
Mail Boxes Etc.	295 Greenwich St.	10007	5:30 p.m.	2
Staples	217 Broadway	10007	6:00 p.m.	2
Staples	488 Broadway	10012	6:00 p.m.	2
Staples	350 Broadway	10013	6:00 p.m.	2
Complete Mail Centers	28 Vesey St.	10007	6:30 p.m.	3
FedEx Drop Box	11 Park Pl.	10007	8:30 p.m.	3
FedEx Drop Box	158 Church St.	10007	6:00 p.m.	3
FedEx Drop Box	361 Broadway	10013	6:30 p.m.	3
FedEx Drop Box	401 Broadway	10013	8:30 p.m.	3
FedEx Drop Box	Grand St. & B'way	10013	8:00 p.m.	3
FedEx Drop Box	150 Broadway	10038	8:30 p.m.	3
FedEx World Service Center	4 Barclay St.	10007	9:00 p.m.	3
FedEx World Service Center	175 Water St.	10038	9:00 p.m.	3
Kinko's	105 Duane St.	10007	8:00 p.m.	3
Staples	217 Broadway	10007	6:00 p.m.	3
Staples	488 Broadway	10012	6:00 p.m.	3
Staples	350 Broadway	10013	6:00 p.m.	3
FedEx Drop Box	80 8th Ave.	10011	8:00 p.m.	5
FedEx Drop Box	161 6th Ave.	10013	8:30 p.m.	5
FedEx Drop Box	315 Hudson St.	10013	8:30 p.m.	5
FedEx Drop Box	201 Varick St.	10014	8:00 p.m.	5
FedEx Drop Box	350 Hudson St.	10014	8:30 p.m.	5
FedEx World Service Center	Pier 40	10001	9:30 p.m.	5
FedEx World Service Center	148 Leroy St.	10014	9:30 p.m.	5
FedEx World Service Center	229 W. 4th St.	10014	9:00 p.m.	5
Mail Boxes Etc.	511 6th Ave.	10011	6:00 p.m.	5
The Packaging Depot	48 8th Ave.	10014	7:00 p.m.	5

The latest FedEx dropoff is at 9:30 p.m. M-F at 148 Leroy St. (Grid 5); Pier 40 (Grid 5); 537 W. 33rd St. (Grid 8); and 560 W. 42 nd St. (Grid 11). This list has duplicate entries for locations that are in more than 1 grid. Thank You.

Name	Address	Zip Code	Pick-Up Time (M-F)	Grid #
Your Neighborhood Office	332 Bleecker St.	10014	7:00 p.m.	5
FedEx Drop Box	200 Park Ave. S.	10003	8:15 p.m.	6
FedEx Drop Box	252 Greene St.	10003	7:00 p.m.	6
FedEx Drop Box	45 E. 7th St.	10003	7:00 p.m.	6
FedEx Drop Box	799 Broadway	10003	8:00 p.m.	6
FedEx Drop Box	9 E. 4th St.	10003	8:00 p.m.	6
FedEx Drop Box	74 5th Ave.	10011	7:00 p.m.	6
FedEx Drop Box	225 Lafayette St.	10012	8:00 p.m.	6
FedEx Drop Box	270 Lafayette St.	10012	8:00 p.m.	6
FedEx Drop Box	375 Lafayette St.	10012	8:00 p.m.	6
FedEx Drop Box	580 Broadway	10012	8:00 p.m.	6
FedEx Drop Box	65 Bleecker St.	10012	6:30 p.m.	6
FedEx Drop Box	161 6th Ave.	10013	8:30 p.m.	6
FedEx World Service Center	4 Union Sq. E.	10003	9:00 p.m.	6
FedEx World Service Center	555 Broadway	10012	9:00 p.m.	6
Kinko's	21 Astor Place	10003	8:00 p.m.	6
Kinko's	24 E. 12th St.	10003	8:00 p.m.	6
Little Village Postal	151 1st Ave.	10003	6:00 p.m.	6
Mail Boxes Etc.	168 2nd Ave.	10003	5:00 p.m.	6
Mail Boxes Etc.	511 6th Ave.	10011	6:00 p.m.	6
Readers Stationery	35 E. 10th St.	10003	5:30 p.m.	6
Staples	59 Union Sq. W.	10003	7:00 p.m.	6
Staples	488 Broadway	10012	6:00 p.m.	6
United Shipping & Packaging	200 E. 10th St.	10003	6:30 p.m.	6
A to Z Business Services	84 Clinton St.	10002	5:00 p.m.	7
Kinko's	250 E. Houston St.	10002	8:30 p.m.	7
Little Village Postal	151 1st Ave.	10003	6:00 p.m.	7
FedEx Drop Box	322 8th Ave.	10001	8:00 p.m.	8
FedEx Drop Box	450 W. 33rd St.	10001	7:00 p.m.	8
FedEx Drop Box	547 W. 27th St.	10001	7:00 p.m.	8
FedEx Drop Box	143 8th Ave.	10011	6:00 p.m.	8
FedEx Drop Box	80 8th Ave.	10011	8:00 p.m.	8
FedEx Drop Box	505 8th Ave.	10018	8:00 p.m.	8
FedEx Drop Box	519 8th Ave.	10018	8:00 p.m.	8
FedEx Drop Box	520 8th Ave.	10018	7:00 p.m.	8
FedEx World Service Center	440 9th Ave.	10001	9:00 p.m.	8
FedEx World Service Center	537 W. 33rd St.	10001	9:00 p.m.	8
FedEx World Service Center	538 W. 34th St.	10001	9:30 p.m.	8
Mail Boxes Etc.	655 W. 34th St.	10001	5:00 p.m.	8
Pricom	170 9th Ave.	10011	5:00 p.m.	8
FedEx Drop Box	100 W. 33rd St.	10001	7:00 p.m.	9
FedEx Drop Box	121 W. 27th St.	10001	8:00 p.m.	9
FedEx Drop Box	1225 Broadway	10001	8:00 p.m.	9
FedEx Drop Box	1250 Broadway	10001	7:00 p.m.	9
FedEx Drop Box	21 Penn Plaza	10001	8:00 p.m.	9
FedEx Drop Box	220 5th Ave.	10001	5:30 p.m.	9
FedEx Drop Box	229 W. 28th St.	10001	8:00 p.m.	9
FedEx Drop Box	230 5th Ave.	10001	8:00 p.m.	9
FedEx Drop Box	322 8th Ave.	10001	8:00 p.m.	9
FedEx Drop Box	330 5th Ave.	10001	8:00 p.m.	9
FedEx Drop Box	366 5th Ave.	10001	7:00 p.m.	9
FedEx Drop Box	450 7th Ave.	10001	8:00 p.m.	9
FedEx Drop Box	5 Penn Plz.	10001	9:00 p.m.	9
FedEx Drop Box	50 W. 34th St.	10001	7:00 p.m.	9
FedEx Drop Box	875 6th Ave.	10001	8:00 p.m.	9
FedEx Drop Box	200 Park Ave. S.	10003	8:15 p.m.	9
FedEx Drop Box	1115 Broadway	10010	5:30 p.m.	9
FedEx Drop Box	1133 Broadway	10010	8:00 p.m.	9
FedEx Drop Box	122 E 25th St.	10010	6:30 p.m.	9
FedEx Drop Box	19 W. 21st St.	10010	5:00 p.m.	9
FedEx Drop Box	257 Park Ave. S.	10010	8:00 p.m.	9
FedEx Drop Box	346 Park Ave. S.	10010	8:00 p.m.	9
FedEx Drop Box	41 Madison Ave.	10010	8:00 p.m.	9
FedEx Drop Box	60 Madison Ave.	10010	7:00 p.m.	9
FedEx Drop Box	143 8th Ave.	10011	6:00 p.m.	9
FedEx Drop Box	220 W. 19th St.	10011	8:00 p.m.	9
FedEx Drop Box	233 W. 18th St.	10011	5:00 p.m.	9
FedEx Drop Box	45 W.18th Ave.	10011	7:30 p.m.	9
FedEx Drop Box	74 5th Ave.	10011	7:00 p.m.	9

Directory Assistance-ESSENTIALS

FedEx Locations

Name	Address	Zip Code	Pick-Up Time (M-F)	Grid #
FedEx Drop Box	80 8th Ave.	10011	8:00 p.m.	9
FedEx Drop Box	28 E. 28th St.	10016	7:00 p.m.	9
FedEx Drop Box	3 Park Ave.	10016	7:00 p.m.	9
FedEx Drop Box	444 Park Ave. S.	10016	7:00 p.m.	9
FedEx Drop Box	475 Park Ave. S.	10016	8:00 p.m.	9
FedEx Drop Box	390 5th Ave.	10018	8:00 p.m.	9
FedEx Drop Box	463 7th Ave.	10018	9:00 p.m.	9
FedEx Drop Box	469 7th Ave.	10018	8:00 p.m.	9
FedEx Drop Box	485 7th Ave.	10018	8:00 p.m.	9
FedEx Drop Box	5 W. 37th St.	10018	7:00 p.m.	9
FedEx Drop Box	505 8th Ave.	10018	8:00 p.m.	9
FedEx Drop Box	519 8th Ave.	10018	8:00 p.m.	9
FedEx Drop Box	520 8th Ave.	10018	7:00 p.m.	9
FedEx Drop Box	225 W. 34th St.	10022	8:00 p.m.	9
FedEx World Service Center	125 W. 33rd St.	10001	9:00 p.m.	9
FedEx World Service Center	1328 Broadway	10001	9:00 p.m.	9
FedEx World Service Center	157 W. 35th St.	10001	9:00 p.m.	9
FedEx World Service Center	326 7th Ave.	10001	9:00 p.m.	9
FedEx World Service Center	350 5th Ave.	10001	9:00 p.m.	9
FedEx World Service Center	390 7th Ave.	10001	9:00 p.m.	9
FedEx World Service Center	401 7th Ave.	10001	9:00 p.m.	9
FedEx World Service Center	125 5th Ave.	10003	9:00 p.m.	9
FedEx World Service Center	20 E. 20th St.	10003	9:00 p.m.	9
FedEx World Service Center	4 Union Sq. E.	10003	9:00 p.m.	9
FedEx World Service Center	1 Madison Ave.	10010	8:00 p.m.	9
FedEx World Service Center	8 E. 23rd St.	10010	9:00 p.m.	9
FedEx World Service Center	108 E. 28th St.	10016	9:00 p.m.	9
FedEx World Service Center	149 Madison Ave.	10016	9:00 p.m.	9
FedEx World Service Center	193 Madison Ave.	10016	9:00 p.m.	9
FedEx World Service Center	2 Park Ave.	10016	9:00 p.m.	9
FedEx World Service Center	1 Penn Plz.	10119	9:00 p.m.	9
Kinko's	245 7th Ave.	10001	8:00 p.m.	9
Kinko's	191 Madison Ave.	10016	8:00 p.m.	9
Mail Boxes Etc.	101 W. 23rd St.	10011	5:30 p.m.	9
Mail Boxes Etc.	511 6th Ave.	10011	6:00 p.m.	9
Staples	345 Park Ave. S.	10010	6:00 p.m.	9
Staples	699 6th Ave.	10010	7:00 p.m.	9
Staples	16 E. 34th St.	10016	6:00 p.m.	9
Staples	250 W. 34th St.	10119	6:00 p.m.	9
FedEx Drop Box	200 Park Ave. S.	10003	8:15 p.m.	10
FedEx Drop Box	122 E 25th St.	10010	6:30 p.m.	10
FedEx Drop Box	220 E. 23rd St.	10010	8:30 p.m.	10
FedEx Drop Box	257 Park Ave. S.	10010	8:00 p.m.	10
FedEx Drop Box	30 Waterside Plz.	10010	8:00 p.m.	10
FedEx Drop Box	346 Park Ave. S.	10010	8:00 p.m.	10
FedEx Drop Box	192 Lexington Ave.	10016	7:00 p.m.	10
FedEx Drop Box	200 Lexington Ave.	10016	8:00 p.m.	10
FedEx Drop Box	3 Park Ave.	10016	7:00 p.m.	10
FedEx Drop Box	444 Park Ave. S.	10016	7:00 p.m.	10
FedEx Drop Box	475 Park Ave. S.	10016	8:00 p.m.	10
FedEx Drop Box	530 1st Ave.	10016	8:00 p.m.	10
FedEx Drop Box	545 1st Ave.	10016	8:00 p.m.	10
FedEx Drop Box	660 1st Ave.	10016	6:00 p.m.	10
FedEx World Service Center	4 Union Sq. E.	10003	9:00 p.m.	10
FedEx World Service Center	346 1st Ave.	10009	6:30 p.m.	10
FedEx World Service Center	108 E. 28th St.	10016	9:00 p.m.	10
FedEx World Service Center	2 Park Ave.	10016	9:00 p.m.	10
Mail Boxes Etc.	163 3rd Ave.	10003	4:30 p.m.	10
Mail Boxes Etc.	350 3rd Ave.	10010	6:00 p.m.	10
Mail Boxes Etc.	527 3rd Ave.	10016	7:00 p.m.	10
Staples	59 Union Sq. W.	10003	7:00 p.m.	10
Staples	345 Park Ave. S.	10010	6:00 p.m.	10
FedEx Drop Box	545 8th Ave.	10018	8:00 p.m.	11
FedEx Drop Box	601 W. 50th St.	10019	8:00 p.m.	11
FedEx Drop Box	825 8th Ave.	10019	8:00 p.m.	11
FedEx Drop Box	630 9th Ave.	10036	8:00 p.m.	11
FedEx World Service Center	980 8th Ave.	10019	9:00 p.m.	11
FedEx World Service Center	560 W. 42nd St.	10036	9:30 p.m.	11
Kinko's	677 11th Ave.	10019	8:00 p.m.	11

Another FedEx note: many Manhattan FedEx delivery trucks have a drop-off slot on the side of the truck itself, in case you're on your way to Leroy St. at 9:15 p.m. and see one.

Name	Address	Zip Code	Pick-Up Time (M-F)	Grid #
Mail Boxes Etc.	331 W. 57th St.	10019	6:00 p.m.	11
Fedex	540 Madison Ave.	10022	9:00 p.m.	12
FedEx Drop Box	10 E. 40th St.	10016	8:00 p.m.	12
FedEx Drop Box	335 Madison Ave.	10017	8:00 p.m.	12
FedEx Drop Box	489 5th Ave.	10017	8:00 p.m.	12
FedEx Drop Box	6 E. 43rd St.	10017	8:30 p.m.	12
FedEx Drop Box	60 E. 42nd St.	10017	8:30 p.m.	12
FedEx Drop Box	1370 Broadway	10018	7:00 p.m.	12
FedEx Drop Box	1385 Broadway	10018	6:00 p.m.	12
FedEx Drop Box	1407 Broadway	10018	6:00 p.m.	12
FedEx Drop Box	485 7th Ave.	10018	8:00 p.m.	12
FedEx Drop Box	5 W. 37th St.	10018	7:00 p.m.	12
FedEx Drop Box	545 8th Ave.	10018	8:00 p.m.	12
FedEx Drop Box	58 W. 40th St.	10018	8:00 p.m.	12
FedEx Drop Box	1301 6th Ave.	10019	8:00 p.m.	12
FedEx Drop Box	1325 6th Ave.	10019	8:30 p.m.	12
FedEx Drop Box	1350 6th Ave.	10019	8:00 p.m.	12
FedEx Drop Box	1370 6th Ave.	10019	8:00 p.m.	12
FedEx Drop Box	152 W. 57th St.	10019	8:00 p.m.	12
FedEx Drop Box	156 W. 56th St.	10019	8:00 p.m.	12
FedEx Drop Box	1633 Broadway	10019	8:00 p.m.	12
FedEx Drop Box	1700 Broadway	10019	8:00 p.m.	12
FedEx Drop Box	1775 Broadway	10019	5:00 p.m.	12
FedEx Drop Box	51 W. 52nd St.	10019	8:30 p.m.	12
FedEx Drop Box	712 5th Ave.	10019	8:00 p.m.	12
FedEx Drop Box	787 7th Ave.	10019	8:00 p.m.	12
FedEx Drop Box	825 8th Ave.	10019	8:00 p.m.	12
FedEx Drop Box	1221 6th Ave.	10020	8:00 p.m.	12
FedEx Drop Box	1230 6th Ave.	10020	8:30 p.m.	12
FedEx Drop Box	600 5th Ave.	10020	8:00 p.m.	12
FedEx Drop Box	3 E. 54th St.	10022	7:00 p.m.	12
FedEx Drop Box	444 Madison Ave.	10022	8:30 p.m.	12
FedEx Drop Box	488 Madison Ave.	10022	8:30 p.m.	12
FedEx Drop Box	550 Madison Ave.	10022	8:00 p.m.	12
FedEx Drop Box	555 Madison Ave.	10022	7:30 p.m.	12
FedEx Drop Box	575 Madison Ave.	10022	8:30 p.m.	12
FedEx Drop Box	590 Madison Ave.	10022	7:00 p.m.	12
FedEx Drop Box	600 Madison Ave.	10022	8:30 p.m.	12
FedEx Drop Box	1177 6th Ave.	10036	8:30 p.m.	12
FedEx Drop Box	120 W. 45th St.	10036	8:00 p.m.	12
FedEx Drop Box	1466 Broadway	10036	8:00 p.m.	12
FedEx Drop Box	1500 Broadway	10036	8:00 p.m.	12
FedEx Drop Box	1501 Broadway	10036	8:00 p.m.	12
FedEx Drop Box	1515 Broadway	10036	8:00 p.m.	12
FedEx Drop Box	1345 6th Ave.	10105	8:30 p.m.	12
FedEx Drop Box	500 5th Ave.	10110	8:00 p.m.	12
FedEx Drop Box	745 5th Ave.	10151	8:30 p.m.	12
FedEx World Service Center	261 Madison Ave.	10016	9:00 p.m.	12
FedEx World Service Center	36 E. 40th St.	10016	9:00 p.m.	12
FedEx World Service Center	51 E. 44th St.	10017	9:00 p.m.	12
FedEx World Service Center	112 W. 39th St.	10018	9:00 p.m.	12
FedEx World Service Center	1400 Broadway	10018	9:00 p.m.	12
FedEx World Service Center	1441 Broadway	10018	9:00 p.m.	12
FedEx World Service Center	525 7th Ave.	10018	9:00 p.m.	12
FedEx World Service Center	1290 6th Ave.	10019	9:00 p.m.	12
FedEx World Service Center	1655 Broadway	10019	9:00 p.m.	12
FedEx World Service Center	200 W. 57th St.	10019	9:00 p.m.	12
FedEx World Service Center	233 W. 54th St.	10019	9:00 p.m.	12
FedEx World Service Center	980 8th Ave.	10019	9:00 p.m.	12
FedEx World Service Center	135 W. 50th St.	10020	9:00 p.m.	12
FedEx World Service Center	30 Rockefeller Plaza	10020	9:00 p.m.	12
FedEx World Service Center	10 E. 53rd St.	10022	9:00 p.m.	12
FedEx World Service Center	405 Park Ave.	10022	9:00 p.m.	12
FedEx World Service Center	1114 6th Ave.	10036	9:00 p.m.	12
FedEx World Service Center	1120 6th Ave.	10036	9:00 p.m.	12
FedEx World Service Center	1211 6th Ave.	10036	9:00 p.m.	12
FedEx World Service Center	43 W. 42nd St.	10036	9:00 p.m.	12
Kinko's	16 E. 52nd St.	10022	8:30 p.m.	12
Mail Boxes Etc.	666 5th Ave.	10013	5:30 p.m.	12

Directory Assistance-ESSENTIALS

FedEx Locations

Name	Address	Zip Code	Pick-Up Time (M-F)	Grid #
Staples	1075 6th Ave.	10018	7:00 p.m.	12
Staples	57 W. 57th St.	10019	7:00 p.m.	12
Fedex	201 E. 57th St.	10022	9:00 p.m.	13
Fedex	540 Madison Ave.	10022	9:00 p.m.	13
FedEx Drop Box	353 Lexington Ave.	10016	7:30 p.m.	13
FedEx Drop Box	660 1st Ave.	10016	6:00 p.m.	13
FedEx Drop Box	99 Park Ave.	10016	8:00 p.m.	13
FedEx Drop Box	100 Park Ave.	10017	8:30 p.m.	13
FedEx Drop Box	150 E. 42nd St.	10017	8:30 p.m.	13
FedEx Drop Box	211 E. 43rd St.	10017	8:30 p.m.	13
FedEx Drop Box	220 E. 42nd St.	10017	8:30 p.m.	13
FedEx Drop Box	280 Park Ave.	10017	8:30 p.m.	13
FedEx Drop Box	299 Park Ave.	10017	7:00 p.m.	13
FedEx Drop Box	335 Madison Ave.	10017	8:00 p.m.	13
FedEx Drop Box	420 Lexington Ave.	10017	8:30 p.m.	13
FedEx Drop Box	60 E. 42nd St.	10017	8:30 p.m.	13
FedEx Drop Box	630 3rd Ave.	10017	8:30 p.m.	13
FedEx Drop Box	633 3rd Ave.	10017	8:30 p.m.	13
FedEx Drop Box	866 U.N.Plaza	10017	8:00 p.m.	13
FedEx Drop Box	110 E. 59th St.	10022	8:30 p.m.	13
FedEx Drop Box	115 E. 57th St.	10022	7:30 p.m.	13
FedEx Drop Box	135 E. 57th St.	10022	7:00 p.m.	13
FedEx Drop Box	150 E. 58th St.	10022	8:30 p.m.	13
FedEx Drop Box	350 Park Ave.	10022	7:00 p.m.	13
FedEx Drop Box	40 E. 52nd St.	10022	8:00 p.m.	13
FedEx Drop Box	444 Madison Ave.	10022	8:30 p.m.	13
FedEx Drop Box	488 Madison Ave.	10022	8:30 p.m.	13
FedEx Drop Box	500 Park Ave.	10022	7:00 p.m.	13
FedEx Drop Box	55 E. 59th St.	10022	5:00 p.m.	13
FedEx Drop Box	550 Madison Ave.	10022	8:00 p.m.	13
FedEx Drop Box	555 Madison Ave.	10022	7:30 p.m.	13
FedEx Drop Box	575 Lexington Ave.	10022	7:00 p.m.	13
FedEx Drop Box	575 Madison Ave.	10022	8:30 p.m.	13
FedEx Drop Box	590 Madison Ave.	10022	7:00 p.m.	13
FedEx Drop Box	600 Madison Ave.	10022	8:30 p.m.	13
FedEx Drop Box	805 3rd Ave.	10022	7:00 p.m.	13
FedEx Drop Box	885 3rd Ave.	10022	8:00 p.m.	13
FedEx Drop Box	979 3rd Ave.	10022	8:00 p.m.	13
FedEx World Service Center	261 Madison Ave.	10016	9:00 p.m.	13
FedEx World Service Center	36 E. 40th St.	10016	9:00 p.m.	13
FedEx World Service Center	600 3rd Ave.	10016	9:00 p.m.	13
FedEx World Service Center	90 Park Ave.	10016	9:00 p.m.	13
FedEx World Service Center	312 E. 46th St.	10017	9:00 p.m.	13
FedEx World Service Center	405 Lexington Ave.	10017	9:00 p.m.	13
FedEx World Service Center	480 Lexington Ave.	10017	9:00 p.m.	13
FedEx World Service Center	51 E. 44th St.	10017	9:00 p.m.	13
FedEx World Service Center	750 3rd Ave.	10017	9:00 p.m.	13
FedEx World Service Center	820 2nd Ave.	10017	9:00 p.m.	13
FedEx World Service Center	10 E. 53rd St.	10022	9:00 p.m.	13
FedEx World Service Center	405 Park Ave.	10022	9:00 p.m.	13
FedEx World Service Center	405 Park Ave.	10022	9:00 p.m.	13
FedEx World Service Center	560 Lexington Ave.	10022	9:00 p.m.	13
FedEx World Service Center	880 3rd Ave.	10022	9:00 p.m.	13
FedEx World Service Center	938 3rd Ave.	10022	9:00 p.m.	13
FedEx World Service Center	230 Park Ave.	10169	8:30 p.m.	13
Kinko's	305 E. 46th St.	10017	8:30 p.m.	13
Kinko's	153 E. 53rd St.	10022	7:00 p.m.	13
Mail Boxes Etc.	847A 2nd Ave.	10017	5:00 p.m.	13
Mail Boxes Etc.	865 1st Ave.	10017	5:30 p.m.	13
Mail Boxes Etc.	1040 1st Ave.	10022	4:00 p.m.	13
Mail Boxes Etc.	208 E. 51st St.	10022	6:00 p.m.	13
Staples	205 E. 42nd St.	10017	6:00 p.m.	13
Staples	425 Park Ave.	10022	6:00 p.m.	13
Copy Usa	491 Amsterdam Ave.	10024	8:00 p.m.	14
FedEx Drop Box	211 W. 61st St.	10023	6:00 p.m.	14
FedEx Drop Box	2112 Broadway	10023	7:30 p.m.	14
FedEx Drop Box	24 W. 61st St.	10023	7:00 p.m.	14
FedEx Drop Box	517 Amsterdam Ave.	10024	8:00 p.m.	14
FedEx World Service Center	156 W. 72 St.	10023	9:00 p.m.	14

FedEx Locations

Name	Address	Zip Code	Pick-Up Time (M-F)	Grid #
Mail Boxes Etc.	163 Amsterdam Ave.	10023	7:00 p.m.	14
Mail Boxes Etc.	2124 Broadway	10023	5:30 p.m.	14
Mail Boxes Etc.	459 Columbus Ave.	10024	6:00 p.m.	14
Staples	2248 Broadway	10024	5:00 p.m.	14
The Padded Wagon	215 W. 85th St.	10024	6:00 p.m.	14
Faster Image	415 E. 72nd St.	10021	6:00 p.m.	15
FedEx Drop Box	1114 1st Ave.	10021	5:30 p.m.	15
FedEx Drop Box	1275 York Ave.	10021	8:30 p.m.	15
FedEx Drop Box	1300 York Ave.	10021	8:30 p.m.	15
FedEx Drop Box	1343 2nd Ave.	10021	8:30 p.m.	15
FedEx Drop Box	428 E. 72nd St.	10021	6:00 p.m.	15
FedEx Drop Box	667 Madison Ave.	10021	8:30 p.m.	15
FedEx Drop Box	695 Park Ave.	10021	7:00 p.m.	15
FedEx Drop Box	968 Lexington Ave.	10021	8:30 p.m.	15
FedEx Drop Box	110 E. 59th St.	10022	8:30 p.m.	15
FedEx Drop Box	500 Park Ave.	10022	7:00 p.m.	15
FedEx Drop Box	55 E. 59th St.	10022	5:00 p.m.	15
FedEx Drop Box	650 Madison Ave.	10022	7:30 p.m.	15
FedEx Drop Box	979 3rd Ave.	10022	8:00 p.m.	15
Kinko's	1122 Lexington Ave.	10021	8:30 p.m.	15
Mail Boxes Etc.	1173 2nd Ave. # A	10021	5:30 p.m.	15
Mail Boxes Etc.	1275 1st Ave.	10021	5:30 p.m.	15
Mail Boxes Etc.	1461 1st Ave.	10021	6:00 p.m.	15
Mail Boxes Etc.	1562 1st Ave.	10028	6:00 p.m.	15
Postal Express Bus	1382 3rd Ave.	10021	6:00 p.m.	15
The Padded Wagon	1431 York Ave.	10021	6:00 p.m.	15
Copy Usa	491 Amsterdam Ave.	10024	8:00 p.m.	16
FedEx Drop Box	517 Amsterdam Ave.	10024	8:00 p.m.	16
Foxy Graphic Services	211 W. 92nd St.	10025	7:30 p.m.	16
Mail Boxes Etc.	2472 Broadway	10025	6:00 p.m.	16
Mail Boxes Etc.	2565 Broadway	10025	6:00 p.m.	16
The Padded Wagon	215 W. 85th St.	10024	6:00 p.m.	16
FedEx Drop Box	1216 5th Ave.	10029	5:30 p.m.	17
FedEx Drop Box	225 E. 95th St.	10128	8:30 p.m.	17
FedEx World Service Center	208 E. 86th St.	10028	9:00 p.m.	17
Mail Boxes Etc.	217 E. 86th St.	10028	6:00 p.m.	17
Mail Boxes Etc.	1369 Madison Ave.	10128	5:00 p.m.	17
Mail Boxes Etc.	1636 3rd Ave.	10128	5:30 p.m.	17
Mail Boxes Etc.	1710 1st Ave.	10128	6:00 p.m.	17
Staples	1280 Lexington Ave.	10028	8:00 p.m.	17
FedEx Drop Box	3022 Broadway	10027	8:00 p.m.	18
FedEx Drop Box	435 W. 116th St.	10027	8:00 p.m.	18
FedEx Drop Box	525 W. 120th St.	10027	8:00 p.m.	18
FedEx Drop Box	475 Riverside Dr.	10115	6:00 p.m.	18
FedEx World Service Center	600 W. 116th St.	10027	9:00 p.m.	18
Kinko's	2872 Broadway	10025	8:30 p.m.	18
FedEx Drop Box	163 W. 125th St.	10027	7:00 p.m.	19
FedEx Drop Box	355 W. Lenox Ave.	10027	5:00 p.m.	19
FedEx Drop Box	55 W. 125th St.	10027	6:30 p.m.	19
FedEx Drop Box	2261 A. C. Powell Bd.	10030	7:00 p.m.	19
FedEx Drop Box	1824 Madison Ave.	10035	7:00 p.m.	20
FedEx Drop Box	1879 Madison Ave.	10035	7:00 p.m.	20
FedEx Drop Box	100 Haven Ave.	10032	7:00 p.m.	23
FedEx Drop Box	1051 Riverside Dr.	10032	7:00 p.m.	23
FedEx Drop Box	161 Ft. Washing. Ave.	10032	7:00 p.m.	23
FedEx Drop Box	177 Ft. Washing. Ave.	10032	7:00 p.m.	23
FedEx Drop Box	3960 Broadway	10032	7:00 p.m.	23
FedEx Drop Box	60 Haven Ave.	10032	7:00 p.m.	23
FedEx Drop Box	622 W. 168th St.	10032	7:00 p.m.	23
FedEx Drop Box	630 W. 168th St.	10032	7:00 p.m.	23
FedEx Drop Box	710 W. 168th St.	10032	7:00 p.m.	23
FedEx Drop Box	722 W. 168th St.	10032	7:00 p.m.	23
FedEx World Service Center	1541 St. Nich. Ave.	10040	5:00 p.m.	24
FedEx Drop Box	1 Battery Park Plaza	10004	8:30 p.m.	BPC
FedEx World Service Center	250 Vesey St.	10281	9:00 p.m.	BPC

Hospitals

The most infamous of NYC Hospitals, Bellevue, is the nation's oldest public hospital, and in 1869 it became the first hospital in the nation to have an ambulance service. There have been a number of significant mergers of the major hospitals lately (Mt. Sinai/NYU, Columbia/Cornell). It shouldn't be long before there's only one (very big) hospital in NYC. Maybe it has something to do with the HMOs. Who knows?

Hospitals	Address	Phone No.	Grid
American Association For Bikur Cholim Hospital	156 5th Ave.	989-2525	9
American Friends of Laniado Hospital	18 W. 45th St.	944-2690	12
Babies & Children's Hospital Of New York	3959 Broadway	800-245-5437	23
Bellevue Hospital Center	462 1st Ave.	562-4141	10
Beth Israel Medical Center	281 1st Ave.	420-2000	10
Beth Israel Medical Center: North Division	170 East End Ave.	870-9000	17
Beth Israel Medical Center:			
Phillips Ambulatory Center/Cancer Center	10 Union Sq. E.	844-8288	9, 10
Cabrini Medical Center	227 E. 19th St.	995-6000	10
Columbia-NY Presbyterian Allen Pavilion	5141 Broadway	932-4000	25
Columbia-Presbyterian Medical Center	622 W. 168th St.	305-2500	23
Gouverneur Hospital	227 Madison St.	238-7000	4
Gracie Square Hospital	420 E. 76th St.	988-4400	15
Harlem Hospital Center	506 Lenox Ave.	939-1000	22
Hospital for Joint Diseases	301 E. 17th St.	598-6000	10
Hospital for Special Surgery	535 E. 70th St.	606-1000	15
Lenox Hill Hospital	100 E. 77th St.	434-2000	15
Manhattan Eye, Ear & Throat Hospital	210 E. 64th St.	838-9200	15
Manhattan Eye, Ear & Throat Hospital	55 E. 124th St.	987-1360	20
Memorial Sloan-Kettering Cancer Center	1275 York Ave.	639-2000	15
Metropolitan Hospital	1901 1st Ave.	423-6262	17
Mt. Sinai Medical Center	5th Ave. at 100th St.	241-6500	17
National Jewish Center for			
Immunology & Respiratory Medicine	535 Fifth Ave.	297-0857	12
New York Eye & Ear Infirmary	310 E. 14th St.	979-4000	6, 7, 10
New York Foundling Hospital	590 Ave. of the Americas	633-9300	9
New York Hospital-Cornell Medical Center	525 E. 68th St.	746-5454	15
North General Hospital	1879 Madison Ave.	423-4000	20
NYU Downtown Hospital	170 William St.	312-5000	3
NYU Medical Center: Tisch Hospital	560 1st Ave.	263-7300	10
Renaissance Health Care Network	215 W. 125th St.	932-6500	19
Roosevelt Hospital Center	1000 10th Ave.	523-4000	11
St. Vincent's Senior Health at Penn South	365 W. 25th St.	463-0101	8
St. Clare's Family Health Center	350 W. 51st St.	265-8950	11, 12
St. Clare's Hospital & Health Center	426 W. 52nd St.	586-1500	11
St. Luke's Hospital Center	1111 Amsterdam Ave.	523-4000	18
St. Vincent's AIDS Center	412 Ave. of the Americas	604-1576	5, 6
St. Vincent's Hospital & Medical Center	153 W. 11th St.	604-7000	5
The Floating Hospital	Pier 11	514-7447	1
The Paul Robeson Family Medical Center	140 W. 125th St.	316-3800	19
V.A. Hospital	408 1st Ave.	686-7500	10

Libraries

In addition to the regular branch system of the New York Public Library, there are several specialized "research" libraries in Manhattan. The Schomburg Center for Research in Black Culture contains an incredible amount of material relating to the history of African-Americans. The Science, Industry, and Business Library is perhaps the newest and swankiest of all Manhattan's libraries. The Library for the Performing Arts contains a wonderful archive of New York City theater on film and tape.* And, of course, the main branch of the New York Public Library (one of Manhattan's architectural treasures designed by Carrere and Hastings in 1897) has several special collections and services, such as the Humanities and Social Sciences Library, the Map Division, Exhibition galleries, and divisions dedicated to various ethnic groups. It contains 88 miles of shelves and has over 10,000 current periodicals from almost 150 countries. You can check out the full system on-line at www.nypl.org.

Libraries	Address	Phone No.	Grid
115th St.	203 W. 115th St.	666-9393	19
125th St.	224 E. 125th St.	534-5050	20
58th St.	127 E. 58th St.	759-7358	13
67th St.	328 E. 68th St.	734-1717	15
96th St.	112 E. 96th St.	289-0908	17
Aguilar	174 E. 110th St.	534-2930	17, 20
Andrew Heiskell Library for The Blind	40 W. 20th St.	206-5400	9
Bloomingdale	150 W. 100th St.	222-8030	16
Chatham Square	33 E. Broadway	673-6344	3
Columbia	514 W. 113th St.	864-2530	18
Columbus	742 10th Ave.	586-5098	11
Countee Cullen	104 W. 136th St .	491-2070	22
Donnell Library Center	20 W. 53rd St.	621-0564	12, 13
Epiphany	228 E. 23rd St.	679-2645	10
Fort Washington	535 W. 179th St.	927-3533	23
George Bruce	518 W. 125th St.	662-9727	18
Hamilton Fish Park	415 E. Houston St.	673-2290	7
Hamilton Grange	503 W. 145th St.	926-2147	21
Harlem	9 W. 124th St.	348-5620	19
Hudson Park	66 Leroy St.	243-6876	5
Inwood	4790 Broadway at Academy	942-2445	25
Jefferson Market	425 Ave. of the Americas	243-4334	5, 6
Kips Bay	446 3rd Ave.	683-2520	10
Macomb's Bridge	2650 A. C. Powell Jr. Blvd.	281-4900	22
Mid-Manhattan Library	455 5th Ave.	340-0833	12
Muhlenberg	209 W. 23rd St.	206-5480	8, 9
New Amsterdam	9 Murray St.	732-8186	2, 3
New York Public Library for the Performing Arts	40 Lincoln Center Plaza	870-1630	14
Ottendorfer	135 2nd Ave.	674-0947	6
Riverside	127 Amsterdam Ave.	870-1810	14
Schomburg Center for Research in Black Culture	515 Malcolm X Blvd.	491-2200	22
Science, Industry, and Business Library	188 Madison Ave.	592-7000	9
Seward Park	192 E. Broadway	477-6770	4
St. Agnes	444 Amsterdam Ave.	877-4380	14
Terence Cardinal Cooke-Cathedral	560 Lexington Ave.	752-3824	13
Tompkins Square	331 E. 10th St.	228-4747	7
Washington Heights	1000 St. Nicholas Ave.	923-6054	23
Webster	1465 York Ave.	288-5049	15
Yorkville	222 E. 79th St.	744-5824	15

*Currently closed for renovation until February 2001. Its archive collection of theater on film and tape may be viewed at the library's annex at 521 W. 43rd St. (870-1639) between 10th and 11th Aves.

Directory Assistance-ESSENTIALS

Police Precincts

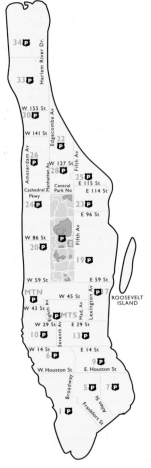

Important Phone Numbers:
All Emergencies: 911
Wanted Persons: 800-777-TIPS
Rape Victims Hotline: 212-267-7273
Crime Victims Hotline: 212-577-7777
Missing Persons Squad: 212-374-6914
Sex Crimes Report Line: 212-267-0013
Noise Complaints (EPA): 718-337-4357
Complaints (Internal Affairs): 212-741-8401
website: www.ci.nyc.ny.us/html/nypd/home.html

Statistics
• 38,574 uniformed personnel
• NYC ranks 166th out of 217 U.S. cities in crime
  (population over 100,000)
• 1998: 629 murders
• 1998: 2,485 rapes
• 1998: 39,005 robberies
• 1998: 28,852 felony assaults
• 1998: 47,150 burglaries
• 1998: 51,427 grand larcenies
• 1998: 43,347 grand larcenies (automobiles)

PRECINCT	ADDRESS	PHONE	GRID
1	16 Ericsson Pl.	334-0611	2
5	19 Elizabeth St.	334-0711	5
6	233 W 10th St	741-4811	5
7	19 1/2 Pitt St	477-7311	4, 7
9	321 E 5th St.	477-7811	7
10	230 W 20th St.	741-8211	9
13	230 E 21st St.	477-7411	9
Mid-Town So.	357 W 35th St.	239-9811	8
17	167 E 51st St.	826-3211	13
Mid-Town No.	524 W 42nd St.	767-8400	11
19	153 E 67th St.	452-0600	15
20	120 W 82nd St	580-6411	14
Central Pk.	86th St. & Transverse Rd	570-4820	C. Pk.
23	162 E 102nd St.	860-6411	17
24	151 W 100th St.	678-1811	16
25	120 E 119th St.	860-6511	20
26	520 W 126th St.	678-1311	18
28	2271-89 8 Ave.	678-1611	18, 19
30	451 W 151st St.	690-8811	21
32	250 W 135th St.	690-6311	22
33	2120 Amsterdam Ave.	927-3200	23
34	4295 Broadway	927-9711	24

Zip Codes/Post Offices

BRANCH	ADDRESS	PHONE	GRID
Ansonia Finance	40 W 66 St.	362-7488	15
Ansonia Sta.	211 W 61 St.	765-2469	14
Appraisers Stores	580 5 Ave. Suite 407	768-8530	12
Audubon	515 W 165 St.	568-3311	23
Bowling Green	25 Broadway	264-8112	1
Bryant	23 W 43 St.	279-5960	12
Canal St.	350 Canal St.	925-3378	2
Cathedral	215 W 104 St.	662-9191	16
Central Parcel Post	325 W 15 St.	243-4608	9
Cherokee	1539 1 Ave.	288-3724	15
Chinatown	6 Doyers St.	267-3510	3
Church St.	90 Church St.	330-5247	1, 2
College Sta.	217 W 140 St.	283-2235	22
Colonial Park	99 Macombs Pl	368-4211	22
Columbus Circ.	27 W 60 St.	285-7858	11,14
Columbus Univ.	1123 Amsterdam Ave.	864-1874	18
Cooper	93 4 Ave.	254-1389	6
Dag Hammarskjold	884 Second Ave.	751-5716	13
Eastside Parcel Post	500 E 132 St.	718-292-2315	18
Empire State	19 W 33 St.	736-8282	9
Fort Washington	3771 Broadway	368-7302	21
Fort George	4558 Broadway	942-0052	24
Franklin D Roos.	909 3 Ave.	330-5549	13
Gracie	229 E 85 St.	330-5551	15, 17
Grand Central Sta.	450 Lexington Ave.	330-5552	13
Greeley Sq.	40 W 32 St.	330-5553	9
Hamilton Grange	521 W 146 St.	330-5554	21
Hell Gate	153 E 110 St.	330-5555	17, 20
Inwood	90 Vermilyea Ave.	330-5556	25
*JA Farley GPO	421 8 Ave.	330-5557	8,9
Knickerbocker	130 E Broadway	330-5558	4
Lenox Hill	221 E 70 St.	330-5559	15
Lincolnton	2265 5 Ave.	330-5560	22
London Terr.	234 10 Ave.	330-5561	8
Madison Sq.	149 E 23 St.	330-5562	10
Manhattanville	365 W 125 St.	330-5563	18,19
Midtown	223 W 38 St.	330-5564	9, 12
Morgan G M F	341 9 Ave.	330-5565	8
Morningside	232 W 116 St.	330-5566	19
Murray Hill	205 E 36 St.	330-5567	10
Murray Hill Fin.	115 E 34 St.	330-5568	10
Old Chelsea	217 W 18 St.	330-5569	9
Park West	693 Columbus Ave.	330-5570	16
Patchin	70 W 10 St.	330-5571	6
Peck Slip	1-15 Peck Slip	330-5572	1, 3
Peter Stuyvesant	432 E 14 St.	330-5573	6, 7, 10
Pitt Sta.	185 Clinton St.	330-5574	4
Planetarium	131 W 83 St.	330-5575	14
Port Authority	75 9 Ave.	330-5576	8
Prince	103 Prince St.	330-5577	6
Radio City	322 W 52 St.	330-5578	11
Rockefeller Ctr.	610 5 Ave.	330-5579	12
Roosevelt Island	694 Main St	752-5564	R.I.
Sta. 138 (Macy's)	151 W 34 St.	330-5581	10
Times Square	340 W 42 St.	330-5582	11
Tomkins Sq.	244 E 3 St.	330-5583	7
Triborough	167 E 124 St.	330-5584	20
Tudor City	5 Tudor City Pl.	330-5585	13
United Nations	405 E 42 St.	330-5586	13
Village	201 Varick St.	330-5587	5
Wall Street	73 Pine St.	330-5588	1
Washington Bridge	555 W 180 St.	330-5589	23, 24
West Village	527 Hudson St.	330-5590	5
Yorkville	1619 3 Ave.	330-5591	17

* 24-Hour Service

Directory Assistance-ESSENTIALS

24-Hour Services

Newsstands	Grid
49th St. and 8th Ave.	11, 12
42nd St. and 7th Ave.	12
23rd St. and 3rd Ave.	10
3rd Ave. (34/35th Sts.)	10
6th Ave. (South of 8th St.)	5, 6
St. Marks Pl.(8th St.)/Bowery (3rd Ave.)	6
6th Ave. and 3rd St.	5, 6
2nd Ave. and St. Marks Pl.	6
Delancey and Essex Sts.	4, 7
1st Ave. and 57th St.	13
Broadway and 50th St.	11, 12
59th St. and 3rd Ave.	13, 15
2nd Ave. (60/61st Sts.)	13, 15
72nd St. and Broadway	14
76th St. and Broadway	14
79th St. and York (1st Ave.)	15
86th St. and Lexington Ave.	15, 17
1st Ave. and 63rd St.	15
Columbus Ave. and 81st St.	14
Broadway and 116th St.	18

Pharmacies	Address	Phone Number	Grid
CVS	342 E. 23rd St.	473-5750	10
CVS	1400 2nd Ave.	249-5062	15
CVS	1 Columbus Pl.	245-0611	11
Duane Reade	224 W. 57th St.	541-9708	11, 12
Duane Reade	2465 Broadway	799-3172	16
Duane Reade	378 6th Ave.	674-5357	5, 6
Duane Reade	1279 3rd Ave.	744-2668	15
Duane Reade	485 Lexington Ave.	682-5338	13
Duane Reade	625 8th Ave. (Port Authority)	967-8110	11, 12
Duane Reade	1 WTC	912-0998	1
Genovese	1229 2nd Ave.	772-0104	15
Kaufman Pharmacy	Lexington Ave. and 50th St.	755-2266	13
Rite Aid	2833 Broadway	663-3135	16, 18
Rite Aid	408 Grand St.	529-7115	4
Rite Aid	282 8th Ave.	727-3854	8, 9

24-Hour Services

Rite Aid	144 E. 86th St.	876-0600	15, 17
Rite Aid	200 W. 70th St.	787-2903	14
Town Total Health	45 E. 30th St.	213-5570	9

Gas Stations

	Address	Grid
Amoco	Broadway and Houston	6
Amoco	8th Ave. and 110th St.	16, 18, 19
Amoco	Amsterdam Ave. and 165th St.	23
Amoco	10th Ave. and 207th St.	25
Citgo	Bowery and 3rd St.	6
Gaseteria	Houston and Lafayette Sts.	6
Gaseteria	West End Ave. and 59th St.	11
Gaseteria	Broadway and 193rd St.	24
Getty	8th Ave. and 13th St.	5
Getty	10th Ave. and 20th St.	8
Gulf	10th Ave. and 23rd St.	8
Jerusalem	10th Ave. and 201st St.	25
Merit	7th Ave. and 145th St.	22
Mobil	Allen and Division Sts.	4
Mobil	6th Ave. and Spring St.	5, 6
Mobil	Houston St. and Ave. C	7
Mobil	11th Ave. and 51st St.	11
Mobil	11th Ave. and 57th St.	11
Mobil	7th Ave. and 145th St.	22
Shell	Amsterdam Ave. and 167th St.	23
Shell	Amsterdam Ave. and 181st St.	23, 24

Veterinarian

	Address	Phone Number	Grid
Animal Medical Center	510 East 62nd St.	838-8100	15

Car Washes

	Address	Phone Number	Grid
Broadway Car Wash	614 Broadway (Houston St.)	673-5115	6
Eastside Car Wash	1770 1st Ave. (92nd St.)	722-2222	17
Westside Highway Car Wash	638 W. 47th St.	757-1141	11

Car Rental

	Address	Phone Number	Grid
Avis	217 E. 43rd St.	593-8378	13

Garages/Repair

	Address	Phone Number	Grid
Auto Center	303 10th Ave.	947-7159	8
Yellow Box of Tin	300 Lafayette St.	925-0228	6

Directory Assistance-ESSENTIALS

24-Hour Services

Delivery and Messengers	Address	Phone Number	Grid
Moonlite Courier	125 E. 23rd St.	473-2246	9
Able Motorized Deliveries	65 W. 36th St.	687-5515	9

Billiards	Address	Phone Number	Grid
Chelsea Billiards	54 W. 21st St.	989-0096	9

Gyms	Address	Phone Number	Grid
World Gym (Mon. - Fri. only)	Broadway and 64th St.	874-0942	14
Crunch (Mon. - Fri. only)	Lafayette and 4th St.	614-0120	6

Locksmiths	Address	Phone Number	Grid
A Alpha Locksmith	45 Ave. A	228-1070	6, 7
A&M Locksmith	215 1st Ave.	242-4733	6, 7, 10
Aaron-Hotz Locksmith	Multiple locations	243-7166	N/A
Abbey Locksmiths	1558 2nd Ave.	535-2289	15
American Locksmiths	247 E. 50th St.	888-8888	13
ATB Locksmith & Hardware	1603 York Ave.	(800) 774-4364	15, 17
Big A Locksmith	Multiple locations	860-2400	N/A
Big John Locksmith	N/A	333-3740	N/A
CBS Locksmith	Multiple locations	410-0090	N/A
Champion Locksmiths	Multiple locations	362-7000	N/A
Citi Security Locksmiths	Multiple locations	483-9494	N/A
Eagle Master Locksmiths	43 E. 28th St.	532-1075	9, 10
East Manhattan Locksmith	160 E. 88th St.	369-9063	17
Emergency Locksmith 24 Hours	Multiple locations	369-4107	N/A
Lockmasters Locksmith	532 W. 145th St.	690-4018	21
Locksmith, Inc.	Multiple locations	319-7657	N/A
Major Locksmith	Multiple locations	799-8808	N/A
Manhattan Budget Locksmiths	Multiple locations	831-8500	N/A
Manhattan Locksmiths	2449-A Broadway	877-7787	16
Master Locksmith	Multiple locations	579-2050	N/A
Mobile Locksmith	Multiple locations	315-2020	N/A
Night and Day Locksmith	1335 Lexington Ave.	722-1017	17
Presto Lockout Service	Multiple locations	831-9667	N/A
S&L Locksmith	Multiple locations	799-9490	N/A
West Side Locksmiths	Multiple locations	564-7070	N/A

Plumbers	Address	Phone Number	Grid
New York Plumbing & Heating Service	244 5th Ave.	496-9191	9
RR Plumbing (Roto-Rooter)	N/A	687-1661	N/A

24-Hour Services

Sanitary Plumbing & Heating	211 E. 117th St.	734-5000	20
Pipeline of New York	2014 2nd Ave.	267-4241	17
Express Plumbing, Heating & Gas	183 E. 104th St.	427-9000	17

Copying	Address	Phone Number	Grid
ADS Copying	29 W. 38th St	398-6166	12
Blumberg Excelsior Copy	66 White St.	343-2400	2
Copycats	1646 2nd Ave.	734-6104	15, 17
Copycats	968 Lexington Ave.	734-6236	15
Copycats	216 E. 45 St.	557-2110	13
Kinko's	2872 Broadway	316-3390	18
Kinko's	16 E. 52nd St.	308-2679	12
Kinko's	191 Madison Ave.	685-3449	9
Kinko's	24 E. 12th St.	924-0802	6
Kinko's	245 7th Ave.	929-2679	9
Kinko's	1122 Lexington Ave.	628-5500	15
Kinko's	13-25 Astor Pl.	228-9511	6
Kinko's	105 Duane St.	406-1220	2
Kinko's	1211 Ave. of Americas	391-2679	12
Kinko's	233 W. 54th St.	977-2679	12
Kinko's	250 E. Houston St.	253-9020	7
Kinko's	305 E. 46th St.	319-6600	13
Kinko's	600 3rd Ave.	599-2679	13
Kinko's	100 Wall St.	269-0024	1
Kinko's	153 E. 53rd St.	753-7580	13
Metro Copying & Duplicating	222 E. 45th St.	687-6699	13
National Reproductions	130 Cedar St.	619-3800	1
National Reproductions	25 W. 45th St.	840-3091	12
On-Site Sourcing, Inc.	443 Park Ave. S.	252-9700	9
Sir Speedy	234 W. 35th St.	451-0440	9
Sir Speedy	225 W. 34th St.	451-0440	9
The Village Copier	420 Lexington Ave.	599-3344	13
The Village Copier	20 E. 13th St.	675-1360	6
The Village Copier	25 W. 43rd St.	869-9665	12

Photo Developing	Address	Phone Number	Grid
Duggal (Mon. - Fri. only)	3 W. 20th St.	242-7000	9

Post Office	Address	Phone Number	Grid
JA Farley GPO	421 8th Ave.	330-5557	8, 9

Directory Assistance-TRANSIT

Airlines

Airline	Phone	JFK	Newark	LaGuardia	Airline	Phone	JFK	Newark	LaGuardia
Aer Lingus	888-474-7424	X	X		British Airways	800-538-2942	X	X	
Aeroflot	800-340-6400	X			Canadian	800-426-7000	X		
Aerolineas Argentinas	800-333-0276	X			Cathay Pacific	800-233-2742	X		
Aeromexico	800-237-6639	X			China Airlines	800-227-5118	X		
Air Afrique	800-456-9192	X			Colgan	800-272-5488		X	X
Air Alliance	800-776-3000		X		Continental (Domestic)	800-523-3273	X	X	X
Air Aruba	800-882-7822		X		Continental Express	800-523-3273		X	X
Air Atlantic Dominicana	800-776-7155	X			Continental (International)	800-231-0856		X	
Air Canada	800-776-3000		X	X	Czech Airlines	212-765-6022		X	
Air China-CAAC	212-371-9898	X			Delta (Domestic)	800-221-1212	X	X	X
Air Europa	888-772-4699	X			Delta Connection	800-345-3400	X		X
Air France	800-237-2747	X	X		Delta Express	800-221-1212		X	
Air India	212-751-6200	X			Delta (International)	800-241-4141	X		
Air Jamaica	800-523-5585	X	X		Ecuatoriana	212-398-6020	X		
Air Nova	800-776-3000		X		Egyptair	212-315-0900	X		
Air Plus Comet	877-999-7587	X			El Al	800-223-6700	X	X	
Air Tran Airlines	800-247-8726			X	Ethiopian Airlines	212-867-0095		X	
Air Ukraine	800-857-2463	X			Eva Airways	800-695-1188		X	
Alitalia	800-223-5730	X	X		Finnair	800-950-5000	X		
All Nippon	800-235-9262	X			Frontier Airlines	800-432-1359			X
Allegro Airlines	800-915-7551	X	X		Ghana Airways	800-404-4262	X		
America West	800-235-9292	X	X	X	Guyana	800-242-4210	X		
American	800-433-7300	X	X	X	Iberia	800-772-4642	X		
American Eagle	800-433-7300	X	X	X	Icelandair	800-223-5500	X		
Asiana	800-227-4262	X			Japan Airlines	800-525-3663	X		
ATA (Domestic)	800-435-9282	X	X	X	Kiwi	800-538-5494		X	
ATA (International)	800-435-9282	X			KLM	800-374-7747	X	X	
Austrian Airlines	800-843-0002	X			Korean Air	800-438-5000	X	X	
Aviacsa	718-656-3018	X			Kuwait Airways	800-458-9248	X		
Avianca	800-284-2622	X	X		Lacsa	800-225-2272	X		
Balkan Bulgarian	800-822-1106	X			Lan Chile	800-735-5526	X		
					Lot Polish	800-528-7208	X	X	
Biman Bangladesh	212-808-4477	X			LTU	800-888-0200	X		

Airlines

Airline	Phone	JFK	Newark	LaGuardia
Lufthansa	800-645-3880	X	X	
Malaysia	800-552-9264			X
Malev Hungarian	800-223-6884	X		
Martinair (Seasonal)	800-627-8462		X	
Mexicana	800-531-7921		X	
Miami Air	305-871-3300		X	X
Midway	800-446-4392		X	
Midwest Express	800-452-2022		X	X
Myrtle Beach Jet Express	800-386-2786	X	X	
North American	718-656-2650	X	X	
Northwest (Domestic)	800-225-2525	X		
Northwest (International)	800-447-4747			
Northwest/ KLM	800-225-2525		X	
Olympic	800-223-1226	X		
Pakistan	212-370-9158	X		
Pro Air	888-477-6247		X	
Qantas	800-227-4500	X		
Royal Air (Seasonal)	800-344-6726		X	
Royal Air Maroc	800-344-6726	X		
Royal Jordanian	212-949-0050	X		
Sabena	800-955-2000	X		
Saeta Ecuador	800-827-2382	X		
SAS	800-221-2350	X	X	
Saudi Arabian Airlines	800-472-8342	X		
Servivensa	718-244-6857	X		
Singapore Airlines	800-742-3333	X	X	
Sky Trek	609-671-0220		X	
South African Airways	800-722-9675	X		
Spirit	800-772-7117			X
Sun Country	800-359-5786	X		
Sunjet International	800-478-6538	X	X	
Swissair	800-221-4750	X	X	
TACA	800-535-8780	X		
TAM	888-235-9826	X		
Tap Air Portugal	800-221-7370	X	X	
Tarom Romanian	212-687-6013	X		
Tie Aviation	888-244-8922	X		
Tower Air	800-221-2500	X		
Trade Winds	718-656-2222	X		
Trans Meridian	770-732-6900	X		
Turkish	800-874-8875	X		
TWA	800-221-2000	X	X	X
TWA Express	800-221-2000	X		
TWA (International)	800-892-4141	X		
United Airlines (Domestic)	800-241-6522	X	X	X
United Airlines Express	800-241-6522	X	X	X
United Airlines (International)	800-241-6522		X	
United Airlines (SFO/LAX)	800-241-6522	X		
US Airways	800-428-4322	X	X	
US Airways Express	800-428-4322		X	
Uzbekistan	212-489-3954	X		
Varig	800-468-2744	X		
VASP	800-900-8277	X	X	
Virgin Atlantic	800-862-8621	X	X	

Directory Assistance-TRANSIT

JFK Airport

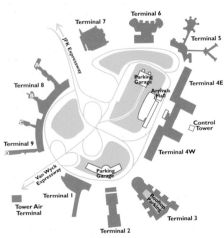

AIRLINE	TERMINAL	
	departure	arrival
KLM	4E	4
Korean Air	1	1
Kuwait Airways	4E	4
Lacsa	2	3
Lan Chile	7	7
Lot Polish	8	8
LTU	4E	4
Malev Hungarian	3	3
Miami Air	4E	4E
Myrtle Beach		
Jet Express	9	9
North American	4E	4
Northwest	4	4
Olympic	1	1
Pakistan	4W	4
Qantas	9	9
Royal Air Maroc	1	1
Royal Jordanian	5	5
Sabena	3	3
Saeta Ecuador	2	3
SAS	7	7
Saudi Arabian Airlines	2	3
Servivensa	4W	4W
Singapore Airlines	1	1
South African Airways	8	8
Sun Country	5	5
Sunjet International	4E	4E
Swissair	3	3
TACA	2	3
TAM	8	8
Tap Air Portugal	3	3
Tarom Romanian	3	3
Tie Aviation	9	9
Tower Air Domestic	T.A	T.A
Tower Air	T.A	4E/
Trans Meridian	4E	4
Trade Winds	4E	4
Turkish	1	1
TWA (Domestic)	5	5
TWA (International)	5	5
TW Express	5	5
United Airlines	7	7
United Express	7	7
United Airlines		
(SFO/LAX) Flights	6	6
US Airways	7	7
Uzbekistan	4W	4W
Varig	4W	4W
VASP	4W	4W
Virgin Atlantic	4W	4W

AIRLINE	TERMINAL	
	departure	arrival
Aer Lingus	4E	4E
Aeroflot	3	3
Aerolineas Argentinas	9	8
Aeromexico	3	3
Air Afrique	1	
Air Atlantic		
Dominicana	4E	4E
Air China-CAAC	3	3
Air Europa	5	5
Air France	1	1
Air India	4W	4W
Air Jamaica	2	3
Air Plus Comet	4E	4E
Air Ukraine	3	3
Alitalia	4E	4E
Allegro Airlines	4E	4E
All Nippon	3	3
America West	6	6
American (Domestic)	9	9
American		
(International)	8	8
American Eagle	9	9
Asiana	8	8

AIRLINE	TERMINAL	
	departure	arrival
ATA (Domestic)	6	6
ATA (International)	4E	4E
Austrian Airlines	3	3
Aviacsa	4W	4
Avianca	3	3
Balkan Bulgarian	4E	4E
Biman Bangladesh	4E	4E
British Airways	4E	4E
Canadian	9	9
Cathay Pacific	3	3
China Airlines	3	3
Continental	4W	4
Delta	3	3
Delta Connection	3	3
Ecuatoriana	4W	4
Egyptair	4E	4E
El Al	4W	4
Finnair	2	3
Ghana Airways	4E	4
Guyana	4W	4
Iberia	8	8
Icelandair	7	7
Japan Airlines	1	1

JFK Airport

Ah, JFK. Let's face it: it sucks. Nonetheless, it's expected that 35 million people will annually use JFK by the year 2000. Expansion and modernization plans are moving forward, but all we can say is: If you've got the choice, go to Newark.

How to Get There—Driving

You can take the lovely and scenic Belt Parkway straight to JFK as long as it's not rush hour. This is about a 30-mile trip, even though JFK is only 15 or so miles from Manhattan. You can access the Belt by taking the Brooklyn-Battery Tunnel to the Gowanus (the best route), or by taking the Brooklyn, Manhattan, or Williamsburg Bridges to the Brooklyn-Queens Expressway to the Gowanus. We of course do not recommend this, because the idea of driving 30 miles to go 15 miles makes us nuts. Instead, get to Atlantic Avenue in Brooklyn and drive east until you hit Conduit Ave. You can take this straight to JFK. It's direct and fairly simple. You can get to Atlantic Ave. from any of the three downtown bridges (look at a map first, though!) From midtown, you can take the Queens Midtown Tunnel to the Long Island Expressway to the Van Wyck Expressway South (there's never much traffic on the LIE, of course...). From uptown, you can take the Triboro Bridge to the Grand Central Parkway to the Van Wyck Expressway South.

How to Get There—Mass Transit

This is your chance to finish "War and Peace." Take the A train going to Far Rockaway. When you arrive at the Howard Beach/JFK Airport stop 17 hours later, you can take the free JFK shuttle bus (which does run pretty often). A better option is to take a bus from either Grand Central or the Port Authority on either Olympia (or New York Airport Service Express (buses for $11-13).

How to Get There—Car Services

Two words: Car Service. Call them, they'll pick you up at your door, drop you at the terminal, and you're done. Some car services are: Allstate Car and Limousine: 212-333-3333 ($39 + tolls from Union Square before 7 p.m., $30 + tolls after 7 p.m.); SABRA: 212-777-7171 ($32 + tolls from Union Square; best to call in the morning); Tel Aviv: 212-777-7777 ($32 +tolls from Union Square; $37 + tolls from 3 p.m. to 6 p.m.).

Parking

Public parking rates are similar to LaGuardia's and actually cheaper for long-term parking. Rates are $2 for the first half-hour, $4 for up to 2 hours, $2 for every hour after that, and $24 per day. Long-term parking is $8 per day.

● Rental Cars (on-Airport)

1. Avis, 718-244-5200
2. Budget, 718-656-6010
3. Dollar, 718-656-220
4. Hertz, 718-656-7600
5. National, 718-632-8300

Phone Numbers

Recorded Information: 718-244-4444
Police/ Lost and Found: 718-244-4225/6
Medical Services: 718-656-5344
Radio Station: 530 AM (traffic updates near airport)
Website: www.panynj.gov/aviation/jfkmain.htm

H Hotels

1. Four Points Sheraton • 151-20 Baisley Blvd • 718-489-1000
2. Hilton JFK Airport • 138-10 135th Ave•718-322-8700
3. Holiday Inn JFK Airport • 144-02 135th Ave • 718-659-0200
4. Pan American Hotel • 79-00 Queens Blvd • 718-446-7676
5. Ramada Plaza Hotel • Van Wyck Expwy • 718-995-9000

Directory Assistance-TRANSIT

La Guardia Airport

Airlines by Terminal:

CENTRAL-A
Air Canada 800-776-3000
America West 800-235-9292
Continental 800-523-3273
Continental Express 800-523-3273

CENTRAL-B
Colgan 800-272-5488

CENTRAL-C
Air Tran Airlines 800-247-8726
ATA 800-435-9282
Frontier Airlines 800-432-1359
Midwest Express 800-452-2022
Spirit 800-772-7117
TWA 800-221-2000
United 800-241-6522
United Express 800-241-6522

CENTRAL-D
American 800-433-7300
Canadian Airlines 800-426-7000
Midway 800-446-4392

DELTA
Delta 800-221-1212
Delta Connection 900-221-1212
Northwest 800-225-2525

US AIRWAYS
US Airways
US Airways Express

US AIRWAYS SHUTTLE
US Airways Shuttle

MARINE
Delta Shuttle 800-221-1212

PHONE NUMBERS
Recorded Info: 718-533-3400
Lost and Found: 718-533-3935
Police Emergency: 718-533-3900
Website: http://www.panynj.gov/aviation/lgaframe.HTM

La Guardia Airport

The best thing we can say about LaGuardia Airport is that it is named for a most excellent (and, unfortunately, dead) New York City mayor, Fiorello LaGuardia. After that, it's pretty much all downhill, except for its easy access (by car) to a major highway, the Grand Central Parkway. LaGuardia is inconvenient to public transportation, since the nearest subway station is miles away. And it has almost no amenities once you're there: The food is gross, the bookstore's been closed for two years, and you can't even get to the gate to greet your loved ones—you've got to wait in an uncomfortable passageway with no seating, or get mobbed along with all the car-service hacks downstairs at the baggage belts. However, it's many miles closer to the city than Kennedy, especially from the Upper West or Upper East Sides. In the end, though, saying it's better than Kennedy is hardly a compliment.

How to Get There-Driving

LaGuardia is mere inches away from the Grand Central Parkway, which can be reached from both the Brooklyn-Queens Expressway (BQE) or from the Triboro Bridge. From lower Manhattan, take the Brooklyn, Manhattan, or Williamsburg bridge to the BQE to the Grand Central Parkway East. From midtown Manhattan, take the FDR Drive to the Triboro to the Grand Central. A potential alternate route (and money-saver) would be to take the 59th Street Bridge to 21st Street North in Queens. Once you're heading north on 21st Street, you can make a right on Astoria Boulevard and follow it all the way to 94th Street, where you can make a left and go straight into LaGuardia. This can be used if the FDR and/or the BQE is jammed, though that probably means that the 59th Street Bridge won't be much better.

How to Get There-Mass Transit

Alas, no subway line goes to LaGuardia (although there should be one that runs across 96th Street in Manhattan, through Astoria, and ending at LaGuardia—but that's another story). The closest the subway gets is the 7/E/F/G/R Jackson Heights/Roosevelt Ave/74th Street stop in Queens, where you can then transfer to the Q33 bus that goes to LaGuardia. Sound exciting? It stinks, actually. A better bet would be to pay the extra few bucks and take the New York Airport Service Express Bus ($10) from Grand Central Station. It runs every 15-30 minutes, only takes half an hour, and doesn't stop anywhere else. You can get it on Park Avenue between 41st and 42nd streets. It also runs from Penn Station and the Port Authority Bus Terminal. A taxi will cost you at least $20.

How to Get There-Really

Two words: Car Service. Call them, they'll pick you up at your door, drop you at the terminal, and you're done. Some car services are: Allstate Car and Limousine: 212-333-3333 (20 + tolls from Union Square); SABRA: 212-777-7171 ($20 + tolls from Union Square; best to call in the morning); Tel Aviv: 212-777-7777 ($20 +tolls from Union Square after 6 p.m.; $25 + tolls before 6 p.m.).

Parking

Typically usurious, parking rates at LaGuardia are $2 for the first half-hour, $4 for up to 2 hours, $2 for every hour after that, and $24 per day. Long-term parking is $24 maximum for the first day and then $10 per day thereafter.

Rental Cars

① Avis • LGA • 800-831-2847
② Budget • 83-34 23rd Ave. • 800-527-0700
③ Dollar • 90-05 25th Ave. • 718-779-5600
④ Enterprise • 104-04 Ditmars Blvd. • 718-457-2900
⑤ Hertz • LGA • 800-654-3131
⑥ National • Ditmars Blvd. & 95th St. • 800-227-7368

Hotels

① Airway Motor Inn • 82-80 Astoria Blvd. • 718-565-5100
② Kings Inn • 87-02 23rd Ave. • 718-672-7900
③ Marriott Hotel • 102-05 Ditmars Blvd. • 718-565-8900
④ Quality Motor Inn • 94-00 Ditmars Blvd. • 718-335-1200
⑤ Skyway Motel • 102-10 Ditmars Blvd. • 718-899-6900
⑥ Westway • 71-11 Astoria Blvd. • 718-274-2800

Directory Assistance-TRANSIT

Newark Airport

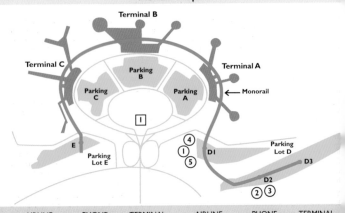

AIRLINE	PHONE	TERMINAL departure	arrival	AIRLINE	PHONE	TERMINAL departure	arrival
Aer Lingus	888-474-7424	A	B	Korean Air	800-438-5000	B	B
Air Alliance	800-776-3000	A	A	Lot Polish	800-528-7208	B	B
Air Aruba	800-882-7822	B	B	Lufthansa	800-645-3880	B	B
Air Canada	800-776-3000	A	A	Malaysia	800-552-9264	B	B
Air France	800-237-2747	C	B	Martinair (Seasonal)	800-627-8462	A	B
Air Jamaica	800-523-5585	B	B	Mexicana	800-531-7921	B	B
Air Nova	800-776-3000	A	A	Miami Air	305-871-3300	B	B
Alitalia	800-223-5730	C	B	Midway	800-446-4392	A	A
Allegro Airlines	800-915-7351	B	B	Midwest Express	800-452-2022	B	B
America West	800-235-9292	C	C	Myrtle Beach Jet Exp.	800-386-2786	B	B
American (Dom.)	800-433-7300	A	A	North American	718-656-2650	B	B
American (Intl.)	800-433-7300	A	B	Northwest/KLM	800-225-2525	B	B
ATA	800-435-9282	B	B	Pro Air	888-477-6247	A	A
Avianca	800-284-2622	B	B	Royal Air (Seasonal)	800-344-6726	B	B
British Airways	800-247-9297	B	B	SAS	800-221-2350	B	B
Colgan Air	800-272-5488	A	A	Singapore Airlines	800-742-3333	B	B
Continental (London)	800-231-0856	B	B	Sky Trek	609-671-0220	B	B
Continental (Dom.)	800-523-3273	C	C	Sunjet International	800-478-6538	A	A
Continental O'Hare/Atl.	800-523-3273	A	C	Swissair	800-221-4750	B	B
Continental Express	800-523-3273	C	C	Tap Air Portugal	800-221-7370	B	B
Continental (Intl.)	800-231-0856	C	B	TWA	800-892-2000	A	A
Czech Airlines	212-765-6022	B	B	United (Dom.)	800-241-6522	A	A
Delta	800-221-1212	B	B	United (Intl.)	800-241-6522	A	A
Delta Express	800-221-1212	B	B	United Express	800-241-6522	A	A
El Al	800-223-6700	B	B	US Airways	800-428-4322	A	A
Ethiopian Airlines	212-867-0095	B	B	US Airways Express	800-428-4322	A	A
Eva Airways	800-695-1188	B	B	VASP	800-900-8277	C	B
Kiwi	800-538-5494	A	A	Virgin Atlantic	800-862-8621	B	B
KLM	800-374-7747	B	B				

Newark Airport

Newark Airport is easily the nicest of the three major metropolitan airports. A new monorail that efficiently connects terminals and the availability of actual human food in its food court makes a layover in Newark much more palatable than one in La Guardia or Kennedy. And Newark's burgeoning international connections are increasing its popularity. And Countrafy to popular belief, Newark is just as close to Manhattan as JFK is.

How to Get There–Driving

By car, the route to Newark Airport is easy—just take either the Holland Tunnel or the Lincoln Tunnel to the New Jersey Turnpike South. You can use either Exit 14 or Exit 13A. If possible, check a traffic report before leaving Manhattan—sometimes there are viciously long tie-ups, especially at the Holland Tunnel. It's always worth it to see which outbound tunnel has the shortest wait.

How to Get There–Mass Transit

If you're allergic to traffic, try taking New Jersey Transit trains which go right into Newark's Penn Station from Penn Station in New York. However, if you're leaving from downtown Manhattan, a clever alternative is to take the PATH train from the World Trade Center to Newark's Penn Station. Once there, frequent buses and cheap taxis will get you to the airport within twenty minutes.

You can also take direct buses from Port Authority Bus Terminal (which has the advantage of a bus-only lane running right out of it into the Lincoln Tunnel), Grand Central Terminal, and Penn Station (the New York version) on Olympia (for $10). A taxi will cost you close to $40.

How to Get There–Car Services

Car services are always the simplest option, although they're a bit more expensive for Newark Airport than they are for La Guardia. Some car services are: Allstate Car and Limousine: 212-333-3333 ($32 + tolls from Union Square); SABRA: 212-777-7171 ($30 + tolls from Union Square; best to call in the morning); Tel Aviv: 212-777-7777 ($30 + tolls from Union Square between 6 p.m. and 3 p.m.; $35 + tolls between 3 p.m. and 6 p.m.).

Parking

Regular parking rates are $2 for the first half-hour, $4 for up to 2 hours, $2 for every hour after that, and $24 per day. Long-term parking $12 per day for monorail–serviced lots (recommended if they're not full). Parking lots G and H are a lot farther away, are only serviced by a shuttle bus and are $8 per day.

Rental Cars (on-Airport)

1) Avis, 800-831-2847
2) Budget, 800-527-0700
3) Dollar, 973-824-2002
4) Hertz, 800-654-3131
5) National, 800-227-7368

Phone Numbers

Recorded Information: 973-961-6000
Police/Lost and Found : 201-961-6230
Medical Services : 201-961-2525
Radio Station: 530 AM (traffic reports near airport)
Website: www.panynj.gov/aviation/ewrframe.HTM

Hotel (on-Airport)

☐ Marriott Hotel, 973-623-0006

Directory Assistance-TRANSIT

Driving in Manhattan

Driving in Manhattan

Hardware requirements: Small, durable car with big, wide tires. New York plates. Plenty of dents and scratches. Loud, obnoxious horn. Stick shift. Semi-automatic tripod-mounted tommy gun.

Software requirements: NFT. Hagstrom 5-Borough Atlas. EZ-Pass. Sweet 'n Low. Fix-a-flat can.

Basic rules: Never look in your rear-view mirror.
        Always assume that the cab that looks like it's about to cut you off, will.
        Always assume that the bus that looks like it's about to cut you off, will.
        Never, ever pull into an intersection unless you're SURE you can make it all the
        way through before the light turns red.
        Never let them see the whites of your eyes.

But seriously, driving in Manhattan is not for the timid, clueless, or otherwise emotionally fragile. Following are some tips that we've encountered over the years:

Hudson River Crossings

The George Washington Bridge is by far the best Hudson River crossing. It's got more lanes and better access than the two crappy tunnels. If you're going anywhere in the country that's north of central New Jersey, take it. The Lincoln Tunnel is pretty good inbound, but check 1010 AM (WINS) if you have the chance—even though they can be horribly inaccurate and frustrating. If you have to take the Holland Tunnel, try the Broome Street approach.

East River Crossings

Brooklyn

Pearl Street to the Brooklyn Bridge is the least-known approach to the Brooklyn Bridge. Only the Williamsburg Bridge has direct access (i.e. no traffic lights) to the northbound BQE in Brooklyn, and only the Brooklyn Bridge has direct access to the FDR Drive in Manhattan. Again, listen to the radio if you can but all three bridges can suck hard simultaneously, especially since all are perpetually being worked on. The Williamsburg Bridge's reconstruction, when complete, may become the best route into Brooklyn, but it will never be great for coming into Manhattan since all lanes spill out onto Delancey Street and immediately hit a row of traffic lights. Your best option to go anywhere in Brooklyn is usually the Brooklyn-Battery Tunnel, which can be reached from the FDR. It's not free ($3.50) but you've got EZ-Pass anyway (if you're not a schmuck).

Queens

There are three options for crossing into Queens by car. The Queens Midtown Tunnel is under construction and is usually miserable, since it feeds directly onto the always-busy Long Island Expressway The 59th Street bridge is the only free crossing to Queens. The best approach to it is First Avenue to 57th Street. If you're in Queens and want to go downtown in Manhattan, you can take the lower level of the 59th Street Bridge since it will feed directly onto 2nd Avenue, which of course goes downtown. The Triborough Bridge is usually the best option (especially if you're going to LaGuardia, Shea, or Astoria for Greek food). The FDR to the Triborough is good except for rush hour—then try 3rd Avenue to 124th Street.

Harlem River Crossings

The Triborough ($3.50) will also get you to The Bronx in pretty good shape, especially if you're then heading east on the Bruckner to go towards 95 or the Hutchinson (which will take you to eastern Westchester and Connecticut). To get to Yankee Stadium, take the Willis or the Macomb's Dam (which

Driving in Manhattan

are both free). The Henry Hudson Bridge will take you up to western Westchester along the Hudson, and, except for the antiquated and completely unnecessary toll plaza, is pretty good. Always attempt to avoid the Cross Bronx Expressway at all costs.

Manhattan's "Highways"

There are two so-called highways in Manhattan, the Harlem River Drive/FDR Drive (which prohibits commercial vehicles), and the Henry Hudson Parkway/West Side Highway. The main advantage of the FDR is that it has no traffic lights, while the West Side Highway has lights from Battery Park up through 57th Street. If there's been a lot of rain, both highways will flood so you're out of luck. We also think that FDR Drive drivers are one percent better than West Side Highway drivers.

Driving Uptown

The 96th Street transverse across Central Park is usually the best one. If you're driving on the West Side, Riverside Drive is the best route, followed next by West End Avenue. People drive like morons on Broadway, and Columbus jams up Columbus Circle. Amsterdam is a good uptown route if you can get to it. For the East Side, you can take Fifth Avenue downtown to about 65th Street, whereupon you should bail out and cut over to Park Avenue for the rest of the trip. The 96th Street entrance to the FDR screws up First and Third Avenues going north and the 59th Street Bridge screws up Lexington and Second Avenues going downtown. Getting stuck in 59th Street Bridge traffic is one of the most frustrating things in the universe because there is absolutely no way out of it.

Driving in Midtown

Good luck! Sometimes, Broadway is best because everyone's trying to get out of Manhattan, jamming up the West Side (via the Lincoln Tunnel) and the East Side (via the 59th Street Bridge and the Queens Midtown Tunnel). The "interior" city is the last place to get jammed up—it's surprisingly quiet at 8 a.m. At 10 a.m., however, it's a parking lot.

Driving in the Village

If you're coming into the Village from the northwest, 14th Street is the safest crosstown route heading east. However, going west, take 13th Street. Houston Street is usually okay in both directions and has the great benefit of having direct access to the FDR Drive, both getting onto it and coming off of it. If you want to get to Houston Street from the Holland Tunnel, take Hudson Street to King Street to the Avenue of the Americas to Houston Street (this is the ONLY efficient way to get to the Village from the Holland Tunnel). First Avenue is good going north and 5th Avenue is good going south. Washington Street is the only way to make any headway in the West Village.

Driving Downtown

Don't do it unless you have to. Western Tribeca is okay and so is the Lower East Side—try not to "turn in" to Soho, Chinatown, or City Center unless you have to. Canal Street is a complete mess during the day (avoid it at all costs), since on its western end everyone is trying to get to the Holland Tunnel, and on its eastern end everyone is mistakenly driving over the Manhattan Bridge (your only other option when heading east on Canal is to turn RIGHT on the Bowery!)

General Information

EZ-PASS Information: 800-333-TOLL
Radio Station Traffic Updates: 1010 WINS
DOT Website: http://www.ci.nyc.ny.us/html/dot/html/travroad/travroad.html
Real-Time Web Traffic Information: www.metrocommute.com

Directory Assistance-TRANSIT

Parking in Manhattan

Information:
Department of Transportation: (DOT): (212) 225-5368 (24 hours)
TTY Deaf or Hearing-Impaired: (212) 442-9488
Website:www.ci.nyc.ny.us/calldot
Parking Violations Help Line: (718) 422-7800
TTY Automated Information for the Hearing Impaired: (718) 802-3555
Website: www.ci.nyc.ny.us/finance
A Hernate Side Parking Suspension Calender

Parking Meter Zones
All No Parking signs in meter zones are suspended on ASP and MLH days; however, coins must be deposited during posted hours.

Meters
At a broken meter, parking is allowed ONLY up to one hour (60 minutes). Where a meter is missing, parking is still allowed for the maximum time on the posted sign. (An hour for a one-hour meter, 2 hours for a two-hour meter, etc.).

Signs
New York City Traffic Rules state that one sign per block is sufficient. Check the entire block and read all signs carefully before you park. Then read them again.

If there is more than one sign posted for the same area, the more restrictive one is the one in effect (of course). If a sign is missing on a block, the remaining posted regulations are the ones that are in effect.

The Blue Zone
The Blue Zone is a "No Parking" (Mon-Fri 7am - 7pm) area in lower Manhattan. Its perimeter has been designated with blue paint; however, there are no individual "Blue Zone" signs posted. Any other signs posted in that area supersede Blue Zone regulations. Confused yet??

General
- All of NYC was designated a Tow Away Zone under the State's Vehicle & Traffic Law and the NYC Traffic Rules. This means that any vehicle parked or operated illegally, or with missing or expired registration or inspection stickers, may and probably will be towed.

- On major legal holidays stopping, standing and parking are permitted except in areas where stopping, standing and parking rules are in effect seven days a week (for example, "No Standing Anytime").

- Double parking of passenger vehicles is illegal at all times, including street cleaning days, regardless of location, purpose or duration. Everyone of course does this anyway.

- It is illegal to park within 15 feet of either side of a fire hydrant. The painted curbs at hydrant locations do not indicate where you can park. Isn't New York great?

- If you think you're parked legally in Manhattan, you're probably not, so go and read the signs again.

Parking in Manhattan

HOLIDAY	DATE	RULES
NEW YEAR'S DAY	1/1/00 (Sat)	MHL
Martin Luther King, Jr.'s Birthday	1/15 (Sat)	ASP
Martin Luther King, Jr.'s Birthday (Observed)	1/17 (Mon)	ASP
Idul-Fitr, 1st/2nd/3rd Day	1/8-9 (Sat-Mon)	ASP
Lincoln's Birthday	2/12 (Sat)	ASP
Washington Birthday	2/22 (Tue)	ASP
Idul Adha 1st/2nd/3rd Day	3/16-18 (Thur-Sat)	ASP
Holy Thursday	4/20 (Thur)	ASP
Good Friday	4/21 (Fri)	ASP
Passover, 1st/2nd Day	4/8-9 (Sat-Sun)	ASP
Passover, 7th/8th Day	4/14-15 (Sat-Sun)	ASP
Holy Thursday (Orthodox)	4/27 (Thur)	ASP
Good Friday (Orthodox)	4/28 (Fri)	ASP
Solemnity of Ascension	6/1 (Thur)	ASP
Shavout, 1st/2nd Day	5/28-29 (Sun-Mon)	ASP
MEMORIAL DAY	5/30 (Tue)	MHL
INDEPENDENCE DAY	7/4 (Tue)	MHL
Assumption of Blessed Virgin	8/15 (Tue)	ASP
Labor Day	9/4 (Mon)	MHL
Rosh Hashanah, 1st/2nd Day	9/30-10/1 (Sat-Sun)	ASP
Yom Kippur	10/9 (Sun)	ASP
Succoth, 1st/2nd Day	10/14-15 (Sat-Sun)	ASP
Shemini Atzereth	10/21 (Sat)	ASP
Simchas Torah	10/22 (Sun)	ASP
Columbus Day	10/9 (Mon)	ASP
All Saints Day	11/1 (Wed)	ASP
Election Day	11/7 (Tue)	ASP
Veterans Day (Observed)	11/10 (Fri)	ASP
Veterans Day	11/11 (Sat)	ASP
Thanksgiving Day	11/23 (Thur)	MHL
Immaculate Conception	12/8 (Fri)	ASP
CHRISTMAS DAY	12/25 (Mon)	MHL

- **Street Cleaning Rules (SCR)**
  Most SCR signs are clearly marked with the " P " symbol with the broom through it. Some SCR signs are the traditional 3-hour ones ("8am to 11am" etc.) but many others vary considerably. Check the times before you park. Then check them again.

- **Alternate Side Parking Suspended (ASP)**
  No Parking signs in effect one day a week or on alternate days are suspended on days designated ASP; however, all No Stopping and No Standing signs remain in effect.

- **Major Legal Holiday Rules in Effect (MLH)**
  No Parking and No Standing signs that are in effect fewer than 7 days a week are suspended on days designated MLH in the above calendar.

Directory Assistance-TRANSIT

Bus Lines

General Information on the Bus System

Phone Number: 718-330-1234

website: www.mta.nyc.nyus

Fare: $1.50 per trip, but there are

Metrocard discounts available

Times: 24/7, just like we like it

Ridership: 1.2 million people per day
600 million people per year

1 — 5 & Madison Avs
2 — 5 & Madison Avs/Powell Blvd
2 — 5 & Madison Avs/Powell Blvd
3 — 5 & Madison Avs/St Nicholas Av
4 — 5 & Madison Avs/Broadway
5 — 5 Av/Av of Americas/Riverside Dr
5 — 5 Av/Av of Americas/Riverside Dr
6 — 7 Av/Broadway/Av of Americas
7 — Columbus/Amsterdam/Lenox/6/7Avs/B'way
8 — 8/9 Sts Crosstown
9 — Av B/E Broadway
10 — 7/8 Avs(Cent Pk w)/.Douglass Blvd
11 — 9(Columbus)& 10 (Amsterdam) Avs
14 — 14 St Crosstown
14 — 14 St Crosstown
15 — 1/2 Avs
15 — 1/2 Avs
16 — 34 St Crosstown
18 — Convent Av
21 — Houston St/Av C
22 — Madison/Chambers Sts
23 — 23 St Crosstown
27 — 49/50 Sts Crosstown
30 — 52/72 Sts Crosstown

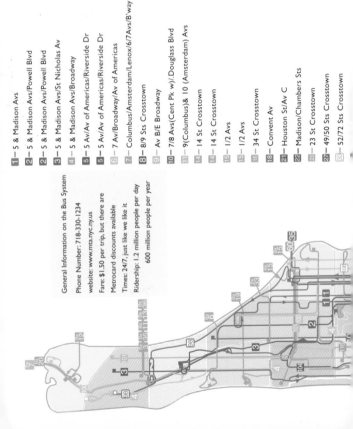

Bus Lines

New York's bus system is pretty good and gets better every year, as more new buses are added—some with clean air technology, even. However, you're likely to only get nauseous (as opposed to home) if you plan on riding the bus very far during the rush hour. The MTA's website publishes a constantly updated list of all temporary and permanent route changes, which occur quite frequently,

M15 — 34 St Crosstown
M35 — Randall's/Ward's Island
42 — 42 St Crosstown
M50 — 49/50 Sts Crosstown
57 — 57 St Crosstown
M60 — Laguardia Airport via 125 St
M66 — 66/67 Sts Crosstown
72 — 72 St Crosstown
79 — 79 St Crosstown
M86 — 86 St Crosstown
96 — 96 St Crosstown
M98 — Washington Heights/Midtown
101 — Amsterdam Av/Broadway/125 St
102 — 3/Lexington/Amsterdam Avs
102 — 3/Lexington/Amsterdam Avs
102 — 3/Lexington Avs/Malcolm X Blvd
103 — 3/Lexington Avs
104 — Broadway/42 St
106 — 96/106 St Crosstown
Bx6 — 116 St Crosstown
Bx6 — E 161/E 163 Sts
7 — Riverdale Av/Broadway
M5 — 125 St Crosstown
19 — 145 St Crosstown
32 — Penn Station-Jackson Heights

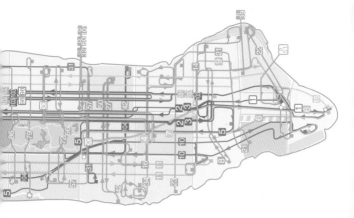

Directory Assistance-TRANSIT

Subway

General Information on the Subway

Phone Number: 718-330-1234

website: www.mta.nyc.nyus

Fare: $1.50 per trip, but there are

Metrocard discounts available

Times: 24/7, just like we like it

every 2-5 minutes during rush hour

every 5-12 minutes non-rush-hour

every 20 minutes overnight

Ridership: 4 million people per day

1.2 billion people per year

F — 6th Ave. Local
- Lexington Ave.
- 5th Ave.
- 47-50 St · Rock Ctr
- 42 St
- 34 St · Herald Sq
- 23 St
- West 4 St
- B'way-Lafayette
- 2nd Ave.
- Delancey St
- East Broadway

N R — Broadway Local
- Lexington Ave.
- 5th Ave.
- 57 St
- 49 St
- 42 St · Times Sq.
- 34 St · Herald Sq.
- 28 St
- 23 St
- 14 St · Union Sq.
- 8 St · NYU
- Prince St
- Canal St
- City Hall
- Cortlandt St
- Rector St
- Whitehall · So Ferry

J M — Nassau St Exp
- Essex St
- Bowery
- Chambers St
- Canal St
- Fulton St · B'way Nassau
- Broad St

Z — Nassau St Local
- Essex St
- Chambers St
- Fulton St · B'way Nassau
- Broad St

E — WTC
- Fulton St · B'way Nassau

E — 8th Ave. Local
- 5th Ave.
- 7th Ave.
- 50 St
- 42 St · Port Authority
- 34 St · Penn Station
- 23 St
- 14 St
- West 4 St
- Spring St
- Canal St
- WTC

B — 6th Ave. Express
- 155 St
- 145 St
- 135 St
- 125 St
- 116 St
- 110 St · Cathedral Pwy
- 103 St
- 96 St
- 86 St
- 81 St
- 72 St
- 59 St · Columbus Circ
- 7th Avenue

B D — 6th Ave. Express
- 47-50 Sts · Rock Ctr
- 42 St
- 34 St · Herald Sq
- West 4 St
- Broadway-Lafayette
- Grand St

D — 6th Ave. Express
- 155 St
- 145 St
- 125 St
- 59 St · Columbus Circ
- 7th Ave.

A — 8th Ave. Express
- 207 St · Inwood
- Dyckman St
- 190 St
- 181 St
- 175 St
- 168 St
- 163 St
- 155 St
- 145 St
- 125 St
- 59 St · Columbus Circ
- 42 St · Port Authority
- 34 St · Penn Station
- 14 St
- West 4 St
- Canal St
- Chambers St
- Fulton St · B'way Nassau

8th Ave. Local
- 168 St
- 163 St
- 155 St
- 145 St
- 135 St
- 125 St
- 116 St
- 110 St · Cathedral Pwy
- 103 St
- 96 St
- 86 St
- 81 St
- 72 St
- 59 St · Columbus Circle
- 50 St
- 42 St · Port Authority
- 34 St · Penn Station
- 23 St
- 14 St
- West 4 St
- Spring St
- Canal St
- Chambers St

Subway

6 Lexington Ave. Local
125 St
116 St
110 St
103 St
96 St
86 St
77 St
68 St
59 St
42 St • Grand Central
33 St
28 St
23 St
14 St • Union Sq
Astor Place
Bleecker St
Spring St
Canal St
B'lyn Bridge•City Hall

3 7th Ave. Express
Harlem St
148 St
145 St

2 7th Ave. Express
135 St
125 St
116 St
110 St
96 St
72 St
42 St • Times Sq
34 St • Penn Station
14 St
Chambers St
Park Place
Fulton St
Wall St

L 14 St-Canarsie Local
8th Ave.
6th Ave.
14 St • Union Sq
3rd Ave.
1st Ave.

S 42 St Shuttle
42 St • Times Sq
42 St • Grand Central

7 Flushing Local
42 St • Times Sq
5 Ave.
42 St • Grand Central

4 5 Lexington Ave. Express
125 St
86 St
59 St
42 St•Grand Central
14 St • Union Sq
B'lyn Bridge • Ciry Hall
Fulton St• B'way Nassau
Wall St
Bowling Green

Other than the incredibly obvious need for another east side line (running down First Ave. to the Lower East Side), the MTA has Manhattan covered pretty well. The simultaneous renovation of many of Manhattan's stations, and the introduction of the Metrocard, have improved the MTA's relations with its ridership, which continues to grow each year. Notes for the future, though: higher ceilings (DC), vending machines (Paris), ETA readouts (London), air-conditioned platforms, continuous cleaning staff, etc. etc. etc.

1 B'way/7 Ave Local
215 St
207 St
Dyckman St
191 St
181 St
168 St
157 St
145 St

9 B'way/7 Ave Local
207 St
191 St
181 St
168 St
145 St

1 9 B'way/7 Ave Local
137 St
125 St
116 St • Columbia U
110 St • Cathedral Pkwy
103 St
96 St
86 St
79 St
72 St
66 St • Lincoln Ct
59 St • Columbus Circ
50 St
42 St • Times Sq
34 St • Penn Sta
28 St
23 St
18 St
14 St
Christopher St
Houston St
Franklin St
Canal St
Chambers St
Cortlandt St
Rector St
South Ferry

Directory Assistance-TRANSIT

LIRR Railroad

General Information: New York City (718) 217-LIRR
Nassau County (516) 822-LIRR
Suffolk County (516) 231-LIRR
TDD (Hearing Impaired) (718) 558-3022
Group Travel and Tours (M-F 8AM-4PM): (718) 558-7498
Mail and Ride (Toll Free): (800) 649-NYNY
Public Affairs (Weekdays 9AM-5PM): (718) 558-8228
MTA Police Eastern Region: (718) 558-3300 or (516) 733-3900
Lost & Found (Weekdays 7:20AM - 7:20PM): (212) 643-5228
Ticket Refunds: (718) 558- 488
Ticket Vending Machine Assistance: (800) 325-LIRR

LIRR Railroad

The Long Island Railroad is the busiest commuter railroad in North America. It has nine main lines and 124 stations stretching from Montauk Point to Manhattan, covering Nassau and Suffolk counties as well as Brooklyn and Queens. If you enjoy traveling on overcrowded, smelly, late trains with intermittent air conditioning, then the LIRR is for you. For further information check out www.ihatethelirr.com or the somewhat tamer site, www.geocities.com/RodeoDrive/Mall/4322.

Fares and Schedules

Fares and schedules can be easily obtained at Penn Station or by calling (718) 217 LIRR. You can also check out their website. If you wait to pay until you are on the train you will have to pay an extra two dollars. The LIRR is a commuter railroad so there is a choice of weekly or monthly passes as well as off-peak ten trips (for trains traveling at non-rush hour times) and on-peak ten trips (for trains traveling at rush hour times). If you are a real fancy pants and need a parlor car reservation call (718) 558 8228.

The Port Jefferson Branch
- Port Jefferson
- Stony Brook
- St. James
- Smithtown
- Kings Park
- Northport
- Greenlawn
- Huntington
- Cold Spring
- Harbor
- Syosset
- Hicksville
- Westbury
- Carle Place
- Mineola
- Merillon Avenue
- New Hyde Park
- Jamaica
- Penn Station (New York)/
- Flatbush Avenue (Brooklyn)

The Ronkonkoma Branch
- Greenport
- Southold
- Mattituck
- Riverhead
- Yaphank
- Medford
- Ronkonkoma
- Central Islip
- Brentwood
- Deer Park
- Wyandanch
- Pinelawn
- Farmingdale
- Bethpage
- Hicksville
- Jamaica
- Penn Station (New York)/
- Flatbush Avenue (Brooklyn)

The Babylon Branch
- Babylon
- Lindenhurst
- Copiague
- Amityville
- Massapequa
- Seaford
- Wantagh
- Bellmore
- Merrick
- Freeport
- Baldwin
- Rockville Centre
- Jamaica
- Penn Station (New York)/
- Flatbush Avenue (Brooklyn)

The Montauk Branch
- Montauk
- Amagansett
- East Hampton
- Bridgehampton
- Southampton
- Hampton Bays
- Westhampton
- Speonk
- Mastic-Shirley
- Bellport
- Patchogue
- Sayville
- Oakdale (Dowling College)
- Great River
- Islip
- Bay Shore
- Jamaica
- Penn Station (New York)/
- Flatbush Avenue (Brooklyn)

The Far Rockaway Branch
- Far Rockaway
- Inwood
- Lawrence
- Cedarhurst
- Woodmere
- Hewlet
- Gibson
- Valley Stream
- Rosedale
- Laurelton
- Locust Manor
- Jamaica
- Penn Station (New York)/
- Flatbush Avenue (Brooklyn)

The Port Washington Branch
- Port Washington
- Plandome
- Manhasset
- Great Neck
- Little Neck
- Douglaston
- Bayside
- Auburndale
- Broadway
- Murray Hill
- Flushing Main Street
- Woodside
- Penn Station (New York)

The Oyster Bay Branch
- Oyster Bay
- Locust Valley
- Glen Cove
- Glen Street
- Sea Cliff
- Glen Head
- Greenvale
- Roslyn
- Albertson
- East Williston
- Jamaica
- Penn Station (New York)/
- Flatbush Avenue (Brooklyn)

The Hempstead Branch
- Hempstead
- Country Life Press
- Garden City
- Nassau Boulevard
- Stewart Manor
- Floral Park
- Bellerose
- Queens Village
- Hollis
- Jamaica
- Penn Station (New York)/
- Flatbush Avenue (Brooklyn)

The West Hempstead Branch
- West Hempstead
- Hempstead Gardens
- Lakeview
- Malverne
- Westwood
- St. Albans
- Jamaica
- Penn Station (New York)/
- Flatbush Avenue (Brooklyn)

The Long Beach Branch
- Long Beach
- Island Park
- Oceanside
- East Rockaway
- Centre Avenue
- Lynbrook
- Valley Stream
- Rosedale
- Laurelton
- Locust Manor
- Jamaica
- Penn Station (New York)/
- Flatbush Avenue (Brooklyn)

Directory Assistance-TRANSIT
Metro North Railroad

General Information (NYC): 212-532-4900
General Information (All other areas): 800-638-7646
Lost and Found (Grand Central Terminal): 212-340-2555
MTA Inspector General Hotline: 800-MTA-IG4U
Website: http://www.mta.nyc.ny.us

Metro North Railroad

Metro North is an extremely accessible and efficient railroad that originates from Grand Central Station in Manhattan. Its three main lines (Hudson, Harlem, and New Haven) form one of the largest commuter railroads in the U.S. There are over 100 stations in its system, and each of the main lines travels more than 70 miles from New York City.

Fares and Schedules

Fares and schedules can be easily obtained at Grand Central Station or on Metro North's website. If you wait to pay until you are on the train, you will pay an extra two bucks, but since Metro-North is a commuter rail line, there are monthly and weekly rail passes available. For more information, use Metro-North's extraordinarily detailed website, which offers in-depth information on each station, full time tables, and excellent maps.

The Harlem Line

- Dover Plains
- Harlem Valley-Wingdale
- Appalachian Trail
- Pawling
- Patterson
- Brewster North
- Brewster
- Croton Falls
- Purdy's
- Golden's Bridge
- Katonah
- Bedford Hills
- Mt. Kisco
- Chappaqua
- Pleasantville
- Hawthorne
- Mt. Pleasant
- Valhalla
- North White Plains
- White Plains
- Hartsdale
- Scarsdale
- Crestwood
- Tuckahoe
- Bronxville
- Fleetwood
- Mount Vernon West
- Wakefield
- Woodlawn
- Williams Bridge
- Botanical Garden
- Fordham
- Tremont
- Melrose
- 125th Street
- Grand Central Station

The Hudson Line

- Poughkeepsie
- New Hamburg
- Beacon
- Breakneck Ridge
- Cold Spring
- Garrison
- Manitou
- Peekskill
- Cortlandt
- Croton-Harmon
- Ossining
- Scarborough
- Philipse Manor
- Tarrytown
- Irvington
- Ardsley
- Dobbs Ferry
- Hastings
- Greystone
- Glenwood
- Yonkers
- Ludlow
- Riverdale
- Spuyten Duyvil
- Marble Hill
- University Heights
- Morris Heights
- 125th Street
- Grand Central Station

The New Haven Line

- New Haven
- Milford
- Stratford
- Bridgeport —
  - Derby Shelton
  - Ansonia
  - Seymour
  - Beacon Falls
  - Naugatuck
  - Waterbury
- Fairfield
- Southport
- Green's Farms
- Westport
- East Norwalk
- South Norwalk —
  - Merritt 7
  - Wilton
  - Cannondale
  - Branchville
  - Redding
  - Bethel
  - Danbury
- Rowayton
- Darien
- Noroton Heights
- Stamford —
  - Glenbrook
  - Springdale
  - Talmadge Hill
  - New Canaan
- Old Greenwich
- Riverside
- Cos Cob
- Greenwich
- Port Chester
- Rye
- Harrison
- Mamaroneck
- Larchmont
- New Rochelle
- Pelham
- Mount Vernon
- Fordham
- 125th Street
- Grand Central Station

Directory Assistance-TRANSIT
NJ Transit

NJ Transit carries hundreds of thousands of New Jersey commuters to New York every morning—well, almost. The main problem is that some lines don't run directly into Penn Station—you have to transfer at Hoboken to another train. Also, while the trains are usually clean (and immune to the weirdness that plagues the LIRR), some lines (such as the Pascack Valley Line) just seem to creep along—and then you have to transfer. However, more "through" lines are in the works, as well as several other projects such as a light rail system which will service the Jersey side of the Hudson River. And while NJ Transit isn't going to compete with Japanese rail systems any time soon, it still beats waiting in traffic at the three measly Hudson River automobile crossings.

General Information: 973-762-5100
Emergency Hotline: 973-491-7400
Newark Lost and Found: 973-491-8792
Hoboken Lost and Found: 201-714-2739
New York Lost and Found: 212-630-7389
Website: www.mta.nyc.ny.us

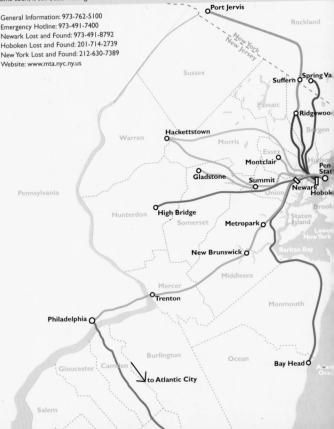

Fares and Schedules

Fares and schedules can be obtained at Hoboken, Newark, and Penn Station, or on NJ Transit's website. If you wait to pay until you're on the train, you'll pay extra for the privilege. However, NJ Transit does have monthly, weekly, weekend, and ten-trip tickets available

The Pascack Valley Line
- Spring Valley
- Nanuet
- Pearl River
- Montvale
- Park Ridge
- Woodcliff Lake
- Hillsdale
- Westwood
- Emerson
- Oradell
- River Edge
- North Hackensack
- Hackensack (Anderson Street)
- Hackensack (Essex Street)
- Teterboro
- Wood-Ridge
- Hoboken

The Port Jervis Line
- Port Jervis
- Otisville
- Middletown
- Campbell Hall
- Salisbury Mills/ Cornwall
- Harriman
- Tuxedo
- Sloatsburg
- Suffern

The Atlantic City Line
- Atlantic City
- Absecon
- Egg Harbor City
- Hammonton
- Atco
- Lindenwold
- Cherry Hill
- Philadelphia

The Northeast Corridor Line
- Philadelphia
- Trenton
- Princeton Junction
  - Princeton
- Jersey Avenue
- New Brunswick
- Edison
- Metuchen
- Metropark
- Rahway
- Linden
- Elizabeth
- North Elizabeth
- Newark
- Penn Station (New York)/ Hoboken

The Main and Bergen Lines
- Suffern
- Mahwah
- Ramsey
- Allendale
- Waldwick
- Ho-Ho-Kus
- Ridgewood
  - Glen Rock
  - Hawthorne
  - Paterson
  - Clifton
  - Passaic
  - Delawanna
  - Lyndhurst
  - Kingsland
- Glen Rock
- Radburn (Fairlawn)
- Broadway (Fairlawn)
- Plauderville
- Garfield
- Rutherford
- Harmon Cove
- Hoboken

The Boonton Line
- Hackettstown
- Mount Olive
- Netcong
- Lake Hopatcong
- Dover
- Denville
- Mountain Lakes
- Boonton
- Towaco
- Lincoln Park
- Mountain View (Wayne)
- Little Falls
- Great Notch
- Montclair Heights
- Mountain Ave. (Montclair)
- Upper Montclair
- Watchung Ave. (Montclair)
- Walnut St. (Montclair)
- Benson St. (Glen Ridge)
- Rowe St. (Bloomfield)
- Arlington (Kearny)
- Hoboken

The Raritan Valley Line
- High Bridge
- Annandale
- Lebanon
- White House
- North Branch
- Raritan
- Somerville
- Finderne
- Bridgewater
- Bound Brook
- Dunellen
- Plainfield
- Netherwood
- Fanwood
- Westfield
- Garwood
- Cranford
- Roselle Park
- Newark
- Penn Station (New York)/ Hoboken

The North Jersey Coast Line
- Bay Head
- Point Pleasant Beach
- Manasquan
- Spring Lake
- Belmar
- Bradley Beach
- Asbury Park
- Allenhurst
- Elberon
- Long Branch
- Monmouth Racetrack
- Little Silver
- Red Bank
- Middletown
- Hazlet
- Matawan
- South Amboy
- Perth Amboy
- Woodbridge
- Avenel
- Rahway
- Linden
- Elizabeth
- North Elizabeth
- Newark
- Penn Station (New York)/ Hoboken

The Morris and Essex Lines
- Hackettstown
- Mount Olive
- Netcong
- Lake Hopatcong
- Dover
- Denville
- Mt. Tabor
- Morris Plains
- Morristown
- Convent Station
- Madison
- Chatham
- Summit
  - Gladstone
  - Peapack
  - Far Hills
  - Bernardsville
  - Basking Ridge
  - Lyons
  - Millington
  - Stirling
  - Gillette
  - Berkeley Heights
  - 986 Murray Hill
  - New Providence
- Short Hills
- Millburn
- Maplewood
- South Orange
- Mountain Station
- Highland Avenue
- Orange
- Brick Church
- East Orange
- Newark
- Penn Station (New York)/ Hoboken
  - Montclair (Bay St.)
  - Glen Ridge
  - Bloomfield
  - Watsessing

Directory Assistance-TRANSIT

Grand Central Station

Grand Central Terminal, designed in the Beaux Arts style by Warren & Wetmore, is by far the most beautiful of Manhattan's major terminals; indeed, it ranks as one of the most beautiful terminals in the world. What's also nice about it is that it's convenient (located right in the heart of Midtown), newly refurbished, and utterly cool. The only bad thing is that it only services Metro North—you have to go to Penn Station for LIRR and NJ Transit trains.

The refurbishment of Grand Central has been taking place over the last few years and it seems to be going quite nicely. The star ceiling has been cleaned and modernized, a second grand staircase has been constructed, and a mall on the lower level is moving towards completion. These improvements, along with Grand Central's existing attractions (the central clock, the Oyster Bar, the catwalks) make it one of New York's most impressive buildings. It's no surprise, then, that there are THREE separate tours of Grand Central; the hour-long LaSalle Tour (212-340-3404), the Municipal Arts Society Tour (212-935-3960), and the Grand Central Partnership Tour (212-818-1777).

General Information:

NFT Grid Number: 13

Address: 42nd Street and Park Ave.

General Information: 212-935-3560

Lost and Found: 212-340-2555

Website: www.grandcentralterminal.com

MTA Subway Stops: 4, 5, 6, 7, S

MTA Bus Lines: 1, 2, 3, 4, 42, 98, 101, 102, 103, 104

Other Rail Lines: Metro North

Newark Airport Bus Service: Olympia (212-964-6233, $10)

LaGuardia Airport Bus Service: NY Airport Express (718-706-9658, $13)

JFK Airport Bus Service: NY Airport Express (718-706-9658, $10)

Year Opened: 1913

Terminal Shops:

America's Coffee
Banana Republic
Chase Bank
Children's General Store
Discovery Channel Store
Douglas Cosmetics
Eastern News
Flowers on Lexington
Godiva Chocolatier
Grand Central Optical
Grande Harvest Wines

Hudson News
Joon Stationery
Kenneth Cole
LaCrasia Gloves
Legends of the Game
L'Occitane
Michael Eigen Jewelers
New York Transit
Museum Gallery & Store
O'Henry's Film Works
Origins

Papyrus
Pink Slip
Starbucks
TOTO
The J. Peterman Company
TrainTunes
Vermont Candle Company
Watch Station
Zaro's Bread Basket

Penn Station

Penn Station, designed by McKim, Mead & White (New York's greatest architects), is a Beaux Arts treasure, filled with light and...oh, that's the one they tore down. Penn Station today is essentially a basement, only without the bowling trophies and the Johnny Walker Black.

BUT...good news seems to be coming from around the corner, in the form of a proposal to convert the eastern half of the Farley Post Office (also designed by McKim, Mead, & White) to a new, above-ground (a novel concept), light-filled station. We can't wait. Until then, Penn Station will just go on being an ugly, crappy underground terminal (citysearch.com says it has "all the charm of a salt mine") under Madison Square Garden, a terminal which services over 600,000 people per day—making it the busiest railway station in the United States.

Penn Station services Amtrak, the LIRR, and NJ Transit trains, which is admittedly a lot of responsibility. Amtrak (800-872-7245), which is surely the worst national train system of any country above the poverty line, administers the station, which may have a lot to do with the fact that it really isn't much of a station. Needless to say, we're hoping this proposal will go through—although we still won't be able to afford the ridiculously high fares that Amtrak charges to go to places like D.C., Philly, and Boston.

General Information:

Address: 7th Avenue and 33rd Street
General Information (Amtrak): 800-872-7245
MTA Subway Stops: 1, 2, 3, 9, A, C, E
MTA Bus Lines: 4, 10, 16, 34, Q32
Train Lines: LIRR, Amtrak, NJ Transit
Newark Airport Bus Service: Olympia (212-964-6233, $10)
LaGuardia Airport Bus Service: NY Airport Express (718-706-9658, $13)
JFK Airport Bus Service: NY Airport Express (718-706-9658, $10)
Passengers per day: 600,000
Year Opened: 1968

Terminal Shops:

If you like Dunkin' Donuts and $2.00 bottles of Evian from Hudson News, then Penn Station is the place for you..

Directory Assistance-TRANSIT

Port Authority Bus Terminal

The Port Authority Bus Terminal is as ugly and characterless as Grand Central Terminal is beautiful and lively. Its neighborhood is perhaps the last genuinely seedy place in Manhattan (although the Port Authority claims that its neighborhood is having a "rebirth"). The Port Authority is, however, a highly functional place, serving 187,000 passengers per day. The chart on the right shows which bus companies run out of the Port Authority and a basic description of their destinations.

Perhaps the Port Authority's saving grace is the presence of its bowling alleys and arcade. You can at least go a bowl a few frames if you've just missed your bus.

On Easter Sunday, Christmas Eve, or Thanksgiving, one can see all the angst-ridden sons and daughters of suburban New Jersey parents joyfully waiting in cramped, disgusting corridors for that nauseating bus ride back to Leonia or Morristown or Plainfield or wherever. A fascinating sight.

General Information:

NFT Grid Number: 11
Address: 41st Street and 8th Avenue
General Information: 212-564-8484
Lost and Found: are you kidding?
Website: www.panynj.gov/tbt/pabframe.HTM
MTA Subway Stops: A, C, E, 7 (Port Authority);
1, 2, 3, 9, 7, N, R, S (Times Square)
MTA Bus Lines: 10, 11, 16, 27, 42, 104
Other Bus Lines: see right-hand page
Newark Airport Bus Service: Olympia (212-964-6233, $10)
LaGuardia Airport Bus Service: NY Airport Express (718-706-9658, $13)
JFK Airport Bus Service: NY Airport Express (718-706-9658, $10)
Passengers per day: 187,000
Passengers since opening: 3 billion
Year Opened: 1950

Terminal Shops:

FOOD
Au Bon Pain
Cafe Metro
Deli Plus
Ditsch Pretzels
Green Tree
Silver Bullet Tavern
Snack on Wheels
Sweet Factory
Timothy's Coffee
Tropica Snack Bar
Worlds Fare
Zaro's Bake Shop

APPAREL
Rainbow Shops

ENTERTAINMENT
Leisure Time Bowling Center
 and Cocktail Lounge

SERVICES
ATM-Fleet
Drago Shoe Repair
Kelly the Film ExpressLab
Hudson News
Marrella Hair Stylists

U.S. Postal Service

CONVENIENCE
B.T. Books & B.T. Lotto
Duane Reade
Hallmark Cards and Gifts
Jay's Hallmark, Inc.
Saks Florist, Inc.
Sunglass Hut

Port Authority Bus Terminal

Bus Company	Phone Number	Area Served
Academy Bus Transportation	800-242-1339	Serves New York City, including Staten Island, Wall St. and Port Authority and New Jersey, including Hoboken.
Adirondack Trailways	800-858-8555	Serves all of New York State with coach connections throughout the U.S.
American Limousine	609-265-2400	Service between Port Authority and Burlington, New Jersey.
Atlantic Express Service	212-962-1122	Service between New York and New Jersey, including Atlantic City, Mammoth & Ocean Counties, South Jersey, and local service in Hudson County. Also offers service between Staten Island and Manhattan.
Bonanza Bus	800-556-3815	Serves many points between New York and New England, including Cape Cod and the Berkshires.
Capitol Bus	800-333-8444/ 800-444-2877	Service between Pennsylvania, Virginia, New York State, and New York City.
Carl Bieber Bus	800-243-2374	Service to and from Port Authority and Wall Street in New York and Redding, Cookston, Wescosville, Hellertown, and Easton in Pennsylvania.
Community Coach	800-522-4514	Service between New York City and W. Orange, Livingston, Morristown, E.Hanover, Whippany, and Floram Park, New Jersey.
DeCamp Bus	800-631-1281	Service between New York City and New Jersey, including the Meadowlands.
Greyhound Bus	800-231-2222	Services most of the U.S. and Canada.
Gray Line BusAirport Travel Info.	800-451-0455	Service offered throughout the U.S. and Canada. Also offers international trips.
Hudson Bus	201-653-2220	Serves 48 states.
Lakeland Bus	201-366-0600	Service between New York and New Jersey.
Leisure Lines	800-524-0275	Services Atlantic City to and from the Bronx/Queens/Washington Heights. Also services Rockland County, Fort Lee, and Spring Valley into Manhattan city streets, including midtown and Wall St. and Bergen County into Port Authority.
Martz Coach	800-233-8604	Service between New York and Pennsylvania.
New Jersey Transit	800-772-2222(NJ)/ 201-762-5100 (all other)	Serves New York, New Jersey, and Philadelphia.
NY Airport Service	212-964-6233	Service between Port Authority and Kennedy and LaGuardia Airports.
Olympia Trails	908-354-3330	Provides express bus service between Manhattan and Newark Airport. Makes stops all over New York City, including World Trade Center, Grand Central, and many connections with hotel shuttles.
Peter Pan Lines	800-343-9999	Serves the East, including N.H., Maine, Philly, DC. Also goes to Canada.
Pine Hill-Kingston	212-967-2900	Services New York state area.
Red Apple Transit	201-222-1062	Services Hoboken to and from New York City.
RocklandCoaches/ Red and Tan Services	201-384-2400	Services New York's Port Authority, GW bridge, and 44th and 8th streets to and from most of Bergen County and upstate New York.
ShortLine Bus	800-631-8405	Serves the New York City airports, Atlantic City, and the Hudson Valley.
Suburban Trails	732-249-1100	Offers commuter service from Central New Jersey to and from Port Authority and Wall Street. Also services between the Route 9 Corridor and New York City.
Susquehanna	800-692-6314	Service to and from New York City and Newark (Greyhound Terminal) and Summerville, New Jersey and many stops in Central Pennsylvania, ending in Williamsport and Lock Haven.
T.C.T. Transit Service	973-589-9044	Between New York City and Jersey City.
Trans-Bridge Lines	800-962-9135	Offers service between New York, Pennsylvania, and New Jersey, including Newark and Kennedy airports.

Directory Assistance-TRANSIT

Ferries, Heliports, & Marinas

Ferries/Boat Tours, Rentals, & Charters

Name	Contact Info	Grid#
Staten Island Ferry	Phone: 718-815-2628 www.ci.nyc.ny.us/html/dot/html/arndtown/ferintro.html Leaves from Battery park every half hour, and goes (obviously) to Staten Island. This service is free.	I
NY Waterway	Phone: 800-53-FERRY www.nywaterway.com This is the largest ferry service in NY. They offer many commuter routes (mostly from New Jersey), sightseeing tours, and very popular shuttles to Yankees and Mets games.	1, 10, 15
Sea Streak	Phone: 800-262-8743 www.seastreakusa.com Catamarans that go pretty fast from the highlands in NJ to Wall Street and E. 34th St.	1,10
Water Taxi	Phone: 201-985-1164 www.watertaxi.com Commuter shuttle from Jersey City and Newport Marina to the World Trade Center.	I
NY Fast Ferry	This ferry (which has no contact info) goes between Highlands, NJ and Pier 11(Wall Street) or East 34th Street, Manhattan	1,10
Circle Line	Phone: 212-563-3200 http://www.circleline.com Circle Line offers many sightseeing tours including the full island cruise (departs from pier 83 at 42nd St. -- $22, no reservations needed), and the visit to Ellis Island (departs from pier 16 at South St. Seaport --$12)	I, 11
Spirit of New York	Phone: 212-727-2789 www.spiritcruises.com Offers lunch and dinner cruises everyday. Prices start at $29.95. Leaves from Pier 61 at Chelsea Piers. Make a reservation at least one week in advance.	8
Loeb Boathouse	Phone: 212-517-2233 You can rent rowboats from April through September at The Lake in Central Park for $10 per hour ($30 cash deposit). M-F 10-5; weekends 10-6:30. No reservations needed.	Central Park
World Yacht Cruises	Phone: 212-630-8100 www.worldyacht.com These very fancy dinner cruises start at $70 per person. They leave from pier 81 (41st St.) and you need a reservation. The cruise boards at 6, sails at 7, and returns at 10.	11

Marinas/Passenger Ship Terminal

Name	Contact Info	Grid#
Surfside III	Phone: 212-336-7873 Dockage at Chelsea Piers. They have daily, weekly, and seasonal (there is a waiting list) per foot rates.	8
North Cove Yacht Harbor	Phone: 212-938-9000 www.northcoveyachts.com A very, very fancy place to park your yacht in Battery Park City.	I
NY Skyports Inc.	Phone: 212-686-4547 Located on the East River at 23rd Street. Transient Dockage is $3 per foot.	10
79th St. Marina	Phone: 212-496-2105 This dock has lots of long-term houseboat residents. It's located at 79th St. and the Hudson River.	14
Dyckman Marine Group	Phone: 212-567-5120 Transient dockage on the Hudson River at Dyckman St.	25
Passenger Ship Terminal	Phone: 212-246-5450 If Love Boat re-runs aren't enough, and you decide to go on a cruise, you'll leave from the Passenger Ship terminal. Take the West Side Highway to Piers 88-94.	11

Helicopter Services

Name	Contact Info	Grid#
Helicopter Flight Services	Phone: 212-355-080 For a minimum of $100, you can hop on a helicopter at one of three locations – E. 34th St., W. 30th St., or the South St. Heliport (pier 6). Make sure you call in advance.	13,8, 10
Liberty Helicopter Tours	Phone: 212-967-4550 Leaves from W. 30th St. or the South St. Heliport (pier 6). Prices start at $51 and you don't need a reservation. Flights depart every 15 mins from 9am-9pm everyday.	3, 8
Wall Street Helicopter	Phone: 212-943-5959 Leaves from the South St. Heliport (pier 6).	3

Empire State Building Lights

The Empire State Building (ESB), designed by the firm of Schreve, Lamb & Harmon, was built in about 14 months by a lot of very committed individuals (at least 5, we think). Its framework was constructed in an unprecedented two-month span. Much of the building was prefabricated, and assembly took place at an average rate of four-and-a-half stories per week. It's no wonder, then, that the mayor gets frustrated when it takes four years to re-do a mile-long stretch of the FDR Drive.

The ESB is a natural lightning conductor and is struck up to 500 times a year. On Valentine's Day, the chapel on the 80th floor houses a giant group wedding for all who show up. The NYC Roadrunners Club hosts an annual Run-Up, where the fastest runners have to bound up all 1,860 steps in under 11 minutes. The Mezzanine is now the scene of "New York Skyride," a giant "thrill ride" simulation of a rooftop helicopter flight, complete with a crash over Wall Street and James Doohan (Star Trek's "Scottie") as the tour guide. There are two observation areas-the open terrace on the 86th floor and the glass-enclosed 102nd floor. The ESB also has an excellent, info-packed website (www.esbnyc.com) that includes history, trivia, and a complete schedule of events.

The Lights

The top 30 floors of the ESB have automated color fluorescent lighting that is lit for holidays and other days of recognition, celebration, and memoriam. Between holidays and events, white lighting is used. The following semi-official lighting schedule lists colors from top to bottom as they appear from the street.

Lighting Schedule (for updates/changes, check www.esbnyc.com)

- January 18 • Martin Luther King, Jr. Day
- February 15 • President's Day
- February 14 • Valentine's Day
- March 17 • St. Patrick's Day
- March • Greek Independence Day
- April • Rain Forest Day
- April 10 to 13 • Spring/Easter Week
- April/May • Israel Independence Day
- May 16 • Armed Forces Day
- May 21-24 • Memorial Day
- May • Police Memorial Day
- June 14 • Flag Day
- June • Portugal Day
- June • Stonewall Anniversary/Gay Pride
- July 1 to 4 • Independence Day
- August 14 to 16 • India Independence Day
- September 3 to 6 • Labor Day
- September • Pulaski Day
- September • Breast Cancer Awareness
- October 12 • Columbus Day
- October 31 until Nov 10 • Autumn
- November 11 • Veterans' Day
- November 24 • United Nations Day
- November • German Reunification Day
- December 1 • AIDS Awareness
- December 1 to Jan 7 • Holiday Season
- December, 1st day of Hannukah • Hannukah
- December 21 • Ramadan
- Yankees • World Series win for the Yankees
- Mets • World Series win for the Mets

General Information

- General Information: 212-736-3100 or info@esbnyc.com
- Observatory Hours: 9:30 a.m. to midnight, last elevator to top is at 11:25 p.m.
- Observatory Admission: $6 for adults, $3 for military, seniors, and children aged 5-12.
- Website: www.esbnyc.com

Directory Assistance-THE ARTS

Movie Theatres

NAME	ADDRESS	PHONE #	GRID #
92nd St.Y	Lexington Ave. at 92nd St.	996-1100	17
A Different Light	151 W. 19th St.	989-4850	9
Aaron Davis Hall	W. 135th St. and Convent Ave.	650-7148	18, 21
Africa Arts Theatre Co., Inc.	660 Riverside Dr.	281-4880	21
American Museum of Natural History	Central Park West at 79th St.	769-5034	14
Angelika Film Center	18 W. Houston	995-2000	6
Anthology Film Archives	32 Second Ave.	505-5110	6
Art Greenwich	97 Greenwich Ave.	929-3350	5
Asia Society	725 Park Ave.	517-ASIA	15
Astor Place Theatre	434 Lafayette	254-4370	6
Black Star Bar	92nd Second Ave.	254-4747	6
Bryant Park Summer Film Festival	Bryant Park, bet 40th & 42nd Sts.	512-5700	12
Cine-Noir Film Society	Pink Pony, 176 Ludlow St.	253-1922	7
Cinema Classics	332 E. 11th St.	675-6692	6, 7
Cinema Village	22 E. 12th St.	924-3363	6
Cineplex Odeon: Beekman	1254 Second Ave.	737-2622	15
Cineplex Odeon: Coronet Cinemas	993 Third Ave.	505-CINE #608	13, 15
Cineplex Odeon: Encore Worldwide	340 W. 50th St.	505-CINE #610	11
Cineplex Odeon: Regency	1987 Broadway	505-CINE #585	14
Circle In The Square	1633 Broadway	581-6371(fax)	12
City Cinemas 1, 2, 3	1001 Third Ave.	753-6022	15
City Cinemas: E. 86th St.	210 E. 86th St.	777-FILM #753	17
City Cinemas: Eastside Playhouse	919 Third Ave.	777-FILM #541	13
City Cinemas: Sutton 1 & 2	205 E. 57th St.	777-FILM #635	13
City Cinemas: Village East	189 Second Ave.	777-FILM #922	6
Civita Colonia Artistica	1633 Broadway	262-7716	12
Clearview's 59th St. East	239 E. 59th St.	777-FILM #615	12, 13, 15
Clearview's 62nd & Broadway	1871 Broadway	777-FILM #864	14
Clearview's Chelsea	260 W. 23rd St.	777-FILM #597	8, 9
Clearview's Chelsea West	333 W. 23rd St.	777-FILM #597	8, 9
Clearview's First & 62nd St.	400 E. 62nd St.	777-FILM #957	15
Clearview's Metro Twin	2626 Broadway	777-FILM #609	16
Clearview's Olympia Twin	2770 Broadway	777-FILM #613	16
Clearview's Park & 86th St. Twin	125 E. 86th St.	777-FILM #604	17
Clearview's Waverly Twin	323 Sixth Ave.	777-FILM #603	5, 6
Clearview's Ziegfeld	141 W. 54th St.	777-FILM #602	12
Coliseum Theatre	Broadway at 181st St	740-1545	23, 24
Common Basis Theater	750 Eighth Ave.	302-5047	11, 12
Crown Gotham Cinema	969 Third Ave.	759-2262	13
Crown Theatres	712 Fifth Ave.	957-7900	12
Czech Center	1109 Madison Ave.	228-0830, ext. 100	15
D.G.A. Theater	110 W. 57th St.	966-3030, ext. 235	12
Embassy 1,2,3	701 Seventh Ave	730-7262	12
Fez	380 Lafayette St.	533-2680	6
Film Forum	209 W. Houston	727-8110	5, 6
Folksbiene Theatre	123 E. 55th St.	755-2231	13
French Institute	Florence Gould Hall, 55 E. 59th St.	355-6160	13, 15
Gavin Brown's Enterprise	436 W. 15th St.	627-5258	8
Goethe Institute	1014 Fifth Ave.	439-8700	15
Guggenheim Museum	1071 Fifth Ave.	423-3500	17
Guild 50th	33 W. 50th at Rockefeller Plz.	757-2406	12
Hudson River Park Conservancy	Pier 25 at North Moore St.	791-2530	2
Hudson River Park Conservancy	Pier 54 at 13th St.	791-2530	5
Instituto Cervantes	122 E. 42nd St.	689-4232	13

w York's movie scene has improved greatly over the past few years—new revival houses such as Cinema Classics, the
e-Noir Film Society, and Tonic compete with outdoor venus at Bryant Park and De Salvo Park, foreign films at the French
itute and the Goethe Institute, and the latest mega-plexes at Union Square and Kips Bay. It still ain't Paris, but it's close.

NAME	ADDRESS	PHONE #	GRID #
Japan Society	333 E. 47th St.	832-1155	13
King Juan Carlos I Center	53 Washington Sq. South	689-4232	6
La Vista	303 E. 8th St.	673-5141	7
Lincoln Plaza Cinemas	30 Lincoln Plz. at B'way & 62nd St.	757-2280	14
Loews 19th St. East	890 Broadway	50-LOEWS #858	9
Loews 84th St.	2310 Broadway	50-LOEWS #701	14, 16
Loews Astor Plaza	44th St. bet. B'way & Eighth Ave.	50-LOEWS #901	12
Loews Kips Bay	Second Ave. & 32nd St.	50-LOEWS #558	10
Loews New York Twin	1271 Second Ave.	50-LOEWS #698	15
Loews Orpheum	1538 Third Ave.	50-LOEWS #964	17
Loews State	1540 Broadway	50-LOEWS #901	12
Loews Tower East	1230 Third Ave.	50-LOEWS #704	15
Loews Village	66 Third Ave.	50-LOEWS #952	6
Manhattan Twin	220 E. 59th St.	935-6420	13
Metropolitan Museum of Art	1000 Fifth Ave.	535-7710	15
Millennium	66 E. 4th St.	673-0090	6
Morgan Library	29 E. 36th St.	685-0008	9
Museum of Modern Art	11 W. 53rd St.	708-9480	12
New Federal Theatre	292 Henry St.	353-1176	4
New Manhattan Repertory, Inc.	1650 Broadway	586-1197	12
New School	66 W. 12th St.	254-8504	6, 9
NY Comedy Film Festival	899 Lexington Ave.	774-1842	15
NY Open Cine	De Salvo Pk, Mulberry & Spring Sts.	252-3465	6
NYPL-Donnell Library Center	20 W. 53rd St.	505-7742	12
NY Society for Ethical Culture	2 W. 64th St.	923-9161	14
Nova Cinema	3589 Broadway	862-5728	21
NYU Cantor Film Center	36 E. 8th St.	998-1795	6
Nyurican Poets Café	236 E. 3rd St.	529-9329	7
Paris Theatre	4 W. 58th St.	688-3800	12
Quad Cinema	34 W. 13th St.	255-8800	6
Reading Entertainment	950 Third Ave.	521-9400	13
Schomburg Center	515 Malcolm X Blvd.	491-2200	20
Screening Room	54 Varick St.	334-2100	2
Show World	675 Eighth Ave.	414-5419	11, 12
Sony 34th St. Showplace	238 E. 34th St.	532-5544	10
Sony Lincoln Square & IMAX Theatre	1992 Broadway	336-5000	14
St. Marks in the Bowery Archives	131 E. 10th St.	533-4650	6
Symphony Space	2537 Broadway	864-1414, ext. 402	16
Thalia	250 W. 95th St.	864-7700	16
The Kitchen	512 W. 19th St.	255-5793	8
The Tripod Room	515 Greenwich	414-4282	2, 5
Tonic	107 Norfolk St.	358-7503	7
United Artists: 64th & 2nd Ave.	1210 Second Ave.	832-1670	15
United Artists: E. 85th St.	1629 First Ave.	249-5100	15, 17
United Artists: Union Sq 14th St.	Broadway at 13th St.	253-2225	6
United Artists: Criterion	1514 Broadway	354-0900	12
Void	16 Mercer St.	941-6492	2
Walter Reade Theater	70 Lincoln Ctr Plz. (65th St.)	875-5600	14
Whitney Museum	945 Madison Ave.	570-3676	15
Womens Projects & Productions	55 West End Ave.	765-1706	14
YWCA	610 Lexington Ave.	735-9717	13
Zanzibar	645 Ninth Ave.	802-7874	11

Directory Assistance-THE ARTS

Museums

Name	Address	Phone No.	Grid
Abigail Adams Smith Museum	421 E. 61st St.	838-6878	15
African American Institute	833 UN Plaza	949-5666	13
African American Wax Museum	316 W. 115th St.	678-7818	18, 19
Alternative Museum	594 Broadway	966-4444	6
American Academy of Arts & Letters	633 W. 155th St.	368-5900	21
American Bible Society Gallery and Archives	1865 Broadway	408-1236	14
American Craft Museum	40 W. 53rd St.	956-6047	12
American Geographical Society	120 Wall St.	422-5456	1
American Museum of Natural History	Central Park West at 79th St.	769-5100	14
American Numismatic Society	Broadway and 155th St.	234-3130	21
Americas Society	680 Park Ave.	249-8950	15
Asia Society	725 Park Ave.	288-6400	15
Asian American Art Centre	26 Bowery	233-2154	3, 4
Black Fashion Museum	155 W. 126th St.	666-1320	19
Carnegie Hall Museum	881 7th Ave.	903-9629	12
Chaim Gross Studio Museum	526 LaGuardia Pl.	529-4906	6
Children's Museum of Manhattan	212 W. 83rd St.	721-1234	14
Children's Museum of the Arts	182 Lafayette St.	941-9198	3, 6
Children's Museum of the Native Americans	550 W. 155th St.	283-1122	21
China Institute	125 E. 65th St.	744-8181	15
Cooper-Hewitt National Design Museum	2 E. 91st St.	849-8300	17
Czech Center	1109 Madison Ave.	288-0830	15, 17
Dahesh Museum	601 5th Ave.	759-0606	12
Dia Center for the Arts	548 and 545 W. 22nd St.	989-5566	8
Drawing Center	35 Wooster St.	219-2166	2, 6
Dyckman Farmhouse Museum	4881 Broadway	304-9422	25
El Museo del Barrio	1230 5th Ave.	831-7272	17
Ellis Island Immigration Museum	Ellis Island, via ferry at Battery Park	363-7620	1
Exit Art / The First World	548 Broadway	966-7745	6
Federal Hall	33 Liberty St.	825-6870	1, 2
Fraunces Tavern Museum	54 Pearl St.	425-1778	1
French Institute	22 E. 60th St.	355-6100	12, 13, 15
Frick Collection	1 E. 70th St.	288-0700	15
Goethe House	1014 5th Ave.	439-8700	15
Gracie Mansion	East End Ave. at 88th St.	570-4751	17
Guggenheim Museum	1071 5th Ave.	423-3500	17
Guggenheim Museum Soho	575 Broadway	423-3500	6
Guiness World Records Exhibit Hall	350 5th Ave.	947-2335	9
Hispanic Society of America	Broadway and 155th St.	926-2234	21
ICP Midtown	1133 6th Ave.	860-1777	12
International Center of Photography (ICP)	1130 5th Ave.	860-1777	17
Intrepid Sea-Air-Space Museum	Pier 86, W. 46th St. at the Hudson River	245-0072	11
Japan Society	333 E. 47th St.	752-3015	13

Museums

Name	Address	Phone No.	Grid
Jewish Museum	1109 5th Ave.	423-3230	17
Lower East Side Tenement Museum	90 Orchard St.	431-0233	4, 7
Merchant's House Museum	29 E. 4th St.	777-1089	6
Metropolitan Museum of Art	5th Ave. at 82nd St.	535-7710	15
Morris-Jumel Mansion	65 Jumel Ter.	923-8008	21, 22, 23
Museum at the Fashion Institute of Technology	7th Ave. at 27th St.	217-5800	8, 9
Museum for African Art	593 Broadway	966-1313	6
Museum of African American History and Arts	352 W. 71st St.	873-5040	14
Museum of American Illustration	128 E. 63rd St.	838-2560	15
Museum of American Financial History	28 Broadway	908-4110	1
Museum of American Folk Art	2 Lincoln Sq. (Columbus Ave. between 65 & 66 St.)	595-9533	14
Museum of Chinese in the Americas	70 Mulberry St.	619-4785	3
Museum of Jewish Heritage	Battery Park City	968-1800	BPC
Museum of Modern Art (MoMA)	11 W. 53rd St.	708-9400	12
Museum of Television and Radio	25 W. 52nd St.	621-6800	12
Museum of the American Piano	211 W. 58th St.	246-4823	11, 12
Museum of the City of New York	1220 5th Ave.	534-1672	17
National Academy of Design	1083 5th Ave.	369-4880	17
National Museum of Catholic Art & History	30 Rockefeller Plz.	957-8866	12
National Museum of the American Indian	1 Bowling Green	668-6624	1
New Museum of Contemporary Art	583 Broadway	219-1222	6
New York City Fire Museum	278 Spring St.	691-1303	2, 5
New York Historical Society	2 W. 77th St.	873-3400	14
Newseum New York	580 Madison Ave.	317-7596	12, 13
Nicholas Roerich Museum	319 W. 107th St.	864-7752	16
Ocean Liner Museum	1158 5th Ave.	369-6076	17
Pierpont Morgan Library	29 E. 36th St.	685-0008	9, 12, 13
Police Academy Museum	235 E. 20th St., 2nd Floor	477-9753	10
Rose Museum	154 W. 57th St.	247-7800	12
School of Visual Arts Museum	209 E. 23rd St.	592-2144	10
Skyscraper Museum	16 Wall St.	766-1324	1
Sony Wonder Technology Lab	550 Madison Ave.	833-8100	12, 13
South Street Seaport Museum	12 Fulton St.	748-8600	1, 2, 3
Statue of Liberty Museum	Liberty Island, via ferry at Battery Park	363-3200	1
Studio Museum in Harlem	144 W. 125th St.	864-4500	19
The Cloisters	Ft. Tryon Park	923-3700	24, 25
Ukrainian Museum	203 2nd Ave.	228-0110	6, 7, 10
Whitney Museum of American Art	945 Madison Ave.	570-3676	15
Whitney Museum of American Art at Philip Morris	120 Park Ave.	878-2550	12, 13
Yeshiva University Museum	2520 Amsterdam Ave.	960-5390	23, 24

Directory Assistance-THE ARTS

Theaters

Broadway

Theater	Address	Phone Number	Grid #
Ambassador Theatre	219 W. 49th St.	212-239-6200	12
Apollo Theater	253 W. 125th St.	212-749-5838	19
Beacon Theater	2124 Broadway	212-496-7070	14
Belasco Theater	111 W. 44th St.	212-239-6200	12
Booth Theatre	222 W. 45th St.	212-239-6200	12
Broadhurst Theatre	235 W. 44th St.	212-239-6200	12
Broadway Theater	1681 Broadway	212-239-6200	12
Brooks Atkinson Theatre	256 W. 47th St.	212-719-4099	12
Carnegie Hall	154 W. 57th St.	212-247-7800	12
Circle in the Square-Uptown	1633 Broadway	212-239-6200	12
City Center Stage II	131 W. 55th St.	212-581-1212	12
Cort Theatre	138 W. 48th St.	212-239-6200	12
Criterion Center	1530 Broadway	212-764-7903	12
Ethel Barrymore Theatre	243 W. 47th St.	212-239-6200	12
Eugene O'Neill Theatre	230 W. 49th St.	212-239-6200	12
Ford Center for the Performing Arts	214 W. 43rd St.	212-556-4750	12
Gershwin Theatre	222 W. 51st St.	212-307-4100	12
Helen Hayes Theatre	240 W. 44th St.	212-307-4100	12
Imperial Theater	249 W. 45th St.	212-239-6200	12
John Golden Theatre	252 W. 45th St.	212-239-6200	12
Judith Anderson Theatre	412 W. 42nd St.	212-564-7853	11
Kit Kat Club	124 W. 43rd St.	212-819-0377	12
Lincoln Center	Broadway & 64th St.	212-875-5000	14
Longacre Theatre	220 W. 48th St.	212-239-6200	12
Lunt-Fontanne Theatre	205 W. 46th St.	212-307-4100	12
Lyceum Theatre	149 W. 45th St.	212-239-6200	12
Majestic Theater	245 W. 44th St.	212-239-6200	12
Marquis Theatre	211 W. 45th St.	212-307-4100	12
Martin Beck Theatre	302 W. 45th St.	212-239-6200	11
Minskoff Theatre	200 W. 45th St.	212-869-0550	12
Music Box Theatre	239 W. 45th St.	212-239-6200	12
Nat Horne Theatre	9th Ave. & 42nd St.	212-279-4200	11
Nederlander Theatre	208 W. 41st St.	212-307-4100	12
Neil Simon Theatre	250 W. 52nd St.	212-307-4100	12
New Amsterdam Theatre	214 W. 42nd St.	212-307-4100	12
New Victory Theatre	209 W. 42nd St.	212-382-4000	12
Palace Theatre	1564 Broadway	212-307-4100	12
Plymouth Theatre	236 W. 45th St.	212-239-6200	12
Radio City Music Hall	1260 6th Ave.	212-247-4777	12
Richard Rodgers Theatre	226 W. 46th St.	212-221-1211	12
Royale Theatre	242 W. 45th St.	212-239-6200	12
Shubert Alley	West of B'way, b/w 44th & 45th Sts.	212-302-4111	12
Shubert Theatre	225 W. 44th St.	212-239-6200	12
St. James Theater	246 W. 44th St.	212-239-6200	12
Studio 54	524 W. 54th St.	212-239-6200	11
The Theater at Madison Square Garden	2 Pennsylvania Plz.	212-307-4111	9
Virginia Theatre	245 W. 52nd St.	212-239-6200	12
Vivian Beaumont Theatre	Lincoln Center, 150 W. 65th St.	212-362-7600	14
Walter Kerr Theatre	219 W. 48th St.	212-239-6200	12
Winter Garden Theater	1634 Broadway	212-239-6200	12

Off-Broadway & Off-Off Broadway

Theater	Address	Phone Number	Grid #
13th Street Theatre	50 W. 13th St.	212-675-6677	6
28th Street Theater	120 W. 28th St., 2nd Fl.	212-727-7765	9
29th Street Repertory Theatre	212 W. 29th St.	212-465-0575	9
47th Street Theatre	304 W. 47th St.	212-265-1086	12
74A	E. 4th St. b/w Bowery & 2nd Ave.	212-475-7710	6
78th Street Theatre Lab	236 W. 78th St.	212-873-9050	14
Access Theater, Inc.	380 Broadway, 4th Fl.	212-501-3909	2, 3
Actor's Playhouse	100 7th Ave. South	212-463-0060	5
The Actors Studio Free Theater at Raw Space	529 W. 42nd St.	212-279-4200	11
Actors Studio Theatre	432 W. 44th St.	212-757-0870	11
All Souls Unitarian Church	1157 Lexington Ave.	212-642-5068	15

Here is, as best we can figure out, all the theaters in Manhattan. the difference between "Off" and "Off-Off," you ask? Size, of course. "Off-Off" is under 100 seats, "Off" is 100-500 seats.

American Jewish Theatre	307 W. 26th St.	212-633-9797	8
American Place Theatre	111 W. 46th St.	212-840-2960	12
American Theatre of Actors	314 W. 54th St.	212-581-3044	11
Angel Orensanz Foundation Center for the Arts	172 Norfolk St.	212-780-0175	7
ArcLight Theatre	152 W. 71st St.	212-595-0355	14
Arno Ristorante	141 W. 38th St.	888-MOB-BOYS	12
Astor Place Theatre	434 Lafayette St.	212-254-4370	6
Atlantic Theater	336 W. 20th St.	212-645-1242	8
Axis Theater	1 Sheridan Sq.	212-807-9300	5
Baby Jupiter	170 Orchard St.	212-982-BABY	7
Bank Street Theater	155 Bank St.	212-633-6533	5
Barter Theatre	62 Perry St.	212-741-9466	5
Blue Heron Arts Center	121 E. 24th St.	212-886-1889	10
Blue Light Theater Co.	136 E. 13th St.	212-279-4200	7
Bouwerie Lane Theatre	330 Bowery	212-677-0060	6
Castillo Theatre	500 Greenwich St.	212-941-1234	5
CBGB's 313 Gallery	313 Bowery	212-677-0455	6
Center Stage NY	48 W. 21st St., 4th Fl.	212-929-2228	9
Centerfold Theater/West End Theatre	263 W. 86th St.	212-866-4454	16
Century Center Theatre	111 E. 15th St.	212-982-6782	10
Chelsea Playhouse	125 W. 22nd St.	212-627-7311	9
Cherry Lane Theater	38 Commerce St.	212-989-2020	5
Chicago City Limits Theatre	1105 1st Ave.	212-888-5233	15
Circle in the Square-Downtown	159 Bleecker St.	212-254-6330	6
Circle Repertory Co.	159 Bleecker St.	212-254-6330	6
Classic Stage Company (CSC Rep)	136 E. 13th St.	212-677-4210	6
Clemente Solo Velez Cultural Center	107 Suffolk St.	212-260-4080	7
Clockworks Theatre	508 E. 12th St.	212-614-0001	7
Club El Flamingo	547 W. 21st St.	212-307-4100	8
Collective Unconscious	145 Ludlow St.	212-254-5277	7
Connelly Theatre	220 E. 4th St.	212-982-2287	7
Context	28 Ave. A	212-505-2702	7
The Creative Place Theatre	750 8th Ave., Suite 602	212-332-9833	11, 12
Currican Theatre	154 W. 29th St., 2nd Fl.	212-736-2533	9
Daryl Roth Theatre	20 Union Square East at 15th St.	212-239-6200	9
Delacorte Theater	Central Park, 81st St.	212-861-7277	16
Dominion Theatre	428 Lafayette St.	212-674-4066	6
Douglas Fairbanks Theatre	432 W. 42nd St.	212-239-4321	11
Duffy Theater	1553 Broadway	212-695-3401	12
Duo Theatre	62 E. 4th St.	212-598-4320	6
Educational Alliance-Mazer Theater	197 E. Broadway	212-780-2300	4
Ensemble Studio Theatre	549 W. 52nd St.	212-247-4982	11
Expanded Arts	85 Ludlow St.	212-253-1813	4
Flatiron Theater	119 W. 23rd St.	212-330-7144	9
Flea Theatre	41 White St.	212-226-0051	2
Fools Company Space	356 W. 44th St.	212-307-6000	11
Fourth Street Theatre	83 E. 4th St.	212-726-1561	6
Franklin Furnace	112 Franklin St.	212-925-4671	2
Gramercy Theatre	127 E. 23rd St.	212-719-1300	10
Gramercy Arts Theatre	138 E. 27th St.	212-889-2850	10
Greenwich House Theater	27 Barrow St.	212-541-8441	5
Greenwich Street Theatre	547 Greenwich St.	212-255-3940	5
Grove Street Playhouse	39 Grove St.	212-741-6436	5
Hamlet of Bank St.	155 Bank St.	212-989-6445	5
Harold Clurman Theatre	412 W. 42nd St.	212-594-2370	11
Harry DeJur Playhouse	466 Grand St.	212-353-1176	4
HERE	145 6th Ave.	212-647-0202	6
House of Candles	99 Stanton Street	212-420-1466	7
Hudson Guild	441 W. 26th St.	212-760-9800	8
Ibis Supper Club	321 W. 44th St.	212-239-6200	11
Impact Theatre Company	612-614 Eighth Ave.	212-592-3172	11, 12
Independent Art Here	145 Spring St.	212-647-0202	6
Intar Theatre	420 W. 42nd St.	212-279-4200	11
Interlude Theatre	45 W. 21st St.	212-388-2260	9
Irish Arts Center	553 W. 51st St.	212-581-4125	11
Irish Repertory Theatre	133 W. 22nd St.	212-727-2737	9
J.E.T. Theatre	134 W. 26th St., 7th Fl.	212-647-8949	9
Jane Street Theatre			

Directory Assistance-THE ARTS

Theaters

at the Hotel Riverview Ballroom	113 Jane St.	212-239-6200	5
Jean Cocteau Rep.	330 Bowery	212-677-0060	5
John Houseman Theater	450 W. 42nd St.	212-967-9077	11
John Montgomery Theater	134 W. 26th St., Studio 1202	212-627-7076	9
Joseph Papp Public Theater	425 Lafayette St.	212-539-8500	6
Kaufman 92nd YMCA	1395 Lexington Ave.	212-996-1100	17
KGB	85 E. 4th St.	212-505-3360	7
The Kitchen	512 W. 19th St.	212-255-5793	8
Knitting Factory-Alterknit Theater	74 Leonard St.	212-219-3055	3
The Kraine Theater	85 E. 4th St.	212-460-0982	6, 7
La MaMa ETC.	74A E. 4th St.	212-254-6468	6, 7
Lambs Theater	130 W. 44th St.	212-997-1780	13
Lark Theatre Studio	939 8th Ave., 2nd Fl.	212-246-2676	16
Lillie Blake Auditorium at P.S. 6	45 E. 81st St.	212-737-9774	15
Lucille Lortel Theatre	121 Christopher St.	212-239-6200	5
Manhattan Class Co.	120 W. 28th St.	212-727-7722	9
Manhattan Theatre Club	311 W. 43rd St.	212-399-3000	11
Mark Goodson Theatre	2 Columbus Circle, A Level	212-841-4100	11,12
Martin R. Kaufman Theater	534 W. 42nd St.	212-279-4200	11
McGinn/Cazale Theatre	2162 Broadway	212-279-4200	14
Medicine Show Theatre	552 W. 53rd St.	212-279-4200	11
The Melting Pot Theatre at Theater 3	311 W. 43rd St.	212-279-4200	11
Metropolitan Playhouse	220a E. 4th St., 2nd Fl.	212-757-4560	7
Miller Theatre-Columbia University	200 Dodge Hall, B'way & 116th St.	212-854-7799	19
Minetta Lane Theatre	18 Minetta Lane	212-420-8000	6
Miranda Theatre	259 W. 30th St.	212-268-9829	8, 9
Mitzi E. Newhouse Theater	Lincoln Center, Broadway at 64th St.	212-362-7600	14
Musical Theatre Works	440 Lafayette St., Space 3-D	212-677-0040	6
Nada	167 Ludlow St.	212-420-1466	4
Nada 45	445 W. 45th St.	212-712-6571	11
National Black Theatre	2031-33 5th Ave.	212-722-3800	19, 20
Neighborhood Playhouse	340 E. 54th St.	212-688-3770	13
New 42nd St. Theatre	348 W. 42nd St.	212-712-6692	11
New York Performance Works	85 W. Broadway	212-566-1500	3
New York Theatre Workshop	79 E. 4th St.	212-460-5475	6, 7
New York Youth Theater	422 W. 57th St.	212-315-1737	11
The Next Stage	145 W. 46th St.	212-354-6121	12
Nuyorican Poets Cafe	236 E. 3rd St.	212-505-8183	7
Oasis Theatre	230 E. 9th St.	212-673-3706	7
Ohio Theater	66 Wooster St.	212-966-4844	6
One Dream	232 W. Broadway	212-274-1450	2
The Ontological-Hysteric Theater at St. Mark's Church	131 E. 10th St.	212-533-4650	6
Orpheum Theater	126 2nd Ave.	212-477-2477	6
P.S. 122	150 1st Ave.	212-477-5288	6, 7
Paradise Theater	64 E. 4th St.	212-253-8107	5
Partners & Crime	44 Greenwich Ave.	212-462-3027	5
Pearl Theatre Co., Inc.	80 St. Marks Pl.	212-598-9802	6
Pelican Studio Theatre	750 8th Ave., Suite 601	212-730-2030	11
Performing Garage	33 Wooster St.	212-966-3651	6
The Piano Store	158 Ludlow St.	212-420-1466	4
Players	115 MacDougal St.	212-254-5076	6
Playhouse 46 at St. Clement's	423 W. 46th St.	212-279-4200	11
Playhouse 91	316 E. 91st St.	212-831-2000	17
Playwrights Horizon Theater	416 W. 42nd St.	212-279-4200	11
The Present Company Theatorium	198 Stanton St.	212-420-8877	7
Primary Stages	354 W. 45th St.	212-333-4052	11
The Producers Club II	358 W. 44th St.	212-315-4743	11
Promenade Theatre	2162 Broadway	212-580-1313	14
Provincetown Playhouse	133 MacDougal St.	212-777-2571	6
Puerto Rican Traveling Theatre	304 W. 47th St.	212-354-1293	11
Raw Space	529 W. 42nd St.	212-643-6399	11
Raymond J. Greenwald Theatre	307 W. 26th St.	212-633-9797	8
The Red Room	85 E. 4th St.	212-279-4200	6
Riant Theatre	161 Hudson St.	212-925-8353	2
Rio's Supper Club	393 8th Ave.	800-MURDER-INC	8, 9
Roundabout/Laura Pels Theatre	1530 Broadway	212-719-9300	12
Saint Clement's Theatre	423 W. 46th St.	212-246-7277	11

Theaters

Saint John's Lutheran Church	81 Christopher St.	212-666-0176	5
Samuel Beckett Theatre	412 W. 42nd St.	212-307-4100	11
Sanford Meisner Theatre	164 11th Ave.	212-206-1764	8
Second Stage Theatre	307 W. 43rd St.	212-246-4422	11
Shooting Star Theatre	40 Peck Slip	212-791-7827	1
Signature Theatre	555 W. 42nd St.	212-244-7529	11
Soho Playhouse	15 Vandam St.	212-691-1555	2
Soho Repertory Theatre/Walker Street Theater	46 Walker St.	212-334-0962	2
Solo Arts Group	36 W. 17th St.	212-463-8732	9
St. Lukes Church	308 W. 46th St.	212-239-6200	11
Stand-Upstairs Theatre	236 W. 78th St.	212-873-9050	14
Stardust Theatre	1650 Broadway	212-239-6200	12
Stella Adler Theatre	419 Lafayette St.	212-260-0525	6
The Studio	145 W. 46th St.	212-354-6121	12
Studio Theater	416 W. 42nd St.	212-279-4200	11
Sullivan Street Lounge	189 Sullivan St.	212-420-1999	6
Sullivan Street Playhouse	181 Sullivan St.	212-674-3838	6
Surf Reality	172 Allen St., 2nd Fl.	212-673-4182	4
Sylvia and Danny Kaye Playhouse	695 Park Ave.	212-772-5207	15
Symphony Space	2537 Broadway	212-864-5400	16
Synchronicity Space	55 Mercer St.	212-925-8645	6
T. Schreiber Studio	151 W. 26th St.	212-741-0209	9
TADA!	120 W. 28th St.	212-627-1732	9
Tenement Theater	97 Orchard St.	212-431-0233	4
Theater for the New City	155 1st Ave.	212-254-1109	6, 7
Theatorium	196 Stanton St.	212-246-7277	7
Theatre East	211 E. 60th St.	212-838-9090	11, 14
Theatre Four	424 W. 55th St.	212-489-7050	11
Theatre of St. Peter's Church	Citicorp Ctr. 619 Lexington Ave.	212-935-2200	13
Theatre Off Park	224 Waverly Pl.	212-627-2556	6
Triad Theater	158 W. 72nd St.	212-362-2590	14
Trilogy Theatre	341 W. 44th St.	212-316-0400	11
UBU Rep	15 W. 28th St.	212-679-7562	9
Union Square Theater	100 E. 17th St.	212-505-0700	10
Variety Arts Center	110 3rd Ave.	212-239-6200	6
Victoria Five Theater	310 W. 125th St.	212-828-7991	20
Vineyard Theatre	108 E. 15th St.	212-353-3366	10
Waterloo Bridge Theatre	203 W. 38th St.	212-330-8879	9, 12
West Park Auditorium	165 W. 86th St.	212-946-5321	14, 16
Westbeth Theatre Center	151 Bank St.	212-691-2272	5
Westside Theatre	407 W. 43rd St.	212-239-6200	11
Wings Theater	154 Christopher St.	212-627-2961	5
Workhouse	41 White St.	212-431-9220	2
Worth Street Theater	33 Worth St.	212-226-1043	2
WOW Cafe	59 E. 4th St.	212-777-4280	6
York Theatre	619 Lexington Ave.	212-935-5820	13

Performing Arts

Theater	Address	Phone Number	Grid #
Amato Opera	319 Bowery	212-228-8200	6
CAMI Hall	165 W. 57th St.	212-841-9650	12
City Center	131 W. 55th St.	212-581-7907	12
Dance Theatre Workshop	219 W. 19th St.	212-924-0077	9
Grace Rainey Rogers Auditorium	Met. Museum, 1000 5th Ave.	212-570-3949	15
Joyce Theater	175 8th Ave.	212-242-0800	8, 9
Juilliard School	60 Lincoln Center Plz.	212-799-5000	14
Manhattan School of Music	120 Claremont Ave.	212-749-2802	18
Merkin Concert Hall	129 W. 67th St.	212-362-8719	14
Music Room	Frick Museum, 1 E. 70th St.	212-288-0700	15
New Museum of Contemporary Art	583 Broadway	212-219-1222	6
Riverside Church	490 Riverside Dr.	212-870-6700	18
St. Mark's Church-in-the-Bowery	131 E. 10th St.	212-674-6377	6
Town Hall	123 W. 43rd St.	212-840-2824	12
Warren St. Performance Loft	46 Warren St.	212-732-3149	2
Washington Square Church	135 W. 4th St.	212-777-2528	6

Directory Assistance-SPORTS

Tennis Courts

There are more tennis courts on the island of Manhattan than you might think, although getting to them may be a bit more than you've bargained for. Most of the public courts in Manhattan (listed in the "Parks" section of the chart below) are either smack in the middle of Central Park, or are on the edges of the city—East River Park, for instance, and Riverside Park. These courts in particular can make for some pretty windy playing conditions.

Public Parks	Address	# of Cts.	Type	Phone No.
Battery Park I	World Financial Center	2	Hard	(212) 374-0973
Central Park Tennis Center	93rd St. & Central Park West	30	Clay/Hard	(212) 280-0205
East River Park Tennis Courts	FDR Dr. No. of Delancey St.	12	Hard	(212) 529-7185
Fort Washington Park	H. Hudson Pkwy. & 172nd St.	10	Hard	(212) 234-9609
F. Johnson Playground	151st Street at 7th Avenue	8	Hard	(212) 234-9609
Inwood Hill Park	207th St. & Seaman Ave.	9	Hard	(212) 304-2381
Octagon Park	Main St., Roosevelt Island	4	Hard	N/A
Randall's Island Sunken Meadow	Randall's Island	11	Hard	(212) 860-1827
Riverbank State Park	W. 145th & Riverbank Dr.	4	Hard	(212) 694-3600
Riverside Park	96th St. & Riverside Dr.	10	Clay	(212) 496-2006
Riverside Park	119th-122nd St. & Riverside Dr.	10	Hard	(212) 496-2103

Private Clubs	Address	# of Cts.	Type	Phone No.
Columbus Tennis Club	795 Columbus Ave.	9	Clay	(212) 662-8367
Crosstown Tennis	14 W. 31st St.	4	Hard	(212) 947-5780
EHCCI/Pasarell YTC	E. 120th St. & First Ave.	4	Hard	N/A
Harlem Tennis Center	40 W. 143rd St.	4	Rubber	(212) 283-4028
HRC Tennis	South Street, Piers 13 and 14	8	Clay	(212) 422-9300
Manhattan Plz. Racquet Club	450 W. 43rd St.	8	Hard	(212) 594-0554
Midtown Tennis Club	341 8th Ave.	8	Clay	(212) 989-8572
River Club	447 E. 57th St.	2	Clay	(212) 751-0100
Roosevelt Island Racquet Club	281 Main St.	11	Clay	(212) 935-0250
Sutton East Tennis Club	488 E. 60th St.	8	Clay	(212) 751-3452
The Tennis Club	15 Vanderbilt Ave.	2	Hard	(212) 687-3841
The Vertical Club	330 E. 61st St.	8	Hard	(212) 355-2052
Town Tennis Club	430 E. 56th St.	3	Hard	(212) 752-4059
UN Plz./Park Hyatt Hotel	1 United Nations Plaza	1	Hard	(212) 702-5016
Village Tennis Court	110 University Place	2	Hard	(212) 989-2300

Schools	Address	# of Cts.	Type	Phone No.
Coles Center, NYU	181 Mercer St.	10	Clay	(212) 998-2020
Columbia U. Tennis Center	575 W. 218th St.	7	Hard	(212) 942-7100
JHS 167 YTC	E. 75th St. (bet. 2nd & 3rd)	4	Hard	(212) 879-7562
PS 125	425 W. 123rd St.	3	Hard	N/A
PS 137	327 Cherry St.	5	Hard	N/A
PS 144	134 W. 122nd St.	4	Hard	N/A
PS 146	421 E. 106th St.	3	Hard	N/A
PS 187	349 Cabrini Blvd.	4	Hard	N/A
Rockefeller University	1230 York Ave.	1	Hard	(212) 327-8000

Getting a Permit

The tennis season, according to the NYC Parks Department, lasts from April 7 to November 30. Permits are good for use until the end of the season at all public courts, and are good for one hour of singles or two hours of doubles play. Fees are:

Juniors (17 yrs and under) $10
Adults (18-61yrs) $50
Senior Citizen (62 yrs and over) $20
Single-play tickets $5

General Information

Manhattan Parks Dept.: (212) 360-8131
website: http://www.ci.nyc.ny.us/html/dpr/html/boomer.html
Permit Locations: The Arsenal, 830 5th Ave. @ 64th St.; Paragon Sporting Goods, Broadway @ 18th St.

Golf Courses

Unfortunately, but not surprisingly, there are no golf courses on the island of Manhattan. Thankfully, there are two driving ranges where you can at least smack the ball around until you can get to a real course. NYC has a number of private and public courses throughout the outer boroughs and Westchester; however, they by no means satisfy the area's huge demand for courses.

Golf Courses

Borough	Name	Address	Par	Phone No.
Bronx	Mosholu Golf Course	3700 Jerome Ave	71	(718) 655-9164
Bronx	Pelham/Split Rock Golf Course	870 Shore Rd(in Pelham Bay Park)	70	(718) 885-1258
Bronx	Van Cortlandt Golf Course	Van Cortlandt Pk S & Bailey Ave	70	(718) 543-4595
Brooklyn	Dyker Beach Golf Course	86th St at 7th Ave	70	(718) 836-9722
Brooklyn	Marine Park Golf Club	2880 Flatbush Ave	71	(718) 338-7113
Queens	Clearview Golf Course	202 - 12 Willets Point Blvd	70	(718) 225-GOLF
Queens	Douglaston Golf Course	6320 Marathon Pkwy	67	(718) 428-1617
Queens	Forest Park Golf Course	101 Forest Park Dr	70	(718) 296-0999
Queens	Kissena Park Golf Course	164 - 15 Booth Memorial Ave	64	(718) 939-4594
Staten Island	LaTourette Golf Course	1001 Richmond Hill Rd	72	(718) 351-1889
Staten Island	Silver Lake Golf Course	915 Victory Blvd	69	(718) 447-5686
Staten Island	South Shore Golf Course	200 Huguenot Ave	72	(718) 984-0101

Fees are generally as follows (Reservations are a must, so call ahead):

Weekdays before 1pm-$21.00
Weekdays after 1pm-$19.00
Weekends before 1pm-$23.50
Weekends after 1pm-$21.50

Also below is where in Manhattan you can at least smack the ball around until you can get out to a real course.

Manhattan Golf Centers

Name	Address	Fees	Phone No.
Chelsea Piers: Pier 59 Golf ClubPier	59, Chelsea Piers (at 23rd Street)	$15.00/large bucket	(212) 336-6400
Randalls Island Golf Center	1 Randalls Rd	$6.00/small bucket $10.00/large bucket	(212) 427-5689

Directory Assistance-SPORTS

Madison Square Garden

Madison Square Garden is home to the Knicks, the Rangers, and the Liberty. If you don't know which sports these teams play, then we can't help you. Either way, we probably can't help you get tickets for the Knicks or the Rangers. Don't worry, though—the Liberty games are the most fun, anyway. MSG also hosts a ton of other events throughout the year, including rock concerts, tennis tournaments, political conventions, and, for those of you with 2+ years of graduate school, monster truck rallies and "professional" wrestling. Check out MSG's web-site for the full calendar of events.

How to Get There—Mass Transit
MSG is right next to Penn Station, so it's extremely convenient to get there. You can take the A-C-E and 1-2-3-9 lines to 34th St. and Penn Station, or the N-R, B-D-F-Q, and PATH lines to 34th St. and 6th Ave.

How to Get Tickets
You can try Ticketmaster for single seats for the Knicks and the Rangers, but a better bet would be to try the "standby" line for these teams (show up a half-hour before game time). There are also the ubiquitous ticket scalpers ringing the Garden for when your rich out-of-town friends breeze in to see a game. You can usually get Liberty tickets (and tickets for other events) through Ticketmaster.

Practical Information
General Information: 212-465-6741
Knicks Hotline: 212-465-JUMP
Liberty Hotline: 212-564-WNBA
Rangers Hotline: 212-308-NYRS
Ticketmaster: 212-307-7171
Website: www.thegarden.com

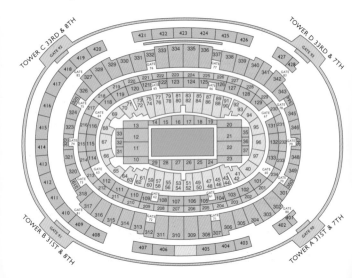

Directory Assistance-SPORTS

Giants Stadium

Giants Stadium, located in the scenic and smelly Meadowlands Sports Complex of New Jersey, is the home of both the New York Giants and New York Jets football teams. They play here on alternating Sundays throughout the fall and the only way to get regular-priced tickets is to inherit them, since both teams are sold out through the next ice age. Giants Stadium also houses Major League Soccer's Metrostars (for which many, many tickets are available) and is the site of several concerts and other sporting and religious events throughout the year.

How to Get There—Driving

Giants Stadium is only 5 miles from the Lincoln Tunnel (closer to mid-town than Shea Stadium, even) but leave early if you want to get to the game on time–remember that the Giants and the Jets are a) sold out for every game and b) have tons of fans from both Long Island and the five boroughs. You can take the Lincoln Tunnel to Route 3 West to Route 120 North to get there, or you can try either the Holland Tunnel to the New Jersey Turnpike (North) to exit 16W, or the George Washington Bridge to the New Jersey Turnpike (South) to exit 16W. Accessing in the stadium from exit 16W allows direct access to the parking areas.

How to Get There—Mass Transit

A less stressful way to get to Giants Stadium than driving is to take a bus from the Port Authority Bus Terminal directly to the stadium. It costs $3.25 each way, and buses usually start running two hours before kickoff.

How to Get Tickets

For the Jets and the Giants, scalpers and friends are the only options. For the MetroStars and for concerts, you can call Ticketmaster or visit Ticketmaster's website.

Practical Information

Giants Stadium Information: 201-935-3900
Ticketmaster: 212-307-3131
Website: www.giantsstadium.com

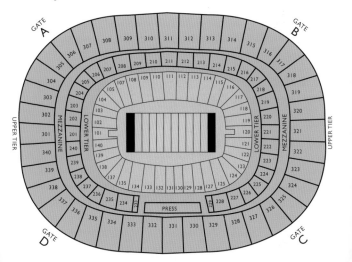

Directory Assistance-SPORTS

Yankee Stadium

Yankee Stadium, or "The House That Ruth Built", has been The Bronx's most famous landmark since the 1920s. Since moving in, the Yankees have won exactly a quarter of the World Series that have been played (24 of 96), making them one of the most successful sports franchises in history. And even Yankee owner George Steinbrenner's infernal meddling can't stop them altogether—they've won four championships since he bought the team in 1973.

How To Get There—Driving
Driving to Yankee Stadium from Manhattan usually isn't that bad. Games don't generally start on weeknights until 7:30, so leaving at around 6:45 from midtown will get you close, if not in your seats, by game time. It's best to take the Willis Ave. Bridge from either 1st Ave. or the FDR Drive and get on the Major Deegan for about one mile until you see the stadium exit. From the upper west side, you can try taking Broadway up to 155th St. and using the Macombs Dam Bridge to cross over to the stadium (avoiding lots of crosstown traffic). Parking (as compared to ticket prices) is usually pretty cheap, especially at those lots that are a few blocks from the stadium.

How To Get There—Mass Transit
Getting to the stadium by subway is easy. The 4 and the D both run express to the stadium, and you can easily hook up with either train at several junctions in Manhattan. It should take you about half an hour from any point in Manhattan. Also, New York Waterway runs a ferry (the "Yankee Clipper") from South Street Seaport, E. 34th St., and E. 94th St.

How To Get Tickets
You can order tickets by phone through Ticketmaster, buy tickets at the box office or at the Yankee store, or buy tickets over the web through either Ticketmaster or the Yankee web site.

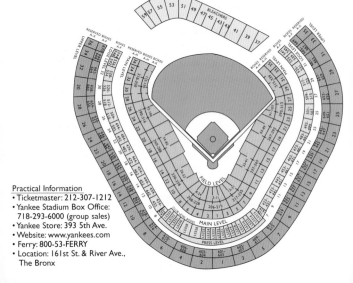

Practical Information
- Ticketmaster: 212-307-1212
- Yankee Stadium Box Office: 718-293-6000 (group sales)
- Yankee Store: 393 5th Ave.
- Website: www.yankees.com
- Ferry: 800-53-FERRY
- Location: 161st St. & River Ave., The Bronx

Shea Stadium

Shea Stadium is the home of the New York Mets. It's painted in those lovely clashing colors of Dodger Blue and Giant Orange (homage to the two baseball teams that deserted New York City for the west coast), and is located in Flushing Meadows in Queens. Although the Mets had one of the most abysmal starts in baseball history in 1962 (going 40-120), since that time, they've won two World Series (in 1969 and 1986), appeared in a third, and have been competitive in at least some portion of every decade.

How To Get There—Driving

Driving to Shea Stadium is easy, although commuter traffic during the week can cause tie-ups. You can take the Triborough Bridge to the Grand Central Parkway; the Mid-Town Tunnel to the Long Island Expressway to the Grand Central; or the Brooklyn-Queens Expressway to the LIE to the Grand Central.

How To Get There—Mass Transit

The good news is that the 7 train runs straight to Shea Stadium. The bad news is: 1) it's the 7 train, usually rated the worst among all train lines; and 2) it's the only train that goes there. However, it will get you there and back (eventually), and the 7 is accessible from almost all the other train lines in Manhattan. Alternately, you can take the E to Roosevelt Ave. and pick up the 7 there, saving about 30 minutes. Also New York Waterway runs a ferry service (the "Mets Express") to Shea from the South Street Seaport, E. 34th St, and E. 94th St.

How To Get Tickets

You can order Mets tickets by phone through the Mets box office, on the internet through the Mets' website, or at the Mets Clubhouse Shop.

Practical Information
• Mets Clubhouse Shop: 143 E. 54th St., Manhattan
• Shea Stadium Box Office: 718-507-8499
• Website: www.mets.com
• Location: 126th St. and Roosevelt Ave., Flushing, Queens

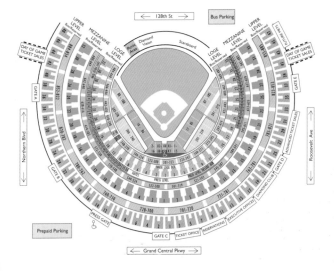

Bibliography

Bibliography/Reference

We have run across many, many great books, pamphlets, magazines, websites, etc. while researching NFT. The following list is by no means complete, but if you're at all interested in New York, each of these selections will provide you with at least one piece of information you didn't know before.

Books

1. The Curious New Yorker, Andrea Kannapell, Jesse McKinley, Daniel B. Schneider, Kathryn Shattuck, and Jennifer Steinhauer; Times Books, New York, NY, 1999.
2. The Encyclopedia of New York City; Kenneth T. Jackson, Editor; Yale University Press, New Haven, CT, 1995.
3. Eyewitness Travel Guides: New York, Elanor Berman; DK Publishing, New York, NY, 1997.
4. The Green Book 1996-97: Official Directory of the City of New York; .E.C. Robbins, Editor; City Publishing Center, New York, NY, 1997.
5. Marden's Guide to Manhattan Booksellers; William Marden; City & Company, New York, NY, 1997.
6. Wild New York; Margaret Mittelbach and Michael Crewdson; Crown Publishers, New York, NY, 1997.
7. Zagat Survey: 1997 New York City Restaurants; Zagat Survey, LLC, New York, NY 1997.

Magazines

Time Out New York—Easily the most comprehensive weekly listings magazine for New York.

Websites

www.citysearch.com—Provides an excellent overview to almost every business, landmark, and attraction in Manhattan.

www.panynj.gov—The Port Authority's excellent website, covering terminals, bridges, tunnels, etc.

Other Publications

New York City Bicycle Master Plan, Department of City Planning & Department of Transportation; City of New York, New York, NY, 1997.

STREET INDEX

STREET INDEX

STREET INDEX

STREET INDEX

STREET INDEX

STREET INDEX